ROUTLEDGE LIBRARY EDITIONS: T. S. ELIOT

Volume 9

T. S. ELIOT

T. S. ELIOT
A Friendship

E. W. F. TOMLIN

LONDON AND NEW YORK

First published in 1988 by Routledge
This edition first published in 2016
by Routledge
4 Park Square, Milton Park, Abingdon, Oxon OX14 4RN
605 Third Avenue, New York, NY 10017

Routledge is an imprint of the Taylor & Francis Group, an informa business

© 1988 E.W.F. Tomlin

All rights reserved. No part of this book may be reprinted or reproduced or utilised in any form or by any electronic, mechanical, or other means, now known or hereafter invented, including photocopying and recording, or in any information storage or retrieval system, without permission in writing from the publishers.

Trademark notice: Product or corporate names may be trademarks or registered trademarks, and are used only for identification and explanation without intent to infringe.

British Library Cataloguing in Publication Data
A catalogue record for this book is available from the British Library

ISBN: 978-1-138-18484-8 (Set)
ISBN: 978-1-315-64488-2 (Set) (ebk)
ISBN: 978-1-138-12252-9 (Volume 9) (hbk)
ISBN: 978-1-138-12256-7 (Volume 9) (pbk)
ISBN: 978-1-315-65042-5 (Volume 9) (ebk)

Publisher's Note
The publisher has gone to great lengths to ensure the quality of this reprint but points out that some imperfections in the original copies may be apparent.

Disclaimer
The publisher has made every effort to trace copyright holders and would welcome correspondence from those they have been unable to trace.

T. S. ELIOT:
A FRIENDSHIP

E. W. F. TOMLIN

ROUTLEDGE
LONDON

First published in 1988 by
Routledge
11 New Fetter Lane, London EC4P 4EE
29 West 35th Street, New York NY 10001

© E.W.F. Tomlin 1988

Photoset by Columns Ltd., Reading
Printed in Great Britain by
Billing and Sons Ltd., Worcester.

All rights reserved. No part of this book may be reprinted or reproduced or utilized in any form or by any electronic, mechanical, or other means, now known or hereafter invented, including photocopying and recording, or in any information storage or retrieval system, without permission in writing from the publishers.

British Library Cataloging in Publication Data
Tomlin, E.W.F. (Eric Walter Frederick), 1913–1988
T.S. Eliot : a friendship.
1. Poetry in English. Eliot, T.S (Thomas Stearns), 1888–1965. Biographies
1. Title
821'.912

ISBN 0 415 02512 5

ACKNOWLEDGMENTS

I wish to express my grateful thanks to Mrs T. S. Eliot for allowing me to reproduce the letters her husband wrote to me. I also wish to thank her for help in many other ways, not least through personal exchanges over the years. Finally, in dedicating the book to her, again with her kind permission, I pay tribute not merely to the wife of a great man but to one who has earned distinction in her own right.

To my sister, Esther Tomlin, I am indebted for granting me permission to reproduce the letters written to her by T. S. Eliot on 3 November 1940, 27 May 1942, and the handwritten letter from Jamaica on 17 January 1961; together with permission to reproduce the copy of the drawing of T. S. Eliot by Mrs Henry Ware (Theresa) Eliot and presented to her by the artist. To George Every I acknowledge with thanks permission to reproduce the photograph taken of T. S. Eliot at Kelham; to the Houghton Library, Harvard University for permission to reproduce the photograph of T. S. Eliot in 1932; to the Felix Mann Estate for permission to reproduce the photograph of T. S. Eliot in his office; to Andrew Sanders for permission to reproduce the photograph of the Chapel at Kelham; and to Graham Hughes and Father Christopher Colven for permission to reproduce the photograph taken in St Stephen's, Gloucester Road.

A few passages from articles of mine in *Agenda* and *The Listener* have been incorporated in the text.

Since the completion of this memoir, in which I have endeavoured to set down everything I remember about T. S. Eliot, further recollections have emerged from the past and must await the opportunity of joining those on record. In this sense, no memoir is ever finished.

E. W. F. Tomlin
London, June 1987

ILLUSTRATIONS

1. The author as a schoolboy.
2. A passport photograph of T.S. Eliot in 1932.
3. T.S. Eliot in his office at Faber & Faber in the early years.
4. Extract from the author's early essay on 'The Younger Generation and Politics', submitted to Faber & Faber when at school, inscribed with T.S. Eliot's notes.
5. T.S. Eliot in his office at Faber & Faber. His room was always crowded with books.
6. T.S. Eliot's visiting card with the address at Harvard given to the author at their second meeting, 1931.
7. T.S. Eliot in the grounds at Kelham, headquarters of the Society of Sacred Mission, taken in the mid-1930s.
8. The chapel at Kelham. T.S. Eliot was a frequent visitor to the monastery.
9. T.S. Eliot's visiting card accompanying flowers sent to the author in Guy's Hospital.
10. Drawing of T.S. Eliot by the author based on a photograph in *The Green Quarterly*, and from observation, 1937.
11. A wartime airgraph to the author from T.S. Eliot.
12. Photograph of the author, taken in Paris, 1947.
13. T.S. Eliot being wheeled into the French Hospital, Shaftesbury Avenue, after being taken ill on an Atlantic crossing. The photograph appeared in the *Evening Standard*, 12 June, 1956.
14. Drawing of T.S. Eliot asleep, Cambridge, Mass., by his sister-in-law, Theresa Eliot.
15. T.S. Eliot in relaxed mood in his office at Faber & Faber.
16. T.S. Eliot and his wife photographed in the early morning, following a celebration of the opening of *The Elder Statesman*, 26 September, 1958.
17. T.S. Eliot's congratulatory letter to the author, 17 June, 1959.
18. The T.S. Eliot memorial tablet in the south transept of St Stephen's, Gloucester Road.

TO VALERIE

INTRODUCTION

The circumstances of my life, which, through no merit of my own, brought me into contact with a number of distinguished men and women, enlarged my perception of what makes a person notable. Above all I observed, even if only in retrospect, that great people had a *presence* which marked them off from the rest. It was as if, in addition to their physical embodiment, they had what might be called – except that it has unnecessary paronormal associations – a psychic presence. Another way of putting it would be to say that they possessed an extra dimension. And if you protest that you cannot fathom what I mean by that, I in turn will reply that in that case you have apparently never met a really great man or woman.

With such a presence and such an extra dimension, T. S. Eliot was a great man in my sense. I was never to meet anyone to whom I could ascribe greatness with such assurance.

This is a personal record. Books on Eliot continue to pour from the press, and there is no sign of the stream diminishing. The majority of these books are concerned with exegesis, as the *oeuvre* lends itself to this sort of approach. Save in order to point or reinforce an allusion, I am not here concerned with interpretation or analysis. I am concerned with the man himself, the personality. Someone as remarkable as Eliot – it is part of the mysterious 'presence' – commands attention in a way that a lesser figure cannot do : for just as we need little detail about a minor figure (save perhaps for the purpose of writing a doctoral thesis), in respect of a major figure we cannot have too much.

To read James Hogg on Shelley and Leigh Hunt on Byron is fascinating, not because they talk of the poetry but rather because they talk of the appearance, the manner, the behaviour of these men.

In the case of persons of great inner life, the outward appearance is still, and perhaps all the more, interesting, because it may serve to reveal something of that inner life in the course of masking it; and the more intensive that life, the more the mask reveals by apparent concealment. Only if behaviourism were true and behaviour were just a mechanistic function would it reveal nothing: it is only because behaviourism is not true, and could not be true, that behaviour becomes significant.

Sometimes when I saw Eliot at a public gathering, I would be seized with wonder that all that extraordinary poetry and prose could have come out of him. Indeed, as we grow older and our contacts multiply, personality becomes a more and more elusive thing. Consequently, anything that can help to shed light upon it, to delineate it, is of interest. And the number of people in a position to do this is, in Eliot's case, diminishing.

This surviving group of friends is placed under particular obligation. Over a fairly long life I have been confronted with evidence, in cases where I was in a position to know the true circumstances, suggesting that the testimony of certain persons, otherwise of known integrity, was suspect: and that, on account of such testimony, a myth had been built up which, without evidence to the contrary, could not easily be demolished. In setting down my own memories, I trust that I may have avoided generating another myth. The precaution seems to me mandatory. For in the case of Eliot, there have been several myths in course of elaboration, and I know how much damage they have already done. But as confirmation of some of the things I myself shall say may not be forthcoming, the reader will have to take my word for them. His own judgment and the judgment of time will test my credibility. Also, I have a suspicion, which may amount almost to superstition, that if one were to exaggerate or to elaborate beyond probability, or to engage in wish-fulfilling surmise, the consequences would ultimately rebound upon one's own head. As it is the record must speak for itself in the hope that, over the years, testimony may accumulate in its support.

In recording TSE's conversation, either from notes or from a fairly retentive memory – which has been further reinforced by constant recollection through the years – I was astonished often how much of value and pungency he was able to crowd into the briefest space. There were, I believe, two reasons for this. As he spoke slowly, and with great deliberation, he released only what was worth saying.

Secondly, he had no small talk. The result is he never squandered his words. It was as if he rationed them. In recounting my friendship with Eliot, one of the most important events of my life, I begin by going back to the period in which his reputation started first to make an impact on me and on my own circle.

Since the reader will have taken up this book in order to find out more about Eliot, it must contain the minimum of me and the maximum about its subject; but the minimum must be an irreducible minimum, and therefore the provision of some background detail is necessary for the purpose of making the course of the friendship intelligible.

Few things are more rewarding in youth than the awakening of common intellectual interests, and the recognition of a mutual, if barely defined, mental need. Looking back, I see this as more crucial by far than sexual awakening, on which so much stress is now placed. For me and for my friends at my school, Whitgift, in the 1920s, books, music, and to a lesser degree art, fed our burgeoning libidos and psyches, and I would not have had it otherwise. Events were propitious. The early BBC opened a new world of music to us : the Croydon Public Library, excellent as it was then, offered us all the books we could need. In fact, 'the Library', as we called it, played a great part in our development. It was not merely a reservoir of books but a meeting-place. Occasionally it could become, however, briefly, a trysting-place too, because it must not be thought that girls played no part in our lives.

CHAPTER ONE

How and when the *name* T. S. Eliot (a striking name at that, because of the combination of initial consonants) first came to my eyes or ears, I cannot now recall. I fancy that he was mentioned in a sermon by the Archbishop of York, then Dr William Temple, as an example of an intellectual who found faith rather than, as was more normal at that time, having abandoned it. Temple, who I was to meet at a weekend for public schoolboys, was closer to the intelligentsia than most other prelates, and certainly he had a powerful mind, even though his Christian Socialism did not appeal to me. My first contact with the Eliot *oeuvre* took place on one of the mid-platforms of East Croydon station, after a visit to the Library for purely bibliophilic purposes. I remember opening the slim volume of *Poems 1909–25*, with its brown jacket, and suddenly realizing that the words that met my eyes were ones I had somehow been waiting for. This was my poetry. This was what I wanted to have written. The result amounted to a kind of conversion. Immediately, as happens when a particular book is sampled, I wanted to read everything by T. S. Eliot. Enthusiasm consumed me, and in many ways it has remained undiminished. The year must have been 1928.

Whether I had communicated my enthusiasm to Burke Trend, almost my exact contemporary at Whitgift who sadly died in 1987, or whether he had made an independent discovery, my next recollection in the field of Eliot awareness was Burke's mentioning the precision of the *prose* of *For Lancelot Andrewes*. We were standing, I remember, in one of the school corridors. At that time I think I had a keener ear for poetry than for prose, because I trace my sensitivity to prose style from Burke's comment. From *For Lancelot*

Andrewes I went back to *The Sacred Wood*. In intellectual matters, as in much else, Burke was far ahead of me; but we found ourselves engaged in that sharing and pooling of experience which I have described as productive of so much elation; and we had something else in common, our mothers had been widowed at an early age, so that for us life was real, life was earnest in a literal sense. We lived – Burke perhaps more than I, as he was an only child, whereas I had an elder sister and brother of similar tastes – on a level of high-mindedness with which I can hardly now credit myself; but it was undoubtedly so. Any form of entertainment was the greatest luxury – a contrast to today when work or study for the schoolchild and the student seems to amount to a tiresome interruption in an endless round of diversion. At any rate, I forthwith devoured *For Lancelot Andrewes*, with its eye-opening preface (of which more anon); and I found especially in the essay on Machiavelli some observations which were permanently to alter my mental viewpoint. I have always regretted that Eliot never wanted that essay republished. But there was more to the spare volume than that: the seminal essay on 'The Humanism of Irving Babbitt', for instance, and evidence of a growing interest in political and social problems. No longer was literature purely literary. No longer was religion divorced from true humanism, which was itself to be distinguished from humanism as a form of *ersatz* religion.

A digressionary paragraph is necessary here in order to set the scene more clearly. I am told by educational experts that candidates for university entrance today have sometimes to be cajoled into recollecting any of the English classics they may have read or glanced at, and also that one of the impediments to their pursuit of study is the emotional turmoil in which they are already enmeshed, or, on arriving at the university, soon become involved. For nothing in youth takes up so much time, or consumes as much valuable psychic energy, as sexual involvement, which must exceed the common cold in the amount of absenteeism it causes. (This, I am told, is especially true behind the Iron Curtain, where so much spare psychic energy has to be discharged in the private sphere.) I am glad to have belonged to a generation which, as I have implied, did not regard an active sex-life to be a sign, or rather *sine qua non*, of sophisticated living. The result was that our 'education sentimentale' was largely brought about by exploring works of imagination and in an, admittedly, sometimes excessively idealistic pursuit of the nature of a just society. This meant above all that we read voraciously. And so, when we presented ourselves to the university interviewers, we could talk, no doubt sometimes with absurd cocksureness, about books and movements and the latest literary or artistic sensation in Paris (for example) in a manner calculated to impress, if sometimes slightly to alarm, our future instructors. I had hardly gone into long trousers (a rite of passage which some fond parents delayed for as long as possible) when, in the train, I would spread a capacious volume such as Spengler's *Decline of the West* on my knees, and cause an almost sensory reaction – not always of approval – from my fellow-passengers, who were mostly of the middle-management type, and therefore belligerently low-brow. In other words, higher education for us – and this applied not merely to Burke, who excelled us all, but to Paul Crowson, Peter Shaw, Philip Martin and Rupert Neville, from each of whom I learnt something of value – implied, when we arrived at the university (which for all of us, as it happened, meant Oxford), a still higher education. It was not a case, as now, of having to be brought up to standard on arrival there, or, as has happened despite indignant denials, of gradually lowering standards to meet the aspiring students half-way. Now, having engaged in a certain measure of self-praise, I must admit to defects. One was the tendency, inseparable from youth, towards mono-enthusiasm. By the time I sat for university entrance, I tended to see everything through the Eliot *oeuvre*. I must have bored everyone to distraction by my championship of original sin, the dissociation of sensibility, and the objective correlative. I must have distressed lovers of the Romantic poets, especially Shelley, or the Georgians, who included most of the dons who had the corvée of dealing with me, by my blanket contempt for these figures, many of whom I have since re-admitted to the pantheon. Above all, I denounced Marx, a figure whom I still exclude; and this sometimes got me into trouble, as many of the dons were convinced Marxians or at least *Marxisants*. But I received the impression then, as indeed I do now, that many of these armchair revolutionaries had, in contrast to myself, never read a word of Marx in their lives. But of that I shall need to speak further.

What I seek to convey to the reader is the truth of Peter Ackroyd's statement in his 1984 biography, that Eliot had emerged in the mid-1920s as 'the new voice' in poetry, the originator of a 'new music', and as something else much less easy to define, namely, the initiator of a sort of cultural mutation. Every now and then this kind of writer-cum-cultural prophet emerges, and as a result there is a shift in the kaleidoscope of taste, the release of a new language of image and sensibility. But it is more than just change. As Eliot said in an early essay 'Sensibility alters from generation to generation in everyone, whether we will or no: but expression is only altered by a man of genius'. Eliot seems to me the most innovative example in English literature since Arnold, a 'cultural' figure if ever there was one. And we heard the music, and sensed the kaleidoscopic shift. Indeed, so great has been Eliot's influence that, if we survey the literary scene prior to the publication of *Prufrock and other Observations*, it seems strangely denuded and bare. Moreover, the Georgians, and not least Masefield, whose attempted resuscitation recently has proved abortive, now make pretty dull reading, with their dream-pastoral-animal-welfare ethos. True, two of my pre-Eliot enthusiasms, Brooke and Flecker, still, for that reason, seem to me to have some merit: the one because he had wit and the other because he, like Eliot, was aware of French poetry, and also because of promise tragically unfulfilled. The other reason no doubt why Eliot excited such interest was because he furnished a new idea of a poet. He was fascinating in not looking the part. Here was an efficient, business-like, personable, and at that time still young-looking individual, writing in a manner different from anyone since the seventeenth century metaphysicals. When years later I saw in the flesh Charles Morgan, not merely Bohemianly cloaked but talking with solemn sententious gravity, it was like a *revenant* – indeed he was a *revenant* – and I realized what a clean sweep Eliot had made of all this literary flummery. Finally, and this was not the least part of the charm, Eliot was by birth American.

Now the oldest of the 'new' countries, the United States was in the 1920s still the land of promise, at least to us tired inhabitants of the Old World. Only a few years earlier, we had seen the Yankees arriving and bringing with them youth and hope. For they all appeared youthful, athletic, early-risers, with a cleanness of look and figure which was hopefulness itself. Then there had been Hollywood. Then there had been jazz, 'everybody's doing it', and something called the blues. Then there had been the breakfast cereals. Then there had been the Rodeo. And then, though to be one of us by naturalization, there had been this equally clean-looking, lean poet, T. S. Eliot. In many ways very English, and perhaps trying a little too hard at first to make himself so, he nevertheless betrayed his American origins by the slight drawl and an occasional American expression – 'the gashouse', 'boost' (then very much a trans-Atlantic word) – and by his regular features, that one associated with some of the stars of the silver screen. Can it be my fancy, or is it a plain fact, that the America of the later twentieth century, weary with world-responsibility and the Vietnam and Watergate traumata, has reflected its anxieties and fatigues in the grey complexions of its menfolk and the dry cosmetic skin of its women, both sexes assuming in old age a cragginess of feature, whereas twenty years into the century Americans had been among the handsomest and most comely people on earth? Or have they acquired this arid look as a result of being slowly cooked, over two generations or so, by excessive central-heating? As for Eliot he first matured as an American, but he aged as an Englishman.

Reverting to schooldays, it was inevitable that we should communicate our enthusiasms not only to our friends (and here I must make a special mention of Ben Weinreb) but also to those few masters who might be expected to sympathize. I think we were lucky at Whitgift in having some highly competent men placed over us. Three of them were exceptionally gifted persons, though differing totally in character: H. G. Woodgate, A. H. Ewen and John Garrett. All were aware of Eliot's growing fame; but being accustomed to the mono-enthusiasm of youth, they received my ardour in particular with certain reservations. The first found *The Waste Land* by no means to his taste, but surprisingly, in view of his agnosticism, he had taken to *Ash Wednesday*. The second, who had an extraordinary knowledge of the 'modern movement' in art, music and literature, was more interested in Eliot's poetic technique than in his ideas, which he found suspect. The last and most enthusiastic, though he may have had less detailed knowledge of the *oeuvre*, was quick to grasp the significance of the man and his achievements. Woodgate and Ewen (in those days we still stuck to surnames and would have regarded the use of first names an intolerable liberty) were rationalists in the Rationalist Press sense. Indeed, Ewen was as near to being a radical behaviourist or reductionist as I have ever encountered. Hardly had I written that sentence when, opening the current school magazine, I came across his photograph, and there he was, the last of the triumvirate, and still, I am sure, interested in practically everything, if as much a thoroughgoing sceptic as ever. It does no harm to a young person to be exposed, at an impressionable age, to a mind that was so corrosive, yet well-stocked; and if, in later life, I have approached theoretical matters with scepticism – in some cases no doubt with undue caution – I owe it partly to 'Percy' Ewen, as we called him. For instance, although my partiality to Eliot's ideas has often caused mild amusement to my friends, and no doubt excited derision in others, I remain far less orthodox in my beliefs than a disciple of Eliot might be expected to be. Nor has my devotion excluded other loyalties. However, the temperate encouragement of these three masters proved fundamental; and a further reason for alluding to them here will soon become apparent. In youth, one's teachers are not so much vibrant personalities as slightly distant archetypal figures. Nor did we wish them to be otherwise. That was how their influence was exerted, across a boundary. They had their personal concerns and we had ours; but of course we regarded ours as the more important, and we judged the value of their instruction by the degree to which it helped to sort out our own preoccupations.

That the intellectual world was ringing with Eliot's name cannot be said at all. Even in the early 1930s, the establishment was largely hostile to him. Many of the detractors have passed into oblivion, though Edmund Gosse has been resurrected owing to a notable biography. Sometimes the hostility reached fever-pitch; and even in the 1950s I heard Lord Dunsany denouncing *The Four Quartets* in terms which he thought, poor man, might, even at that late hour, do something to reverse Eliot's reputation, of which he was almost pathologically jealous. As to Arthur Waugh's description of Eliot and Pound as 'drunken helots', there could hardly have been a more inept description of the patrician Eliot or the Confucian Pound. What seemed slightly amusing about these hostile manifestations was that the new literary movement, with its revolutionary reappraisals, was led by a man who, from another point of view, seemed to be the champion of reaction. And when we – that is to say, our little circle – had first seen Eliot's photograph, I believe in the *Radio Times*, we were intrigued to find a striking-looking man, extremely well-groomed, brows slightly knit, who was as unlike our idea of 'a poet' as could be imagined. It must be remembered that our conventional notion implied someone 'romantic' like Shelley,

Browning, Tennyson or Yeats in appearance. The businessman poet was altogether a novelty.

And then one day, about 3.30 p.m., while wandering in my school cap and blazer round Bumpus's in Piccadilly – at that time the bookshop most frequented in the West End – I spotted a small typewritten notice saying that T. S. Eliot would be giving a lecture on John Marston at King's College, London, at eight o'clock that same evening.

I jumped at the idea of going. My mother, who accompanied me, was equally enthusiastic, because the name of T. S. Eliot had become as familiar to her as a favourite pop idol would be to the modern parent of a star-struck child. Although we were obliged to turn our arrangements upside down, this mattered not at all. What remained in my memory was the extreme difficulty, once we had arrived at King's in the Strand, of finding the right lecture-room. First of all, we encountered an irascible porter, moustacheod with twiddles like the last German Emperor. Of the lecture itself, no one knew anything at all, least of all the porter; and I recall my indignation – kept with difficulty in check – that the most humble lackey was not bursting with excitement that the great poet was due shortly to arrive. On the contrary, the name, even after insistent repetition, meant nothing to anybody, and the additional information 'the poet – you know, the *poet*!' – far from jogging their memories, tended, to my bafflement, to diminish their interest. It was only by chance that, after wandering through the dismal, grubby green, peeling corridors, like those of a decaying hospital, we reached the library, where the lecture was billed to take place. Already there had assembled a few people, mostly academic figures, with Professor F. S. Boas, his moustache (this was an era of moustaches) encircling his mouth like a corona, occupying the chairman's seat. On the right of a room much longer than broad, my eye was on the door. Punctually to the moment, a tall figure in a large lightish-brown overcoat, American cut, swept into view, pausing to verify that he had hit upon the right place. Seeing Boas, whom he evidently knew, and smiling in recognition, he strode in. I at once recognized the 'round of his skull', the abundant brown hair, glossy with brilliantine, and the accurate slashed parting. The yellowish parchment skin was almost wholly unlined. With him was a short woman who seemed to melt into the audience, and on whom I bestowed no more than perfunctory attention.

The chairman, with many 'er-ah' interpolations, introduced the speaker as someone with a 'great reputation'. It reminded me that, at this stage, Eliot had written, with the exception of *The Four Quartets*, almost all his great poetry, and much of his best prose. When he rose to speak, it was with a steady propulsive movement, and I could not help noting the contrast between his spare, athletic figure and the tousled slumped pedants who had come to listen to him. He had a direct look, assisted by face-confidence. He articulated well, and he improvised an opening paragraph in which he stated that Marston was in many ways a difficult writer, and one from whom he had been able to steal only twice. The remark brought a laugh, as one of the subjects of contention and censure had been Eliot's habit, a unique one, of incorporating in his verse odd lines from other people. ('Immature poets imitate : mature poets steal'.) The practice later became common, but with much less success, witness Richard Aldington. Although Eliot was a beautiful verse reader, and the more so because there was no artifice – and certainly no Yeatsian 'low drone' – he experienced difficulty with lines,

> The black jades of swart night trot foggy rings
> 'Bout heaven's brow,

where 'trot foggy rings' stumped him momentarily, and he inserted, with a slow smile that creased his brow, the equally slowly delivered words – 'some of Marston's lines are difficult to read' – which, plain statement though it was, achieved by the slight drawl, the remnant of his southern accent, much greater effect than it could otherwise have done.

The paper, dated in the *Selected Essays* as belonging to 1934 and obviously much revised, was what Boas declared it to be, 'a work of art'. W. J. Lawrence, in broad Scottish accent, and Percy Allen, added, among others, their comments, both with considerable brio; and Boas announced the discovery of new facts about Marston's life, which Eliot duly noted down on the back of an envelope. The information brought a sudden smile to his face, the lips curving, symmetrically, but revealing irregular and nicotine-stained teeth.

Reading the essay in its final form, I realized how much thought had gone into it, and how it contained clues to Eliot's own methods of composition, including those to be exploited in the later drama. He spoke of 'the doubleness of the action' of poetic drama at its most profound, a 'pattern behind the pattern' of the kind that

> we perceive in our own lives only at rare intervals of inattention and detachment, drowsing in the sunlight. It is a pattern drawn by what the ancient world called fate: subtilized by Christianity into mazes of delicate Theology; and reduced again by the modern world into crudities of psychological or economic necessity.

These words have been open to inspection for half a century, but you have no idea what an impact they made at the time, or how extraordinarily stimulating it was to find a literary critic who could pronounce with such authority on matters beyond most 'literary' men's compass, or even conception. Moreover, the passage just quoted has, like much of Eliot, worn well because he was talking, especially in the final sentence, about matters that have become still more relevant. And here was the man himself uttering the words. They included some references to the French neuro-psychologists Ribot and Janet, of the University of Nancy, which he evidently struck out, but which, as one who hung upon his words, I vividly recall. This leads me to hope that the printed version may, in this and in other cases, be checked with the original, if it has survived; for I am convinced that some gems would thereby be recovered. At any rate, my mind, then I suppose at its most receptive, found the talk, by one who looked so much more alive than most of the audience, vibrating at several levels at once, as I was later to perceive happen with so much of Eliot. Nor did I fail to note another of his characteristic habits, that of using one work to shed light on another. He spoke of a

> Marston tone, like the scent of a flower, which by its peculiarity sharpens our appreciation of other dramatists as well as bringing appreciation of itself, as experiences of gardenia or zinnia refine our experiences of rose or sweet-pea.

Again, to my mind, such sensory analogies make Eliot a poet much nearer to sensory experience than those held to be more overtly sensual, like Auden or Dylan Thomas. He had a keen olfactory sense, as his early poems or indeed his very last make clear: and his nostrils were always slightly flared. After the lecture, when comments were being called for, his otherwise smooth brow crinkled and his eyebrows rose, and then he would plunge in thought by directing his eyes to the ground. His gestures were minimal, but they seemed charged with significance.

Then, too soon for my liking, the session was over, and Eliot slid once more – I retain the word used in my diary, struggling as I did to find the *mot juste* – into his large overcoat, and left with the woman. Once outside, my mother, who had a talent for quiet manoeuvre, managed to convey to him that I wanted to ask him a question or two: and I still remember the tall figure pausing and bending over to listen, though I myself was a good six foot. Even with the boldness of youth, I felt a certain awe in his presence, which was never to leave me. I asked him when the three books he had mentioned in the preface to *For Lancelot Andrewes* would be coming out – *The School of Donne*, *The Outline of Royalism* and *Principles of Modern Heresy*. He nodded, smiled, and then, looking at the ground, shook his head. 'I did think of writing them at one time,' he said, 'but now I've changed my mind. Perhaps I'll write something else. I'll try.' Another enquirer then need his attention, but what then took my attention was the short fidgety figure hovering at his side. As she had her face half hidden by a scarf, I could not make out her features, but I noticed that she kept plucking him by the sleeve, as if impatient of the homage he was receiving. To this he appeared to pay no attention whatever. Even though I knew nothing of her at that time, my impression was that she was a bundle of nerves. I recall them going off together, a forlorn pair. This was my first and, so far as I know, my last view of Vivien Eliot.

On 8 December 1931, in the middle of an economic crisis, I took the train to Oxford with Burke Trend. He was to sit for a classical scholarship at Merton: I had switched at the last minute from English to History and was aiming for a scholarship at Brasenose. As this is not an autobiography, I omit details, and confine myself to saying that Burke got the top scholarship at his college and I won a Hulme Exhibition at mine. Seeing that I had prepared so little and have never been good at examinations, this was a source of surprise to me. Burke's success, the prelude to so much else, did not come as a surprise at all. The result was that both of us had the best part of a year at our disposal before going up. I at once sat down to reading all the books that my concentration on topics such as the Tudors and Peter the Great (of which for some reason I had made myself something of an expert) had prevented me from sampling.

One book that came my way was the recently published *Politics and the Younger Generation* by A. L. Rowse, a Fellow of All Souls. It was Percy Ewen who, in addition to so much else, had stimulated my interest in politics. Indeed, he seemed so well informed, and in receipt of so much up-to-date intelligence about both home and foreign affairs, and convinced of the way in which the country should be run, that we sometimes fancied that, one day, he would be summoned by the powers-that-be, desperate for guidance, to assume overall control. On the other hand, I was by this time so deeply read in Eliot – which included studying from cover to cover every issue of *The Criterion* that arrived at the Reference Library in Croydon, and in particular the Commentaries signed 'T. S. E.' – that my views began to take a direction totally different from those of Ewen, which were predictably left-wing. No wonder that when I began reading A. L. Rowse, with his sustained eristic, I found myself even more in disagreement with the left; for in those days he well merited Eliot's description of him as 'our ferocious friend'. Hardly had I finished the book, or even before, but I began writing a sustained refutation chapter by chapter. For this task I considered myself qualified at least to the extent of being decidedly of the younger generation. It proved to be the longest essay I had written: in point of exuberance it was perhaps the best I ever wrote. I am sure it was over-confident and in many ways naive. I decided to call it 'The Younger Generation and Politics'; and because Rowse's book had been published by Faber and Faber, I wrote a letter to that firm explaining that I was a schoolboy and therefore of the younger generation, and that I wanted to 'answer' Rowse's book if possible in the Criterion Miscellany series. To this I received an answer

> E.W.F. Tomlin Esq.,
> Kylemore,
> 157 Brighton Road,
> Purley.   March 22nd 1932.
>
> Dear Sir,
>   Thank you very much for your interesting letter of the 17th. Your suggestion is attractive, and if you are writing the pamphlet anyhow we should like very much to see it. But we have so many

commitments on hand for the Criterion Miscellany that we could not possibly commission anything further.
  Yours faithfully,
   F. Wilberforce.
    Faber & Faber Ltd.

Although I must have been aware that Eliot was in publishing, I did not know at which house; nor could I imagine that a man of his eminence could be other than a lofty adviser or consultant. Nor of course did I know that F. Wilberforce (Lord Wilberforce's sister) was Eliot's secretary. Nevertheless, to have one's letter described as 'interesting', one's suggested project as 'attractive', and the final version one that the firm wanted very much to see, were gratifying to one who had hitherto regarded publishers as remote people who apparently spent most of their time sending out rejection letters. I did not bother too much about the negative ending of the letter, but set to work. That summer, when John Garrett was still a new master at Whitgift, we went at his initiative – that is, Paul Crowson, Peter Shaw, Philip Martin and myself – to the Canterbury Festival, where we saw Tennyson's *Becket*, so soon to be superseded by the Eliot play. I think I confided to John Garrett – whose great gift was enthusiasm and perhaps greater gift was to make us feel for the first time adults – that I had been writing my own 'tract for the times', because he knew Rowse personally. Meanwhile, Percy Ewen, having borrowed my copy of Rowse's book, admired it for the very reasons that I held it in abhorrence. Another excursion that summer was one I made with Burke Trend to Haywards Heath, where we were delegates at a Church of England conference for young people. Burke was at first reluctant to go, as he was at that time an agnostic, but I am glad that he accompanied me. Here we met the Archbishop of York, William Temple, from whom I had first heard Eliot's name; Christie, soon to be made head of Repton, to whom we may have introduced it; and, among others, a young man from Blundells who, as we quickly ascertained, was as enthusiastic about Eliot as I was. I also seem to remember that he was a Buddhist. I mention this in order to underline how the young had taken Eliot as their literary champion, replacing Thomas Hardy, who, as Middleton Murry and many others testified, was during the last decades of his life the Grand Old Man of English Letters. The later Yeats had not yet penetrated our world.

It was in June 1932 that I finally decided that my essay was more or less in shape, and so I dispatched it, a wad of handwritten foolscap, to Fabers.

I did not at that time anticipate anything dramatic; but to my astonishment, there dropped on the mat of our house in Purley on 12 July 1932, a letter about the essay signed by none other than T. S. Eliot himself.

It read as follows

> Dear Mr. Tomlin,
>
> I have read with much interest your essay on the Younger Generation and Politics. Although I am more than doubtful of the possibility of such an essay from a publisher's point of view I was much impressed by your thinking and lucid gift of exposition: I should be very glad if you could find the time to call here and discuss it with me. I suppose that your school work will make this impossible until the end of July, but I expect to be in London throughout August. I will retain the manuscript until I hear from you.
>
> Yours sincerely,
> T. S. Eliot.

The receipt of this letter was, I need hardly say, one of the most momentous occasions of my life – what I am now doing in my eighth decade was partly determined (it is curious to reflect) then and there. That he should wish to see me was sufficiently gratifying. I had always wanted to be, among other things, a writer, and it looked as if my career in that field were about to begin. I immediately replied asking him to name a day, and back came the reply dated 14 July suggesting Wednesday 20 July. Events moved rapidly in those days.

My mother, who always warmed to my enthusiasms and who had been very taken with Eliot when we met him at King's, accompanied me to Russell Square and, so far as I know, walked round that oasis of quiet throughout my interview. This was quite like her: she lived in and through her children, and I do not suppose that any other kind of life ever occurred to her as worth living. As for me, my first personal contact with Fabers was with Ethel Swan, always known as Miss Swan, who inhabited a little box, like an old-fashioned Turkish bath, facing the lift and with whom I came to associate the firm's continuity. Justly so: because, as became apparent when she retired in 1973, after 47 years as receptionist/telephonist, she had acquired considerable personal knowledge of the staff, not least of Eliot. She greatly respected him, and she was aware of something of his troubles, having to handle a tearful and sometimes drugged Vivien. He in turn greatly respected her, called her Swannie, and did her many kindnesses. She was one of those faithful subordinates who wield much greater power than they ever realize. The lift which I was invited to use, knocking and straining on its way to the fourth floor, seems to have remained permanently in that condition, since I never knew it in any other. It did go down but it was quicker to walk. An obscure door confronted me, on which was fixed a brass plate bearing the name 'T. Stearns' – brought, I later gathered, from his maternal grandfather's office in St Louis, Missouri. I knocked on the door and heard a deep 'Come in'. I advanced into a rather dingy room. There he was, in glasses, I noticed, which partially detracted from the direct look, as they flashed disconcertingly. The city suit was very well pressed, with the silk handkerchief flopping out of the breast pocket. My eyes settled first upon the piles of books on the floor, like stalagmites, and then upon the curled and faded snapshots, unframed, on the mantelpiece. One was of a boy in a Red Indian headdress: I wondered if it were himself. The Eliot I then formally met, tall and grave and measured in speech, was in all but the most superficial physical traits the man I knew for the next 34 years. He did not present so young an appearance as I had remembered from the earlier meeting (of which it did not occur to me to remind him), perhaps because of the glasses; but, judging from what I was later to learn, this was hardly surprising. But he was no less well-groomed, his sleek, abundant hair, which was never to thin with age or hardly to change in colour, being pomaded as usual and in the fashion of those days, set off the well-defined parting and the wedge of hair on the left, which on most people's brows fall away too sharply to accommodate. Except in later life, when the hair no longer possessed the old sheen, he always seemed, on meeting, as if he had just come from the barber's. The rather dark room, though no doubt bigger than it seemed, was cluttered, mostly with new books. On this occasion he took a chair to the left of his no less cluttered desk – whereas on later meetings he would sit in his desk chair, swivelled round – and placed me to the right, facing the window. I at once began to find myself at my ease. True, there was still the wonder that there had issued from this man, manipulating pen, pencil (the beginning of *Ash Wednesday* was jotted down on the back of an envelope) or more likely typewriter, those extraordinary poems; but he seemed, at that first prolonged encounter, to be able to place himself on my level without the smallest impression of *de haut en bas*. And this, though heaven knows he must sometimes have been a trifle bored and I often knew him to be dog-tired, was so far as I was concerned, his habitual manner.

As he had so little small talk, which no doubt tended to make him shy and aloof in company, he began at once to refer to my essay. This he approached by way of first commending its legibility. Not at that time possessing a typewriter and belonging as I did to perhaps the last generation to be compelled to write legibly, I had drafted and copied fair a quite presentable manuscript. The fact interested him, because he had lately been afflicted, so he told me, with writer's cramp. By way of demonstration he splayed his fingers slowly. When he wrote down some words at the end of the interview, I noticed that he pressed the pen hard upon the paper, as if he were making incisions instead of inscribing the surface. In the normal way, this produced a very pleasing hand, exactly suited to the ordered prose, just as F. R. Leavis's calligraphic rendering of an electro-cardiogram exactly mirrored a prose of sub-Henry James quality. This led on to his repeating the commendation of my work which he had done in his letter. Today I put this down largely to a wish to encourage a beginner; but at the time, coming from so distinguished a writer, it seemed impossibly high praise. With regard to what he had been good enough to call my 'thinking', he remarked, with a touch of a smile, 'You're on the right side'. This was in allusion to my critique of the armchair Marxism of the period – though, as we now know, it was not all armchair – and the current habit, which today may seem difficult to imagine, of subscribing to the creed without troubling to make acquaintance with the canonical scriptures. Again, largely owing to Percy Ewen's example, I had buried myself in a translation of *Das Kapital*, admittedly following this with speedy exhumation: for I cannot think that anyone not deliberately undergoing penance will have read more than the first of the three tomes. Eliot felt quite sure that few of the young communists had read as much of the Marxist Bible as I obviously had, and this made him chuckle. Although a critique of leftist ideology was very much needed, he felt that my essay was at once too long for a pamphlet and too short for a volume. In any case – and this was said looking firmly at the ground with a last-minute glance up and a quizzical smile – he did not consider that the best way to 'start me off' was by publishing a commentary on 'a bad book'. Coming from the book's publisher, this struck me as rather a bold thing to say. My copy, scored over and commented page by page, has disappeared, like so many other volumes I had wished for sentimental reasons to keep. But the handwritten essay, with Eliot's own marginal comments, is before me as I write, though except for a glance or two, I have never re-read it in its entirety.

He said that he would like to have another look at the text in case it might prove suitable for splitting up into an article or two. In this connection, he used the words *disjecta membra*; and I recall the stress on the first syllable of *membra*, followed by a good rolled 'r'. Meanwhile, some 'trepanning' might be necessary. He would be happy to consider anything else I had available for *The Criterion*. As I had hardly dared to think of becoming a contributor to that periodical, this was ample compensation for any disappointment I might feel over the issue of the essay itself, which I had secretly hoped might still be acceptable for the 'Criterion Miscellany' series, in which *Thoughts after Lambeth* had originally appeared. When he learnt that I was to go up to Oxford in the autumn, he was all the more concerned that I should not want to produce anything calculated to offend the authorities there. At all costs I was not to 'rush into print'. The Marxism I was attacking had become an orthodoxy among many of the young academics; and an undergraduate would not do himself much good – and might incur positive disapproval – if, on arrival, he became identified with the opposition, however minor a figure he might be.

In later life, A. L. Rowse was to become a friend, but he tended, at that time, to hold views which he could not imagine anyone in his right mind opposing. These views were not merely Marxist in politics but a form of 'scientific humanism' in ethics and philosophy; and such views I found as uncongenial then as, perhaps with greater reason, I do now. From what Eliot told me, he (Rowse) had some idea that, with persuasion, he could convert Eliot himself to socialism, which, seeing that the latter had years earlier come to the conclusion that a secular outlook must inevitably lead to despair, was a forlorn hope. What I found interesting during that first interview was that Eliot, while certain that Marxism and indeed any form of totalitarianism was a dead end, had no alternative 'right wing' solution to put forward. He never thought in terms of solutions or wings, least of all solutions by either revolution or reaction. In fact, I think he suspected that anyone who had an 'answer' to the economic problem, as to the spiritual problem which to some extent it masked, had not understood the 'question': and the question was what made life both endurable and worth living at all. A social change-round, quite apart from the chaos it would bring about, would, in his opinion amount to an evasion of the problem. He said this in the quiet way he had when enunciating a fundamental point. There was no gesture, (Ezra Pound had something to say about that in his Introduction to Remy de Gourmont's *Physique de l'Amour*) merely the adoption of the posture of Rodin's 'Thinker' slightly hunched, the round head ducking between his shoulders, with the glance upwards at the end of the remark, with a nod or two to drive the point home.

In those days, social pundits were very quick with 'solutions'. And I suppose I may have thought that, when Eliot touched on the social 'crisis', he would have some solution up his sleeve – one that he had not outlined in his writings – and that I might become privy to it. When he said 'I don't see what is to be done', I remember feeling just a little disappointed. But the reaction was momentary. I at once recalled the line in *Ash Wednesday* – 'Teach us to sit still', and the evocation and elaboration of that same line in *Thoughts after Lambeth*:

> Not only Youth but Middle Age is on the march; everybody at least according to Fleet Street, is on the march: it does not matter what the destination is, the one thing contemptible is to sit still.

There was something doggedly independent in this attitude; but I felt that, compared with his younger contemporaries who were busy enrolling in various political causes – 'taking a ticket', as Eliot put it – and putting their faith in instant remedies, above all 'Revolution', his attitude had a kind of stoic nobility about it. Some years later, in February 1940, he was to write that 'we can have very little hope of contributing to any immediate social change: we are more disposed to our hope in modest local beginnings than in transforming the whole world at once'. Here was a tenable political attitude. It did not mean that we should refrain from action. What it meant was that there was no one, final, permanent remedy, least of all a violent one.

He then spoke of the difficulty of accomplishing consistent and remunerative reading, not just the 'latest' books but the classics; he said he was satisfied if he read one Greek play a year.

A curious feature of this meeting is that I cannot recall anything that I myself said. I suppose I made an adequate impression, because he told me to write or to come and see him whenever I wanted. This was generous, because he was exceptionally busy on two fronts, public and private; and there would come a time when he was so heavily engaged that meetings had to be arranged weeks ahead. I realized that it was time I took my leave; but, seeing my hesitancy, he told me that he would be away in the United States from September to May, but that I was to write to him there and send him anything I fancied. He had not visited the land of his birth for seventeen years. Taking a visiting card from his wallet, he put down his address in firm characters: Eliot House, Cambridge, Mass. It was then that I noticed the pressure he applied in doing so. But he promised to write to me again before his departure.

On emerging from the russet-coloured building, I reflected how, in a comparatively short time, Eliot, simply by talking in a slow, rather plodding way, had managed to communicate so much more than one who discharged a torrent of words, many of them superfluous. I also marvelled at the manner in which, in talking to me on the subject of my essay, he seemed to dismiss from his mind everything else. He made me feel, emerging from 'The Ignominy of boyhood', that I mattered and even mattered to him. Vague rumours had circulated that he had private troubles, which poems like *The Waste Land* and *The Hollow Men* had reflected. What I did not know was that at that particular time, he was going through an acute personal crisis, the worst he was to suffer. There was the anguish of having to decide to leave Vivien. On account of his harassing daily life, he was unable to prepare the lectures at Harvard and at the University of Virginia until he had actually boarded the ship; and, talking of harassment, his vexations continued until the very moment of embarkation; for Vivien managed to get hold of and conceal his passport (it appears that she locked it in the bathroom), and he was obliged to return by taxi to recover it. The wonder is not that the lectures, at least as published, were not up to his expectations (as he later avowed) but that they are as good as they are. Years later I expressed my admiration for both *The Use of Poetry and The Use of Criticism* and *After Strange Gods*. 'There were some brilliant paragraphs', he said resignedly. To my mind, *After Strange Gods* contains prose of a clarity and grace that he rarely equalled, and I was sorry for more reasons than one that he never consented to its republication.

In view of his kindly warnings about stating views in print that might not endear me to my tutors, I began to cast about for a subject less directly political. In fact, I need not have worried: so far as my own instructors were concerned, they were on the whole a disappointing lot, as much lacking in drive and stimulation as the Whitgift masters were enlivening. But that is to anticipate. Apart from Eliot himself, the writer who, though recently dead, had been steadily increasing in reputation, was D. H. Lawrence. Moreover, he was sufficiently daring or shocking, according to the standards of the time, to attract the attention of the young and, as because of that attraction, slightly to scandalize the old. I decided to write a study of him. These thoughts passed rapidly through my mind as, declining to use the lift, I descended the stairs. Otherwise I was in so abstracted a state as almost to forget to make a gesture of farewell to Miss Swan.

My mother, who had all this time been waiting for me, was as anxious to hear my account of what had happened as I was to retail it. She had taken to Eliot. His attractiveness, his gracious manner, his punctiliousness and politeness, and his flashes of humour: these she found endearing. Like most mothers she thought her son in some way specially endowed, and had convinced herself that Eliot must have come to a similar conclusion or would speedily do so. It does no harm to a young man to have one utterly dependable ally, and the most dependable of all is the maternal ally. There will be enough detractors in due course to demolish his conceit. We travelled home on top of a bus; and as 'on top' meant in those days 'uncovered', this was invariably an exhilarating experience, provided the weather were reasonable. Moreover, conversation, unlike that carried on below, could be uninhibited. Our talk was, as often with that dependable ally, of the future, which seemed to hold out infinite promise: and by the time we reached home, we had convinced each other that that day had been the start of something auspicious. In other words, we had had as I came to realize, a typical mother-and-son confabulation, in which the son – especially perhaps the younger son as I was – is as much aware of the mother's exaggerated estimate of his abilities as he is anxious to do his best to fulfil her expectations. The day was nevertheless important because, in addition, I had received Eliot's valued encouragement; and encouragement both at home and from such a source was, at that juncture, a combined gift of inestimable price. If I may venture on an additional beatitude: blessed are they that encourage, for they shall earn more gratitude than they will ever know.

Although I had hoped that Eliot might publish part of my Rowse essay in *The Criterion*, or in its entirety in the *Criterion Miscellany*, I could see that this would be difficult, and perhaps undesirable.

The reader would need to have read Rowse's book; and there was no public then, as there was later, for youthful effusions as such. I realized that I would be better occupied on the Lawrence project, because everyone was beginning to read Lawrence. Meanwhile, the manuscript of the political essay was to become precious because of the marginal pencilled comments which Eliot had made. When he had said that he would read the whole thing again, I knew that he meant it: first, because of his punctiliousness, and secondly because he was, as I found, almost pedestrianly thorough in all that he did. The slapdash and the cursory were totally foreign to his nature: in which respect he differed from some members of the intelligentsia, as I was to find on entering the university.

He was as good as his word. At the beginning of October, just before I went up to Oxford, my spirits were again raised as a result of receiving a letter which was in many ways no less encouraging than the first. What struck me was that he should have taken the trouble to get in touch again when he was obviously more than usually busy. He scarcely knew me, and there must have been many other young people whose work showed far greater promise; but when he said that he had had another look at my manuscript I knew that whatever his disclaimer he had given it close attention, as later events were to prove. He wrote

28th September 1932

Dear Mr. Tomlin,

 I have looked over your Ms. again, but I am very sorry to say that I have not had the leisure to study it carefully enough to make any suggestions. I am leaving for America to-morrow and am afraid, therefore, that I must return the Ms. without further comment. I must add, however, that my opinion of it is in no way diminished on re-reading. If you have the time to adapt part of it in any way, or to write any other short essay, I hope you will let me see it. Please write to me direct at Eliot House, Cambridge, Mass., USA. I dare say that the first few terms at Oxford you will find yourself too busy with other matters, but remember that I shall be immensely interested and I hope you will come and see me after I am back next May.
    Yours sincerely,
    ME.
     pp. T.S. Eliot

P.S. This letter has had to be held over as I was doing Mr Eliot's work while his secretary was away, and was unable to obtain your address.

He went to considerable trouble in another respect. He wrote to several of his friends at Oxford, among others to Father Martin D'Arcy and to Leslie Rowse himself; and, as I found out in due course, he wrote and spoke about me kindly to others. This was to lead, among much else, to a meeting with F. R. and Queenie Leavis at Cambridge, which, by some sort of providence, led to a friendship which remained unimpaired through the next 40 years. Eliot had spoken to me about *Scrutiny* as a possible place for my work, and in fact I was to write articles for that lively journal before I became a contributor to *The Criterion*.

When I returned to school, Percy Ewen, John Garrett and Harry Woodgate wanted to know how the great man had struck me, and – less easily ascertained – how I had struck the great man. In some of them I detected a faint note, if not of envy, then of surprise that their still raw pupil had gained such attention in that quarter. The one in whom this feeling seemed uppermost took the opportunity, some time later, of writing to Eliot for a contribution to a drama magazine which he then edited, using my name without consultation as a reference. It worked. Eliot, though extremely busy, wrote an interesting article for him on 'Religious Drama and the Church'. The publication was called *Rep*, the journal of the newly-formed Croydon Repertory Company, and, so far as I know, the article has not been referred to anywhere save here. In his covering letter Eliot generously referred to me as 'one of whom I have great hope'.

It was nevertheless to John Garrett that we owed the visit to Whitgift of A. L. Rowse himself. He came to speak to our exclusive little society, 'The Fanatics', a title taken from a play by a young local writer called Malcolm Muggeridge. With his shock of black hair and fierce if ascetic countenance, Rowse though gentle in private, was in public something of a firebrand. In a violent denunciation of our social system, he referred to Eliot as politically a simpleton, though he did so in the most friendly terms. Afterwards, when I was introduced to him, he spoke of Eliot's 'simplicity', by which I think he meant his humility. One of his spiritual directors, The Reverend Frank Hillier, spoke of his 'truly childlike heart', which was not incompatible with manliness.

Otherwise I did not trumpet my new acquaintance, exciting though it was. Indeed, I did not for some little time even tell my closest school friends about it. In those days, the taboo on swanking was particularly powerful. It was as powerful as the taboo on swotting. You had to work, but you must not be seen to be working – overmuch. So that although I began to read many of the books which Eliot's writings had brought to my attention – especially Frazer's *Golden Bough* and Jessie Weston's *From Ritual to Romance*, T. E. Hulme's *Speculations* and the much less accessible works of Charles Maurras, quite apart from the poetry of Laforgue and Corbière – I did not parade my industry. What I did parade, with an assertiveness which my companions must have found puzzling and perhaps a source of comic relief, was a new set of beliefs and loyalties.

Today, half a century later, it may be difficult for some people to realize what a renewed impetus Eliot gave to the cause of belief in England, in the otherwise intellectually dreary 1930s. For of the two best known Christian apologists, G. K. Chesterton and Dean Inge, Chesterton was regarded as something of a joke (though I now think he was much more than that), and Dean Inge, as he himself said, was not so much a pillar of the Church as a couple of columns in the *Evening Standard*. And in any case, the two – the one Catholic and the other intransigently Protestant – were at loggerheads for most of the time. Eliot was in a different category. Here was both a 'new voice' in literature, and an intellect at least as powerful as that of Matthew Arnold, Ruskin or Newman of the nineteenth century; indeed, for an exact parallel, he could be compared with some of the major intellects of the thirteenth century. And he had come out of America. To us, the United States, though a country where 'all good fallacies go when they die', was not the place whence great intellects had as a rule sprung. The mentors that had held authority for long were now cut down to size: Wells, Shaw and Russell; Whitehead, Eddington and Jeans; Freud, Jung and Adler: Middleton Murry and and Huxley brothers. Here in *Thoughts after Lambeth*, for example (a much weightier document than its length would suggest), was a wit capable of demolishing the pretensions of humanists, atheists and modernists alike. Here were remarks that seemed to afford a new sort of mental liberation. For 'anyone who has moved in intellectual circles and comes to the Church experiences a sense of exhilaration'. Then there was the striking remark in an article published in

Wyndham Lewis's *Enemy* (1927), that 'Christianity will probably continue to modify itself with something that can be believed in. I do *not* mean conscious modifications like Modernism, which have the opposite effect'. And finally, in the most profound essay called 'Second Thoughts on Humanism (1921)', there was the assertion that you must either be a naturalist or a supernaturalist. 'There is no avoiding that dilemma'. And there isn't.

Coming from a layman, such aperçus brought about in some of us a kind of mental Copernican Revolution, the importance of which I have rarely heard stressed: namely, the possibility of intellectual conviction taking precedence over emotional gropings towards faith, instead of the emotions waiting for an intellectual guarantee that 'science' might some day provide: which might mean waiting indefinitely. It was no longer a question simply of 'being religious'. Anyone, including the unbeliever, could be religious. It was quite the fashion. What was more difficult, but far more satisfying, was to arrive at a view of life which the intellect could consent to, and the emotions gradually learn to accommodate. It was that which Eliot, if I am not mistaken, found exhilarating. It did not take the form of euphoria, or the kind of soul-baring made popular about that time by the Oxford Group.

As I say, I still find *Thoughts after Lambeth*, which Wyndham Lewis tried for some reason to knock out of the ring in *Men without Art*, one of the most readable and powerful of Eliot's prose works. For its argument still applies.

> To put the matter bluntly on the lowest level, it is not to anyone's interest that religion should disappear. If it did, many compositors would be thrown out of work: the audiences of our best-selling scientists would shrink to almost nothing; and the typewriters of the Huxley Brothers would cease from tapping.

It is superb satire, and the kind of satire of which we are still much in need. And if the Huxleyan typewriters have ceased from tapping, it is only because their successors make use of the word-processor. Religion is still the fashion, and those who take leave of it claim to be the most religious of all. Eliot would have called this retention of religious *emotion* without an object a pathological condition.

CHAPTER TWO

I realized how much Eliot was coming to mean to my generation when I attended the Duke of York's camp, where public school boys joined with 'working-class' boys in an experiment which proved more successful than we had expected. Two Manchester grammar school boys I met there, Miller and Bailey, had devoured Eliot's poetry, though they had not espoused his politics or his beliefs. At Oxford, where I was to meet Bailey again (Merton), they became vocal members of the Labour Club, and we drifted apart. But I was able to see how Eliot, the poet, could captivate many, perhaps a majority, who shared neither his politics nor his faith, and whose addiction did nothing to alter their views on these subjects. And this seemed to me to say a great deal about the status, indeed the use, of poetry. A striking example was John Strachey, whose extreme left-wing viewpoint (at that time) did not prevent him writing a moving passage about *The Waste Land* in his book *The Nature of Capitalist Crisis* (1935). Even more striking an example was Prince Mirsky's book, *The Bourgeois Intelligentsia of Great Britain*, published originally in Moscow, in which Eliot, whose opinions were as far removed from those of the author as could be, was singled out as the writer most worthy of contemporary attention.

Finally, there were transient contacts made at Officers' Training Corps camps, at Tidworth or at Strensall in Yorkshire, where it always seemed to rain, especially during night ops. This weather made it possible, though we usually kept it to ourselves, to establish some identity of interest: and I remember encountering an Eliot addict from some other company in the most unlikely circumstance. We were wise to keep our interest secret. To talk of poetry in such a context would never do. Tents were let down, debagging took place, and limbs were daubed with paint, for far less serious offences.

Today, the gap between school and university, being wider, is filled usually with prolonged travel, often to parts of the world to which we, with few facilities and less cash, could not have hoped to venture. In my case, the only foreign journey I made, apart from a dash or two across the Channel, was with some other Whitgiftians to the Rhineland. It was organized by one of those 'Friendship' associations which proliferated before the war, not least with a view to maintaining relations, already precarious, with Germany. Here we found ourselves thrown into the company of a party of girls. With two of these, no doubt because they were pretty, I sought to ingratiate myself; and I did so by forcibly introducing them to Eliot's works – together with the music of Vaughan Williams, which had always seemed to be his musical equivalent – and maintaining the pressure until they gracefully yielded. I remember our drifting past the Lorelei, and the thickset Germans on board bursting into song, and so interrupting my recitation of the opening lines of *The Waste Land*, a passage which I had chosen because of its evocation of Germany. What these contacts proved was that Eliot's poetry, however the tastes were acquired, appealed equally to women and to men, which time has served to confirm. And a decade later, there was a girl at Queen Anne's School, Caversham, whose affection for Eliot's poetry led to a devotion of a more permanent nature.

I am told that, during and immediately after the last war, a poet to excite a similar enthusiasm among the young – a line of the verse declaimed in one room being capped by another along the passage for instance – was Dylan Thomas. But, apart from the fact that Thomas had in my view a minor talent, and that Wales, where the enthusiasm was most strong, had produced poets (and Thomas's for that matter) of higher calibre, I cannot believe that the young bounder evoked a devotion comparable to that commanded by Eliot. To my mind, Eliot was a great poet who was also a great man, a great human being; and that could not possibly be said of Dylan Thomas, as it could hardly be said of poets far superior to Thomas – Thomas Hardy or W. B. Yeats. The encomiums of Thomas, the man, launched by critics like the late John Davenport ('I knew him well'), accompanied as they were by onslaughts against the fuddy-duddys who deplored his moral conduct, leave me with an unimpressive figure, as I am similarly left by a reading of Thomas's letters, and now his widow's reminiscences. Unlike many people of an eminence comparable to Eliot's – and this is one of the justifications for a memoir such as the present – the reputation, far from dipping after his death, has steadily risen, and this despite some attempt on the part of a few detractors to denigrate his character.

Consequently, it was above all Eliot the charismatic character, Eliot the intellectual leader, that enlisted so much of our enthusiasm. As Dr Demant said in his very fine address at the Requiem for Eliot at St Stephen's on 17 February 1965, 'he was the most vigorous interpreter of this age to itself'. Moreover, a guru has to be young enough to be new and old enough to be revered; and Eliot qualified on both counts. Not that we failed to quote the verse, which was all the better when it left the page and which, like all true poetry, seemed to crave that levitation. During a winter journey when pre-war under-heated cars obliged us to put forward every effort to sustain our morale, Philip Martin, who was to become Chancellor of Chichester Cathedral, engaged me in an antiphonic contest in reciting *Ash Wednesday*. I often wondered whether anyone ever tried to do similarly with the poetry of William Empson, or other members of the obscurity-for-obscurity's-sake school.

To look back on one's youthful predilections is an amusing, if slightly wistful and melancholy, experience; but, except for the missionary zeal with which I exercised mine, I see no reason to regret my addiction. It was not more than briefly monomaniac, as I shall show. And it is surely more desirable to come under the influence of a man as big as Eliot than to be caught up, as today, with the little deities of the Pop World. This was a world which Eliot thought might take over the future, though it was 'a future in which we ought not to be interested'. Unfortunately, it is here.

That these latest developments, combined with all the preparations for Oxford, should have left me a trifle exhausted was not perhaps surprising. Besides, apart from the Lawrence study, I had worked very hard at writing an essay on 'Some Implications of the Materialist Theory of Art', which I had promised Eliot and which in due course I dispatched to Harvard for his attention. As most of the intelligentsia was espousing Marxism, I thought I would read up as much about and around it as I could. The essay was chiefly inspired – a word applicable to that work, if to few other Marxist writings – by Trotsky's *Literature and Revolution*. By the time I entered into residence at Brasenose, I was suffering from headaches, due as I now think to eyestrain; for I had come to devour books with a voracity which was probably injudicious, especially as some of them were not directly related to my studies. Elizabethan drama, yes; but Wyndham Lewis's *The Lion and the Fox*, no. Not, that is, if I wanted to please my tutors, for having switched from English to History, I later plumped for Modern Greats; and I suspected that neither the historians nor the Anglicists, still less the philosophers or economists, would approve of Wyndham Lewis. This was assuming that they had heard the name, or did not confuse him with D. B. Wyndham Lewis, a frequent occurrence. In any case, I soon found that my loyalties tended to provoke exasperation among dons for whom A. E. Housman was the 'latest' poet, and Eliot and Pound mere mountebanks. No doubt a more experienced young man would have conveyed his preferences with greater tact; but I remember reflecting how differently Eliot, or Leavis for that matter, or Wyndham Lewis himself, would have treated the too enthusiastic undergraduate; and I have since made up my mind that, unless the hero or heroine was a demonstrable fraud, I would not condemn even the most extreme youthful infatuation. For if the object were on the level assumed, the infatuation would subside into genuine regard, and, if not, it would be extinguished at the first sign of fallibility.

If old people who have themselves never pledged loyalties are tempted to ridicule the dedication of the younger generation, it is usually not so much out of superiority as out of pique, which is offended superiority. In the case of the dons, however, some few of them were not much older than myself; but of these, as of some languid elderly ones who seemed to have had no enthusiasms to lose, I encountered none whose company proved intellectually stimulating. My 'moral tutor' was a chemist with whom, try as I might, I could establish no satisfactory rapport, though he was a genial man with a liking for music. As to my philosophy tutor, he had the least enquiring mind, next after a Labour Lord trained in 'philosophy and scientific method', I have ever encountered. I therefore looked elsewhere; and I found a man who, apart from his outstanding gifts, happened to have known Eliot, because he had tutored him: R. G. Collingwood.

Meanwhile I was looking forward, though with cautious hopes, to receiving some news about my essay on Marxist Art. When it came about on 20 December 1932 it was the best Christmas present I could have been given. The content was in one sense negative, but to receive a letter from T. S. Eliot at all was a bonus. Dated 17

December 1932, the letter came from B-11, Eliot House, Cambridge, Mass., and I fancy that he had typed it himself.

> Dear Tomlin,
>
> I am sorry I did not acknowledge your ms. at once as I should have done, as it is manu- and not typescript. It seems to me a very able piece of work, and quite what I should expect; but I have had my hands too full to give it the detailed criticism that it merits. I hope to be able to attend to it soon after my return from a lecture-tour in January. Meanwhile, with most cordial good wishes for Christmas, I am,
>
> Yours very sincerely,
> T.S. Eliot

That he did give the essay (which I have never re-read) the attention he said it 'deserved', I was to learn in due course.

In view of the general attitude of the Senior Common Room, it was satisfactory to find, within a short while of beginning the first term, several fellow students at Brasenose who were Eliot enthusiasts. There was Gordon Phillips, who became an Anglican priest and who died a few years back partially estranged from the Church, and Martin Jarrett-Kerr, who, after a brilliant degree in English, also took orders, joined the Community of the Resurrection, and kept on with his literary studies. Although we were geographically separated for long periods, we maintained contact and have preserved a friendship to this hour. The third new friend, quite different in both character and temperament, was Michael Cullis, whom I first met at a gathering of the Brasenose Musical Society. He was extolling the merits of Delius's *Sea Drift* against a very loud rendering of the same. He first engaged my attention by revealing a close knowledge of the work of both Eliot and Pound, and a personal acquaintance with the latter. These and related interests, as well as a strong compatibility based on differences of temperament, have bound us together in lifelong friendship.

One day, working in the Radcliffe Camera library, and having ordered a copy of Eliot's translation of *Anabase* by St Jean Perse, I noticed a dark young man hovering near, who conveyed in a whisper that he too was interested in Eliot. His name was Harold Mason, who had come up to Oriel from Hull. This meeting was the beginning of an association which, with many gaps owing to our various travels, lasted for the next half century. Harold was more interested in I. A.

Richards than Eliot, and, being a Humian, did not share Eliot's outlook. He worked for some time on *Scrutiny*, and shared Leavis's early admiration for Eliot.

Eliot had written to A. L. Rowse about me, and he got in touch early, recollecting our meeting in Croydon. My first encounter with him at Oxford was on a walk we took round the city – this was more common a way of making closer acquaintance than it is now. Somewhat to my relief, I soon realized that Eliot had not mentioned my diatribe against *Politics and the Younger Generation*, but Rowse knew that I was not of his political persuasion. And as anyone not adhering to the Labour Party was classified as a reactionary, this was how he referred to me both to my face and to others, though always with a kind of impish geniality. It was as if I were a rather curious, if harmless, insect of an otherwise obsolete phylum. Of Eliot he was obviously very fond, and he was much gratified to be counted among the poet's friends. He spoke feelingly of the 'intense personal unhappiness' which had been the source of much of the verse. At the same time, more debatably, he expressed the view that, but for the personal tragedy, Eliot would never have turned for consolation to religion, or to royalism, or to similar 'reactionary' loyalties. On the contrary, he would no doubt have followed Rowse into the ranks of Labour. I reflected that Eliot seemed then and later as much in demand by the socialists as by the Catholics; it was under a socialist government that he received in 1948 the Order of Merit. Both teams were equally puzzled that he had not joined them long ago, or even cheered them from the side-lines. On the strength of Eliot's introduction, Rowse was good enough to keep in touch with me, and I several times went to tea at All Souls, my fellow-guests being, to a man (there were never any women), of Rowse's political allegiance. I felt that some of these young fellows, with their newly-acquired interest in 'the workers', were not a little puzzled by Rowse's description of the latter as 'the idiot people': a term which had begun to appear in his books, and which was repeated with a certain monotony even when, at the end of the war, he repudiated the left altogether. I felt that a man like Eliot would never talk of his fellow-men – the bulk of his fellow-men – like that. This change of view naturally made relations easier: which, together with my interest in Cornwall, promoted the pleasant acquaintanceship we later maintained.

Rowse's conversation afforded several glimpses of Eliot, one of which remained very much in my mind. He spoke of the occasion when, having lunch together in London, Eliot seemed to become more and more despondent about the state of the world and the human condition, until in his dejection he almost slumped over the table. This prompted Rowse to say: 'Come on, cheer *up*, Eliot!' at which he immediately braced himself, sat up straight, adjusted his tie, and smiled winningly, as he could so readily do. Despite divergences, Eliot must obviously have found Rowse's company stimulating; I suspect it was for just this capacity to revive his sometimes low spirits. In any case, Eliot enjoyed conversation, which did not have to be exclusively intellectual – he liked a bit of gossip – and Rowse was a good conversationalist. Eliot also enjoyed 'dining with the opposition', a phrase he often quoted from F. S. Oliver; and Rowse provided ample opportunity for that. He also liked good food, which Rowse, though accustomed to the high table at All Souls, may not for health reasons have been able sufficiently to appreciate. The truth is that Eliot was emphatically not a solitary, still less a misanthropic person, though circumstances were such that solitude – a solitude which, as he wrote, became 'harder to endure' – was forced upon him. In the strangely thin intellectual atmosphere of London in those days, conversation of a high quality was not easy to come by; and the opposition, subscribing to a faded Fabianism combined with an arid Marxism, was, unless represented by a man of Rowse's volatility, singularly uninteresting to dine with.

It was John Garrett, paying one of his regular visits to Oxford, who brought another admirer of Eliot round to my rooms, Nevill Coghill. Besides being a scholar of *Piers Plowman*, Coghill, a huge teddy bear of a man, was an expert in the drama; and these were the days before Eliot had turned to writing plays, except for the *Wanna go home, Baby* fragments, and before Coghill's own famous production. Meanwhile Garrett and Coghill had become admirers, and more recently friends, of the young W. H. Auden; and I recall that I clashed with Coghill on what I felt to be the disparity of talent between Auden and Eliot. He took the view that, just as Eliot had extended the scope of poetry, Auden had extended it still further. Auden was the kind of man, he declared roundly, who could write a poem about anything – even about the 'blue-bottles on a pile of steaming horse-shit'. This delicate image, I remember, delighted John Garrett. He seemed in his mind's eye to see this poem already in a kind of Platonic heaven, ready to descend with a plop on its rightful place in the anthologies. In those days, four-letter words did not enjoy the circulation that they do today, and I was as shocked at its utterance as I was repulsed by the image. I rather think that Coghill left, after this meeting, feeling that I was rather a solemn young prude.

One of the first Anglo-Catholic Congresses was held in 1933 at the Albert Hall, and Eliot had been billed to speak at it. I do not know how this should have happened, because his American visit had been fixed well in advance. The impression was given by one of the speakers that he had been delayed in returning home on account of some accident. This may have been a euphemism for personal worries connected with the planned legal separation from Vivien, and also to the need to keep his movements secret. I had no idea of that delay until I had taken my seat in the gallery – an insignificant layman in a very crowded auditorium of High Church personnel. At the beginning of the meeting, a letter from Eliot was read out by the Chairman, a bishop I believe, which I hope has been preserved, because it was a most interesting and witty document. I recall that Eliot had been 'introduced' as being 'poet, essayist, and Catholic', pronounced 'Kartholic'; for those were the days when it was the fashion to talk of 'Maas', often with a lingering over the 'M', so that the word had a (to me) rather off-putting nasal ring. Eliot began his letter, I recall, by saying that the general impression of the Church of England, or at least the Anglo-Catholic branch of it, was of a small group of laymen surrounded by a great host of clergy. I doubt whether, at this distance, I have got the words right: all I know is that he had a way of putting things that they immediately evoked mirth, and there was a gale of laughter. That the grave poet could so put the solemn audience in a good and receptive mood from the start was something of an achievement. Of the rest of the session I remember very little. Later that year, when he had first begun his attendance at St Stephen's, he delivered a very impressive address at the Anglo-Catholic summer school at Keble, Oxford, entitled 'Catholicism and the International Order'; but alas, I was unable to be present. Given that this took place a month after his return from America, when he must have been – and, from all accounts, was – in a state of considerable anxiety and even anguish, the finished and well-thought-out prose of that address, to say nothing of its wit, shows that he was able to lift his mind above personal considerations in a manner demonstrating the highest degree of self-discipline.

I wrote a letter or two to Eliot from Brasenose, one in June of some length. Possibly it was a little despondent in tone, as I still had not settled down so well as I had hoped. Moreover, I found the climate of Oxford extremely enervating. I knew that he had been away, and I and my family spent some of the vacation on a tour of the West Country, visiting Morwenstow, Cornwall, with which my life was later to become so closely bound up. He answered my letter on 23 September 1933:

> Dear Mr Tomlin,
> I should have answered your letter of 25th June, which awaited my return; but I did not see any immediate prospect of our meeting, as I have spent the summer out of London. I should be glad to hear from you. When do you go up again? It might be possible to fix a meeting some day when I was coming to town.
> I should be interested to know whether you have done any writing, and have written anything since your essay on 'Materialist Art'.
>   Yours sincerely,
>   T.S. Eliot.

I replied saying that I had been working on an essay provisionally entitled 'D. H. Lawrence and his Critics', an essay on the dimensions of 'The Younger Generation and Politics'. This information prompted him to write again on 7 October 1933:

> Dear Mr. Tomlin,
> I am extremely sorry that I could not arrange a day in town free enough from other engagements to be able to ask you to come and see me. I hope that it will be easier by the time of the Christmas vacation.
> Could you send me the Lawrence article to read? I should very much like to see it. I am of course considerably in accord with your views in 'Some Implications of the Materialist Conception of Art; nevertheless, and in spite of its admirable exposition, I did not feel sure that this was the right piece to start you off on. There is plenty of time. I think I had better send it back to you now, as it is your only copy, and we will discuss it again when we meet.
>   Yours sincerely,
>   T.S. Eliot.

What was encouraging about this letter was its indication that he wanted to launch me as a writer: which, though it might interest few other people, was of some interest to me, a drudging undergraduate.

For I was in no respect a 'brilliant' student; and although I wanted 'to write', as so many others do, I had in mind at that time a career in politics. And this was the beginning of that conflict between the man of thought and the man of action, if I can be said to be either, with which I was to be torn this way and that all my life. If I interject these personal remarks, it is because I always regarded Eliot as more than a mere literary influence, and therefore a figure about whom *any* testimony, even that of my own, was necessarily of value. I hoped he would like the Lawrence essay, to which I had applied myself in the hours left over from Modern Greats. I promptly sent it to him; and when he wrote about it in a letter of 7 December, I heaved a sigh of relief, because I was not sure of his attitude to Lawrence, and not altogether sure of mine either.

> Dear Mr. Tomlin,
> I have been meaning to write to you about your very interesting Lawrence essay, but a talk would be more satisfactory. This is just a line to acknowledge your note, and to ask you to let me know whether I shall find you at your Purley address after this? I should then be glad if you would lunch with me on the first day that we can both arrange.
> Yours in haste,
> T.S. Eliot.
> per TS.

I wrote back full of gratitude for the attention he had given the essay; and grateful I had reason to be. I also expressed the hope that, whatever might be arranged between us, he would also find the time to pay a visit to Oxford. One of the associations which had recently sprung up was the Phoenix Society – I cannot now recall at whose instance it was founded, nor the details of its constitution, but several distinguished writers had been invited down under its auspices, and we very much wanted to persuade Eliot to come. Being a friend, I was commissioned to issue the invitation, so I wrote to him in January 1934. On the 26th he replied:

> Dear Mr. Tomlin,
> Thank you very much for your kind letter of the 22nd. I shall be very glad to come to address the Phoenix Society when I can, but I am afraid that either this term or the summer term will be out of the question. The summer term is not a good time for such

occasions in any case, but I have work in hand which will occupy all of my spare time until June. I think that I could probably come in the Michaelmas term, if that suited the Society.

I must take the occasion for expressing my regret for not having been able to have a talk with you during the Christmas holidays. I should very much like to see you and talk over the Lawrence essay and other things, and if you should be coming up to town during the term, and could let me know a few days ahead, I think we could probably arrange a lunch. I hope that this may happen.
Yours sincerely,
T.S. Eliot.

As I kept few copies of my letters in those days, I do not know what occasioned the word 'kind'. All I know is that it was due to no artificial gush on my part; I have always lacked epistolary exuberance, to the regret of close friends. As to the Phoenix Society, I was later glad that Eliot was unable to come at that juncture. The Society disintegrated in consequence of a financial imbroglio, which involved two distinguished writers. One was of major importance, Wyndham Lewis, who must have suffered a moral lapse; the other was less distinguished, Herbert Read, who suffered the loss of his fee. Fortunately for me, I was appointed treasurer when all this was over; but I believe I am the only one living who is in possession of the full facts.

As to coming to talk with him, the phrase 'I hope that this may happen' was one that only Eliot could have employed. It was on a par with the line from 'Journey of the Magi' – 'It was [you may say] satisfactory'. This interjection of a slightly exaggerated formality of phrase characterized his conversation as well as his writing. It was often only after a *tête-à-tête* session with him that I would realize how capable he was of sustained, if often subdued, wit. I say 'subdued', because he hated showing off; he told me that he found Jean Cockeau's straining after effect scarcely tolerable. The careful choice of words, upon which wit depends, meant that I would come away not merely with wit but with wisdom too; and that is the reason why a single session with Eliot, which did not have to be solemn by any means, was more productive and lasting than a dozen sessions with some other persons of eminence. I felt nearer to him in his formality than in the expansiveness of others. By way of comparison, a few days in Paris looking after Bertrand Russell – who incidentally, could not have been a more easy official guest – gave me the opportunity of listening to him for long periods by myself (for an official programme leaves otherwise tedious gaps). But, despite his charm and fund of persiflage, I could not say I knew him the least bit more at the end than at the beginning. With the supposedly reticent Eliot it was quite the reverse.

Meanwhile, owing to Eliot's thoughtfulness in putting me in touch with persons whom he felt I would like to meet, I had received a letter from Father D'Arcy. This read:

> Campion Hall,
> Oxford.   January 14th 1934
>
> Dear Mr. Tomlin,
>   My friend T.S. Eliot told me during the vacation that I must make your acquaintance, so I should be very glad if you could come to tea here on Thursday next at 4.30.
>   Yours sincerely,
>   M.C. D'Arcy.
>   S.J.

Father D'Arcy, Master of Campion Hall, was already a 'legendary' figure, by which is meant that he was very much a fact, a presence. Indeed, he was at the height of his influence, even though he was to rise to greater authority as Provincial of the Jesuits in England. In the latter post, despite the honour conferred on him, he was unhappy. His almost Afro-head of grey hair, like a silver aureole, furrowed face and sunken though piercing eyes, made him appear patriarchal and much older than he was. In fact, he was at that time under fifty; and fifty then and for a long period, seemed to us a very advanced age.

At that time Campion Hall was a sparsely furnished but well-maintained presbytery type of building, and Father D'Arcy's quarters consisted of a severe but well-polished office-sitting-room with a bedroom adjoining. He possessed a great charm – a combination of Simone Weil's gravity and grace. And he gave the impression, on account of this gravity of manner and a confidential way of talking, of being the keeper of a number of well-selected, patrician consciences. Indeed, this was true. With Father Martindale, whom I never met, he was the most famous intellectual Catholic in the country and, as we all know, he had already made some spectacular converts, among them Evelyn Waugh and Lord Longford. He must have resembled certain of those statesmen-priests for whom France and Spain or indeed the Vatican have been famous: and, except for administrative incapacity, he might have relished exercising similar authority. A book of his called *The Nature of Belief* had attained considerable fame (though not so great as the later *Mind and Heart of Love* which, being mistaken for a handbook for young lovers, or the 1930s version of the 'Joys of Sex' type of book, became a best-seller until the word went round that it was not of much use in that regard), and copies of it were to be seen discreetly relegated to the back shelves of wistful academic agnostics and disillusioned hedonists.

In those days tea was an important event. It was then that much business was done, important information exchanged, and occasionally, due to the starchy crumpets liberally consumed, digestions undermined. Father D'Arcy placed his guests immediately on his left and right, and he usually invited two or three only. In my case, I was for the first hour the only one present; and, given the occasion for my being there, the conversation naturally turned upon Eliot. The first thing that Father D'Arcy told me caused me no little surprise. It was that Eliot had mentioned me in the footnote to his new book, *After Strange Gods*. (He switched my initials, but that did not matter.) He had also been considering publishing my Lawrence article, though somewhat curtailed, in *The Criterion*. You have to be as young as I was then to realize the pleasure this news afforded me. It is to be seen in the context of the Oxford of the time, when dons were inclined to assert their authority by slapping pert undergraduates down, instead of patiently tolerating their whims. What this meant was that Eliot had taken sufficient interest in me to supply these details to his friend. After our meeting, I was to hurry out to Blackwells to buy the slim book, and soon the news of the footnote was to spread among Oxford Eliot enthusiasts, and there was a demand to see the Lawrence essay. This I was unable to meet because, as very often before the days of photocopying, there was only one version and Eliot had it.

That I knew something of Eliot's personal circumstances, D'Arcy seemed to have assumed. He said that Eliot had separated from his wife, though with no intention of divorcing; that he had reached this decision only after prolonged consultation with his spiritual advisers, whose views he regarded as having absolute priority; and that he had been anxious to seek his (Father D'Arcy's) opinion as well. That

Eliot should have consulted him on this delicate issue had gratified him; and he felt that his endorsement was all the more necessary, because – readers must bear in mind that, despite the conversations at Malines, etc., the ecumenical movement had made little headway at that time – the Roman view was that Anglican orders were null and void, as they are still held to be. From certain hints that Father D'Arcy dropped, it was obvious that he entertained the hope, which he may never have abandoned, that Eliot would, especially at this critical moment, decide to submit to Rome: in which case the regulation of his private life was a matter of genuine Catholic concern. Indeed, there was one occasion when, almost in a tone of puzzled petulance – except that he never seemed to give way to ordinary weaknesses – D'Arcy confessed that he 'could not for the life' of him see why such submission had not already taken place. (From time to time, his gravity would give way to liberal gestures with his arms, and this was such a moment.) He had a habit, comprehensible in a member of his Order, of speaking for and on behalf of the Church as a whole : as if the Church had already thrown open its portals to receive the author of *The Waste Land* and not least *Ash Wednesday*, and was wondering why he had not yet turned up. Meanwhile, D'Arcy felt entitled to regard himself as one of the voluntary keepers of the Eliot conscience, which had, so to speak, already entered the public domain. My tone may sound frivolous, but it is not meant to be.

Father D'Arcy, a generous and warm-hearted man, clearly liked Eliot and revered him as a poet; and, regarding the Catholic Church as the repository of truth, outside which there was no salvation, he conceived it his duty to seek to bring this major talent within its fold. Writing so much later, when even the Catholic Church has implicitly admitted the possibility of salvation outside Rome – echoing Jacques Maritain's emendation to the effect that there was no salvation 'outside the truth' – I find something curiously ultra-montane about Father D'Arcy's attitude. In retrospect I find his manner, though endearing, just capable of raising a smile: for sustained gravity, unless during an actual ceremony, is something of which humankind cannot bear very much.

Even at the time, despite a great and continuing respect for the Roman Church, I remember to have had a faint impression of such a feeling. It became obvious to me, likewise, that he hoped from our first meeting – and there were to be a number of others – that I too, though among the smaller fry, would enrol myself among the

Faithful: which made his final remark, 'The Church will pray for you', as overwhelming as it was unexpected.

Father D'Arcy also disclosed that Eliot in an access of confidentiality had told him that he would write no more verse. His conclusion was evidently bound up with the feeling that, as a result of the personal trauma, there was no more in him. At the end of the American lectures that became *The Use of Poetry and the Use of Criticism*, he had reiterated the same theme, ending with the melancholy remark that 'the sad ghost of Coleridge beckons me from the shadows'. The impression he gave me, however, was that he had still certain judgments and pronouncements to make on literary matters, and that the rest of his life was to be devoted to working out the implications, literary and social, of his conversion. And he seems to have conveyed the same impression to Father D'Arcy, who took the view – which proved to be only partly correct – that Eliot's future was as a public figure. As we know, despite the seemingly complete *oeuvre* from 'Prufrock' to 'Marina', Eliot had another productive phase which would vastly extend his public recognition.

I have a feeling that Father D'Arcy wrote to Eliot following our meeting. In those days, before the telephone came into more general use and before the rise in postal costs, correspondence was more intensive, and matters were more conscientiously followed up than they are now. But in any case, Eliot was always scrupulous and reliable; and I knew that as soon as he could find the time, he would make a concrete suggestion about meeting. I was therefore pleased but not surprised when I received a letter dated 13 February 1934, suggesting lunch on 23 February. I duly obtained permission from my tutor to go to London which he readily gave, though I could see that the reason for it meant little to him.

The Oxford and Cambridge Club, which Eliot frequented at that time, has not changed much over the years, including its gastronomic standard, which, compared with some other establishments in Pall Mall and St James's, remains high: but its members were of the most traditional sort, and the guest, especially if he were a stripling, was subject to keen scrutiny as he entered, not least from those who slowly raised their heads above their newspapers. The appointment was at 1.15 p.m. and I was there on the dot. Eliot, who came in shortly after, seemed at home in this atmosphere. This was partly on account of his scrupulous adherence to conventional city dress, which suited his tall spare figure; but I remarked at once on the fact that he looked younger, and appeared to be a good deal better in health, than at our former meeting. Compared to some of the dishevelled human bundles filling the huge armchairs, he was strikingly spry and wholesome-looking. In fact, that old-fashioned word is more appropriate than any other. Consequently, my perturbation at entering on what was only my second visit to a London club instantly vanished.

This proved in many ways a landmark in our relationship, above all in its promise to be a permanent one. To have seen a great man in the flesh – 'Ah, did you once see Shelley plain?', as Browning wrote in *Memorabilia* – is always memorable; and in recording the initial and abiding impression it is posterity one should principally have in mind; and therefore, it is one's duty to set down as accurate a portrait as possible. That Ben Jonson, or Thomas Heywood, or Dr John Hall, or Hemminge and Condell, did not leave their own pen-portraits of Shakespeare is a great pity: pen-portraits not just describing his physical appearance but his manner and deportment, which, as I said at the beginning, is a psycho-physical complex. Eliot must have had hundreds of acquaintances, how many friends he had I do not know, but I have not read any description of him, *as a person*, which brought him back to me plain. This was no doubt because everybody reacts to our 'more particular encounters with persons' (to use his own phrase) in 'a special way'. All I know is that, in respect of an outstanding individual, Browning again applies: 'How strange it seems and new!', because it did so seem in this case.

It was the head which, on early acquaintance, proved most striking. In the days of phrenology (a 'science' which has not quite died out), it would have been an object of fascinating investigation. The size of the brain is no longer thought to determine the level of intelligence: I believe that Turgenev had one of the largest of brains and Anatole France one of the smallest, so that dimensions can mean nothing very much. But the remarkable skull in which the Eliot brain was encased always seemed to me to afford some clue to the efficiency of the mechanism within. For this 'second embryo', as the brain has been aptly called, combined in his case an analytical and imaginative capacity in equal measure and of the first order. Some of his work must have involved a degree of mental concentration which few are capable of sustaining, hence the extraordinarily high standard of the essays. You felt that he needed time to summon up the mental energy, which accounted for the fact that he was slow of speech and devoid of restless movement: and there would be moments when he would bring his words into line with his thought – especially towards the end of some piece of close reasoning – by the series of short nods of which I have spoken: after which he would plunge his head down as if for cerebral recuperation. In listening he would employ the same concentration; and this always seemed to be a compliment to his interlocutor, because, after all, he must have been obliged to attend in his time to some pretty banal and pretentious wordage.

The slowness of movement must not be exaggerated. He was not ponderous. He was in some ways extremely *alert*; and the head could switch round rapidly in response to something unexpected or to a matter which particularly attracted his attention. Given his controlled behavior and evenness of temper, these movements carried all the more significance and seemed to be held in reserve for just such contingencies. Nor did I ever see the slightest hint of a blush suffuse his face, perhaps because there was no cause.

As to his habitual expression, I find it difficult to select the right word. 'Kind' or 'benevolent' is too broad, though in later life the latter would have been appropriate. I think the *mot juste* is applicable also to his prose style, which Edmund Wilson described as 'pleasing'. I would say that his composed expression was pleasing, just as the composition of his sentence gave pleasure, at least to anyone sensitive to style. He held his mouth closed longer than most, which seemed to reinforce the face-confidence. I would not put him among those persons – rare enough in any case – who are fun to be with. But he was comfortable and reassuring to be with, as the funsters sometimes are not, or, being hard put to it to sustain their conviviality, change easily to moodiness. Except when exhibiting slight signs of fatigue, he maintained an evenness and stability of disposition which permitted the relationship to resume, after however long a break, on the former basis : there was no reaching or manoeuvering after the old familiarity, because it had never been extinguished.

On this occasion, as on some others, he looked at me searchingly for a second or two after shaking hands. It was as if he wished to reassert some prior subliminal understanding. Indeed, this whole operation was more prolonged than would normally have been the case, as greeting seemed to mean a great deal to him. We sat down and he ordered two sherries. Again there was no preliminary fumbling conversation (perhaps because of the subliminal understanding), and he asked me directly about Oxford. Apart from work, what was I doing? I replied that I had taken up rowing; but I explained that, unlike my brother at University College, who was to become a Blue, I had not so far achieved much success. If I had established any record, it was that of breaking an oar in two, due to an impulsive desire to get in more strokes than my opponent (I have since been assured that an immense, but totally misdirected, show of strength must have been the cause of such a feat). Eliot found this very funny. He manifested his amusement as much by a kind of jerky, almost spasmodic chuckle which I was to hear him utter frequently, for I do not recall him ever laughing outright, and I wonder if anybody else did. The subject was of interest to him because, while at Merton in 1914, he too had taken up rowing; but he had found that he was too thin-skinned. Here he gestured – one of the quick gestures – to his backside, with a look of mock agony which creased his brow and which I was to recall in other such disclosures.

It was then time for us to begin lunch. At the table, where we sat side by side, he explained, as if it were the most natural of conditions, that, it being Friday, he would abstain from meat and drink only beer, but that I was on no account to follow his example. I did not. He was so solicitous of my welfare that he insisted on my eating what even to me, at that period of unashamedly hearty appetite, was an enormous meal. Among the vegetables, he highly recommended onion, and there was a little contretemps when the waiter failed to bring it. The brow creased again, while a gentle admonition was administered, with the result that shortly after there was levered on to my plate an onion of unusual proportions. It proved rather difficult to demolish; and I was in great fear that I would send it flying, as had happened one day when I was lunching with a company director who wanted me to tutor his son. No doubt Eliot observed my momentary unease, but he helped to quieten it by talking steadily about undergraduate politics, about which he had sought my views.

He was always interested in what youth was thinking. Although it was not true, I told him, that everyone, don and undergraduate, was on the left, there certainly were some very left-wing dons, quite apart from A. L. Rowse. I mentioned that I was attending some lectures by Rowse on Political Theory, but I deliberately refrained from alluding to Rowse's reference to his essay on John Bramhall, with the comment: 'Not that T. S. Eliot knows anything about political theory, as I *well* know.' (I fancy Rowse had spotted me in the audience, which was not large, and wanted to launch a missile at the 'reactionary'.) Eliot was also anxious to hear about the writers in whom the students were taking interest, and we spoke about Auden, Spender and Day Lewis, and also Empson. To us, these were new 'voices'; but they did not seem to me to be as new as all that, and Empson's 'voice' was, and to me has remained, somewhat incoherent. Referring to *Seven Types of Ambiguity*, Eliot said he thought Empson ought to re-write it from start to finish. Eliot, who had been responsible for launching Auden and Spender, made some comment about the different reading habits of the new generation. Whereas he and his contemporaries had been familiar with a poet like Byron, especially the Byron of the dramatic poems, from early youth, Auden seemed only just to have discovered him – as was apparent from the *Letters from Iceland*, which was due shortly to appear. In fact, the habit of reading itself was not what it had been: there was, he thought, too much preoccupation with modern writers and not enough with the established ones. This always worried him. The reading of contemporary works had become an *excuse* for neglecting the old. He hinted that some of his own remarks on Shelley and Keats had apparently been responsible for persuading many that, as 'romantic poets', they were not worth bothering about. He was right. He spoke as one with authority. I did not read Shelley for several decades. Keats was another matter. As for Browning, he squeaked in because of Ezra Pound.

We must have talked at considerable length, because by the time we had finished – and I in my repletion had refused the cheese, while he judiciously selected some rare variety, as was his wont – the dining-room was empty. Our converse was interrupted by his going to the cashier's desk at the far end of the room and settling up : and I had an opportunity of watching another example of his laborious but thorough method of doing business. It began by some searching of pockets in both trousers and waistcoat, and issuing of coins as if he were discharging some reluctant obligation – the word 'tender', otherwise absurdly artificial, seemed almost exactly appropriate in this case.

Back in the sitting-room, where he ordered coffee, we embarked upon the more detailed business of the day, which concerned my essay on Lawrence. When it came to literary matters, he was usually forthright, feeling perhaps that here, in contrast to personal concerns, he could speak with authority. To the novice, the fact that he apparently felt it worthwhile to go through one's work with such care, and to criticize what he considered to be defects (which usually consisted in the pretentious and the 'clever'), was itself sufficiently satisfying : because one felt that if he were frank enough to isolate particular failings, he would not have hesitated, had it been necessary, to condemn the whole. He considered the Lawrence essay to be a much more mature piece of work than 'The Younger Generation and Politics'. He even said it was 'good stuff'. The trouble was that is was a good deal too long. As it slightly exceeded the length of the previous essay, which therefore also placed it outside consideration for the ordinary periodical, he cautioned me against acquiring the habit of writing at inconvenient length. He himself had accustomed himself to writing the length of a *Times Literary Supplement* article, and he had found that once this habit had become ingrained, it was extremely difficult to break it.

As he had made reference to the essay in *After Strange Gods* and as he had evidently spoken to Father D'Arcy about using it in part or parts for *The Criterion*, I was slightly disappointed that he made no mention of publication in our talk; but from some remarks he dropped in an apparent aside it was clear that as with the case of the Rowse article, he had chiefly my career in mind and the necessity of obtaining a good degree. Meanwhile, writing, though to be encouraged, must remain a by-product. Indeed, it was not before I had left Oxford, but then almost straightaway, that he invited me to write for *The Criterion*. As he had said before, he was against 'rushing into print'.

He did, however, put out the suggestion that I should try to condense the Rowse essay into an article, which he would then examine in the light of my position at the University, because he felt that Rowse's book needed a *riposte* from the younger generation which he claimed to be addressing or for whom he claimed to be speaking. I said that I would set to work on this. We then resumed the political theme on which we had touched before lunch. I told him I had been reading Georges Sorel, an interest which Harry Woodgate had originally kindled, and this led me to ask him whether he had met Charles Maurras, a man of much the same mould. He had not, though it was clear that Maurras had greatly influenced him. He knew, and was in touch with, Maurras's disciple, Léon Daudet. Maurras had of course helped to form his ideas on royalism, but he was quite clear in his mind that the *Action Française*, the organ of the royalist movement, was much too intemperate and vituperative for his taste. I feel it is important to stress this; for at the time of writing, a book has been noticed in the press which deplores Eliot's submission to the views of that periodical, adducing one more argument that Eliot was a fascist. On the occasion of which I am speaking he seemed to me to go out of his way to underline his reservations about *political* royalism, perhaps because he knew that youth tends, in forming an opinion, to embrace the whole. He nevertheless offered to lend me his copy of Maurras's book, *Enquête sur la Monarchie*, which he believed he had among the books in his room. This was a reference for the first time to what many people, Wyndham Lewis included, regarded as a kind of secret abode which he would refer to with extreme reluctance. Of this I shall speak later, not because I ever visited it – few ever did, George Every could confirm that – but because in due course he informed me where it was; and I have often thought that a plaque ought to be placed there, similar to that set up at Kensington Court Gardens.

It was the reference to Charles Maurras that first brought me to notice Eliot's knowledge and pronunciation of French. He was a very good linguist and knew the language well, as he knew German and Italian. Moreover, he took care to attain the most exact rendering of any out-of-the-way word. Thus he rightly pronounced Maurras, Maurra*s* : but his accent tended to be influenced by what he had been taught at school – presumably Smith Academy, St Louis – and not what his ear must have been tuned to during his stay in Paris in 1912. It therefore jarred a little to hear him say, with great emphasis on the second syllable, *Action Franzsayz*, with an Anglo-Saxon accent of which he was obviously quite unaware. Otherwise, he was a man who rarely committed an error of this kind, either in language, dress or protocol. Indeed, he was something of an expert on the first two. It was always the 'bench of bishops'. Herbert Read, in receiving a knighthood, had been 'gazetted' as having rendered services to literature (not art); an inhabitant of Scotland was 'a Scot'. The 'advowson' at St Stephen's (i.e. the right of presenting the benefice) was 'in the hands of trustees'. And so on.

I realized that it was time that I took my leave, and he rose to his feet with the familiar gravity. I remember that we went on talking while we were putting on our coats in the cloakroom, which in this case assumed the sliding effect I had noticed at King's. His final words were that we must meet again at Easter, and that I should send him anything I had written in the meantime. All this greatly cheered me, for in an unequal relationship of this kind, it was never clear until the last moment what new direction it would take, or whether it was to be taken further at all. As I felt elated and that in any case he had had enough of my company, I watched to see if I could judge which way he was going, so that I might make off in the opposite direction. He went away at a quick, striding pace towards his office, and I walked up Pall Mall and into St James's.

Reflecting on this meeting as I went, I realized for the first time that in his company I had felt completely at ease. First of all, he talked in a language I could understand; for however subtle might be his prose, his speech was thoroughly straightforward and even simple. Secondly, he was simple and straightforward, displaying a quiet charm that called forth an immediate response. Male to male contact of this kind necessarily differs from male to female contact, in which the awareness of sexual difference is rarely absent, and therefore can give rise to faint tension. Having no experience of homosexual feeling, except conceivably in early adolescence, and then in the most rarefied form, I cannot report that such tension is present in contact of that order. All I know is that male to male contact of the kind I experienced with Eliot, and with one or two other close male friends, is successful, rewarding, and in fact intimate, only *because* it is devoid of sexual feeling. Indeed, if such feelings were for some reason to intrude, the charm would be lost. I insert these remarks because of the persistent insinuations that Eliot, owing to his friendship with Jean Verdenal and perhaps with others, was either homosexual or, as one fellow-poet remarked, suppressed homosexuality. From this early meeting, I became aware of an attachment that presumably he must partly have reciprocated, despite disparity of age – he was twenty-five years older than me – and my own slightly withdrawn temperament. The latter itself may have partially commended me to him, as he shunned forced intimacy, though I may occasionally have appeared a little over-solemn. That many people found him solemn too, as well as shy and too wrapped up in himself, I am aware. So far as I am concerned, he was none of these things. And as I have never found coping with shy men easy – shy women are different : they somehow arouse the chivalrous instincts – I can the more readily testify to his lack of embarrassing reserve. I felt that I could ask him anything; and, on account of his assurance, I took care, wisely I now believe, not to presume too far on his privacy.

Then there was another rather curious fact. With other creative figures I knew, like Wyndham Lewis or James Joyce, or, if he can be classed as such, Arnold Toynbee, the work seemed easy to associate with their physical presence. Lewis, for instance, was himself like one of his characters, and even like one of his portraits, as if he had had a hand in creating himself. Joyce spoke very much as he wrote. With Eliot the work possessed an impersonality, or a transcendence of personality which was difficult to trace back to the man in the city suit who moved between Russell Square and clubland and St Stephen's, Gloucester Road. No wonder he was called – or a film about him was named – the Mysterious Mr Eliot. But with this mysterious man I now felt a kinship which I somehow knew would last.

CHAPTER THREE

The Rowse essay having been completed, I dispatched it to Fabers and received Eliot's comment in a letter dated 19 April. He wrote:

Walter Tomlin Esq.,
Kylemore,
97 Brighton Road,
Purley, Surrey.

Dear Mr. Tomlin,
    I have read your essay dealing with Rowse's book, and although I must read it again before committing myself to a formal opinion, I must say that from practical points of view it seems to me a great improvement over anything previous. On the first reading it seemed to me that I agreed with everything you said but this is such an uncommon experience that I must read it again before taking my oath on that point.
    I wonder how you feel about publication. The essay will no doubt annoy Mr. Rowse, who doesn't always find it easy to understand why everybody doesn't think as he does. But I don't know that that matters very much from any point of view, even his own. You are not, I take it, in any way a pupil of his but only attend his lectures. I can imagine any man being rather hurt at having his ideas publicly attacked by anyone who was at the time in the status of being his pupil; and it would hardly be good form on the pupil's part. But I am under the impression that your relations with him consist of no more than attending his lectures, and that you have very little to do with him personally. Is he likely, for instance, to be one of your examiners in any subject? I really ask this sort of question in consideration of your interests.

I don't know the book of George Sorel which you mention. Indeed, I believe that the only one which I have read is the 'Reflexions sur la violence'. I think the best thing that I can do is to get hold of a copy and read it myself first. In general translations of French books do very badly unless they are very popular works, for the reason that the majority of people who are interested are usually able to read them in French; furthermore, some of the leading periodicals will already have reviewed the French text. But I should like to read anything that you recommend so warmly, and if I see any chance for a translation I will write to you again about it.
                Yours very truly,
                T.S. Eliot.

Of course I saw that, in his appraisal of the situation, he was right. Publication of the essay, presumably in *The Criterion*, would understandably have hurt Rowse's feelings; it might, at the same time, have shown me up as an impertinent upstart. I presume that Eliot, perhaps overestimating my powers, had thought that I could somehow write a piece which would have avoided causing offence. Also, I may have given him the impression, with the urgency of youth possessed of strong convictions, that I wanted at all costs to have something published on this subject. True, I was not Rowse's student: but I had met him chiefly through Eliot's introduction, and he had been civil enough, and even, despite marked differences of viewpoint, encouraging. I did not believe that he was likely to be one of my examiners in Finals, and this turned out to be true. As irony would have it, however, an examiner that I did have passed on to Rowse the information that, in the paper on Political Institutions, in which I did badly, I had vigorously attacked Rowse's pamphlet on 'The Question of the House of Lords'. Rowse began his pamphlet, if I remember rightly, with the words: 'What is there to do with the House of Lords except to abolish it?' whereas I had followed J. S. Mill in regarding its most salutary function as that of 'a check on precipitancy'. But, in those days, to defend the House of Lords was to be dubbed a shameful reactionary. For me, it was sufficient satisfaction that Eliot had approved my essay; that he considered it the best thing I had done; and that I had been one of the few to express opinions which had his total concurrence.

From a letter to my mother dated 2 May, which has escaped

destruction, it is clear that I had just written to Eliot explaining that I realized the undesirability of publication, unless indeed Rowse himself were prepared to give it his endorsement. I mentioned this in view of the fact that Eliot had wanted Rowse to read the original essay, and I was anxious to see whether he still recommended this. Rowse was at that time in London, or I might (I said) have asked him to tea and taken some soundings. In the end, perhaps because I was embarking on other work, the matter was quietly dropped. On the whole, I was glad. I did later show Rowse an essay of mine, but this was not a personal onslaught. He clearly disapproved of it and that was that.

Thereafter I never attacked Rowse's political views in print, and, when I came to know him better, I no longer felt I had reason to do so. I trust that he will not mind my reproducing a letter from a mutual friend containing personal criticism. In this I do not think that Eliot exaggerated. If he exaggerated at all, it was in supposing that anything I might say mattered all that much.

As to the projected translation mentioned in the last paragraph, it referred to Sorel's *Illusions du Progrès*. This was a book I had thought far superior to the *Reflexions sur la Violence*. Looking back on it today, however, I perceive how dated it is; but, in the 1930s it might just have excited interest, simply as illustrating one direction in which a Marxian might, in his disillusionment, turn. (Sorel, beginning as a revolutionary syndicalist, gravitated towards the *Action Francaise* movement, which was the reason why I thought the book might interest Eliot.) I heard no more on the subject; and if this meant that I had failed to persuade Eliot to devote precious time to reading the book, I was more relieved than otherwise.

We, on the other hand, were at that stage of life when we felt we could find time for anything that took our fancy. There was a great deal of extra- or para-curricular activity. Burke, I remember, helped to establish an Education Society: Harold Mason and I and a girl called Alethea wanted to publish a kind of politico-literary manifesto. This would be a counterblast to the growing propaganda of the Left, not only in Oxford but outside – in fact, I suggested that it should be called *Counterblast*, with Wyndham Lewis's 'puce monster', *Blast*, in mind – but we were as anxious to dissociate ourselves from the Right. A feminist magazine called *Lysistrata* was also one of our targets. The idea was to bring in some big names: two we had in mind were Eliot and Leavis. I had by this time met the latter. Having appeared to saddle Eliot with reading Sorel's book, I was reluctant to impose further tasks on him. An essay of his I had read at school entitled 'Religion without Humanism', from a symposium published under the title of *Humanism and America* (1930), edited by Norman Foerster, had excited scant interest on this side of the Atlantic. It occurred to me that its republication in our Symposium might both appeal to him and attract public attention: for I considered it an authoritative statement of the *value* of Humanism (the title was a little misleading) in its relation to religion. Moreover, it was written in Eliot's early style: pleasing, pungent and persuasive. Accordingly, I wrote to Eliot asking whether he would agree to lend us his assistance and his authority in this way. As he told me he did not possess the book and had lost sight of the paper, I hurried to London, located it at the National Central Library, as it then was, copied out the essay in longhand (being fed with sheet after sheet of paper by the rather puzzled girl at the reception-desk), and called with it at Faber's.

As he was a very busy man, I was grateful that Eliot should have been prepared to see me without any notice at all. True, he had become used to being interrupted – there were, in the category of interrupters, young feckless poets who thought nothing of calling and expecting to be subsidised without there being any thought of reimbursement. Dylan Thomas was one such suppliant. I know, because Eliot told me: he also disclosed, what he usually kept to himself, that after the poet had drunk himself to death, and hearing that his widow was in difficulties, he had provided liberal help, though whether she was aware of the fact I do not know. Another interrupter, especially at this time, was of course Vivien herself, who, despite the legal separation, would continue to pester him, causing great embarrassment to Miss Swan and to his secretary. The one most called upon to handle the situation was Brigid O'Donovan, and she seems to have managed very well. Yet, when I saw him on this occasion, he seemed more than usually calm and quiet, which, given that the most painful of interrupters might arrive at any hour, showed that when, in the very essay I was delivering to him, he had talked about the necessity for the 'discipline and training of the emotions', he meant what he said and practised it. It was this habit of self-mastery which made one expect him always to maintain a standard of behaviour which other people felt themselves excused from emulating. For the trouble with the great and the good is that we expect them to be on duty the whole time.

Indeed, quite early on, I tried to work out in my mind what it was that made his personality (though he did not like the word) so compelling; and I came to the conclusion that it was because he did not let me down in my own estimation of him. When we are first trying to establish our values and standards in life, there are certain people, or it may be institutions, upon which we decide we have at all costs to rely. This means that they must on no account fail us, just as, to take a different level, the woman whose beauty we find captivating must be seen to maintain her attractions: so much so that we 'will' her to display a beauty that she does not always possess, or perhaps has never possessed. It was the steady reliability, the unfailing support, which I knew I could count on, which distinguished Eliot from so many others. I did not have to pretend that he was a great man: by his acts, his understanding, and his solicitude, and by the example he set and maintained of standards higher than those of his fellows, he showed himself to be one.

He was in any case visibly touched that I should have gone to the lengths of copying the essay; but in those days no other method of putting him in possession of it was available. Of its contents he retained only the haziest notion; and he explained that he would have been reluctant to contribute to such a volume – his *Second Thoughts on Humanism*, published a year earlier, had consisted of a devastating criticism of the editor – save that it represented a tribute to Irving Babbitt, whom he had always revered as one of his masters and about whom he felt that his early criticism had been misunderstood, not least by Babbitt himself. In any case, he felt he ought to stop making too many major pronouncements of this kind. I noticed that he pronounced the name B'bbitt. He moved round the room – in so far as it was possible in such cramped quarters – glad to be relieved momentarily of desk work but perhaps by way of indicating that the interview must be conducted as if we were both on the move; and this meant that certain remarks were addressed to the window or the mantelpiece. In fact, he liked standing, especially when telephoning, which, as he disliked that form of communication, may have rendered it less irksome. But then, having exhausted his recollections of the circumstances of his writing the paper, he switched to more personal matters and enquired carefully how I was getting on in a way that made me feel that my mission had been worthwhile and that I had by no means wasted his morning.

Meanwhile, having appealed to Leavis, we received from him almost by return a literary essay, and we set to work to write our own pieces. To our gratification, Blackwells, whom we had approached, expressed interest in the project, something we had not dared to expect.

Nevertheless, we soon found that producing a publication of the required length, and assembling a representative group of writers, was no easy task. To find enough opponents of the left who were not too far committed in the other direction proved more difficult than we had imagined. Also, we were in much too much of a hurry. Even now, I remain uncertain who was supposed to be doing what. Our spirits were already beginning to flag when I received a letter from Eliot dated 2 June:

2 June 1934

Walter Tomlin Esqre.,
Brasenose College
Oxford.

My dear Tomlin,

I must apologise humbly for my delay in dealing with what I know is an urgent matter; I can only plead that I have been extremely busy. It was several days before I could read carefully the paper which you had taken the trouble to copy out; and more than several days before I could make up my mind about it. I hoped that I might be able to pass the little article after only a few minor changes; but now I must face the fact that, with the exception of one or two points worth making, I want to scrap the whole thing.

I remember now that the article was written for a special purpose. I had no desire to associate myself with that group of 'humanists' at all: it was only out of courtesy and regard for my old master Irving Babbitt that I took part. I considered it only as a volume in honour of Babbitt; and I took the only possible line that I could at the moment, in his support. To reprint now what is in any case a rather feeble piece of writing, would give it a stamp of my own endorsement which I don't want it to have.

I do not see furthermore that the essay has any close relevance to the subject of your symposium. If I had not been so busy during these recent weeks, or if your book was to appear in the autumn instead of immediately, I would gladly try to write something new for you. But I am busy all the coming week, and am then taking a holiday of a fortnight, during which I must get done two other pieces of work. So I can only wish you the best of success with your other contributors, and hope to see a brilliant book.

> Your ever sincerely,
> T.S. Eliot.

I am very sorry indeed about this, esp. after the trouble you have been put to.

Naturally I was disappointed that the most notable name of which we could boast had to be excluded: and although I knew that he disliked re-reading his prose works, I was as sorry that he felt the essay to be below standard as I was to regret his later repudiation of *After Strange Gods*. I still think his essay, far from being 'a rather feeble piece of writing', to be a powerful piece of advocacy; and it contained some remarks about culture and religious observance for which in penetration and acuteness I can recall no exact parallel. I fear that he greatly over-estimated our combined literary and administrative abilities. I wrote a little later to say that, while his repudiation of the essay was in no way responsible for the decision, we had deferred our project. I expressed the hope that one day he would include the piece in a volume or volumes of collected essays: a collection I still feel is very much needed.

He was quick to respond. On 13 June, he wrote:

Dear Tomlin,

I am sorry to hear that your enterprise has fallen through for the moment: but I am not surprised. My knowledge of book ventures, especially of works of collaboration or including contributions by various hands, tells me that such things are seldom done so quickly as you and your friends hope. I shall be glad to try my hand at something else in the autumn; and I should like you to tell me, when you can, more exactly about the intended and the expected contents, as I might find a subject more suitable.

I am out of town for the rest of this month, but after that I expect to be in town.

> Yours sincerely,
> T.S. Eliot.

When I look back, I am amazed that Eliot should have even contemplated going to such trouble on our behalf. It is now clear – and, in view of the final lines of his letter of 2 June, it was sufficiently plain by then – that he was writing under great pressure: which up to his last years was the condition in which he produced most of his work, including some of his best. Although writing under pressure is how many authors are best able to function, Eliot set himself so high a standard that his achievement, given its quantity, was the more remarkable. There were moments when he took on too much; and although I pursued the matter of our volume only because he had invited me to do so, I soon realized that I was asking more than I should have done, especially as I was uncertain at any moment whether my collaborators saw eye to eye with me about the scope of our project. We still cherished the idea of putting together a 'counterblast'; but I perceived in due course that we had begun to differ regarding the objective to be demolished. Still bearing in mind the essay in the humanist volume, I wrote to Eliot during the summer suggesting as a theme for his consideration one based on the statement: 'The problem of nationalism and the problem of disassociated personalities may turn out to be the same'. This seemed to me to be one of the most perceptive remarks in the essay, about which some elaboration on his part would be of considerable interest. As I kept little of my side of any correspondence in those days, I am not sure whether I explained more clearly what we were trying to do, as he had requested. All I know is that by the time we had entered into residence again that autumn, we found we had made so little progress, and had remained so vague about our aims that, one evening, Harold Mason and I, who had seen more of each other than we did anyone else in the group, resolved to abandon the project altogether; and I therefore wrote to Eliot, from whom I had not heard further, telling him that our plan had made so little headway that I felt it my duty to tell him not to trouble himself any more. At the same time, I renewed the invitation on behalf of the Phoenix Society, as there was a consensus that this should be revived.

He replied on 2 November:

Walter Tomlin, Esq.,
Brasenose College,
Oxford.

Dear Tomlin,
   Excuse my delay in answering your letter of the 18th October. I was in bed last week with a cold and am a good deal in arrears with my correspondence.
   First of all, may I tell you that although I am sorry in general that your volume has, at any rate for the moment, fallen through, it comes as a considerable relief to my conscience. I have had my hands pretty full lately and it would have been more than doubtful whether I could have got ready in time such an essay as you wanted. In fact, I had really bitten off more than I could chew and there is a considerable amount of reading which I ought to do before I attempted an essay of that kind.
   I should be delighted to assist the Phoenix to a reincarnation to the best of my ability, but I simply haven't the time for another lecture this term, and am not yet certain how I shall be fixed at the beginning of next term. Could we leave this for a bit; and will you let me know as soon as you come down for the holidays so that we may meet and discuss it?
                    Yours ever sincerely,
                    T.S. Eliot.

I could see that, had he embarked upon the paper, it would have left me conscience-stricken in my turn. That anything he undertook or contemplated would be a thorough piece of work, I knew; but I do not suppose I appreciated how much preparation he would have considered necessary, including intensive readings. I imagined he could just sit down, perhaps at the typewriter to which he had recourse even for poetry, and produce the requisite text. It was true of Eliot, as it was true of Dr Johnson, that he needed to read himself into a writing disposition; and that is perhaps why some of his best essays were produced under the stimulus of a particular kind – a review-book or some text which would 'tie him down'. He used some such expression in the text of an unpublished essay that I later found at Harvard. An essay or a lecture on some general theme did not always have the required effect, as some of the otherwise magisterial addresses delivered when he was a world-figure tend to show.

That same November, I escaped from Oxford life by securing permission – I do not know whether such authorization is needed these days – to go to a performance in London by the Group Theatre in Great Newport Street, under Rupert Doone, of *Sweeney Agonistes*. I could wish, incidentally, that Eliot had retained the original title of *Wanna Go Home, Baby?*, which always seemed to me exactly right. The Group Theatre, as it name implied, was considered to be slightly advanced or progressive. The ladies wore their underwear, which, far from revealing anything, seemed rather like a ribbed pink carapace, but did in some measure convey the sordidness of their profession. I thought it was a good performance. What I did not know was that Vivien Eliot was in the audience. At least I did not recognize her; but then she was such a shrinking, washed-out-creature – when later I had lunch with one of Eliot's former doctors he described her as 'an ugly little thing', which was rather unkind and hardly accurate – that she could easily have escaped notice.

Discontent with our literary projects seem to have provoked in me discontent of another, more general, kind: for I found my philosophical tutelage increasingly unsatisfactory. I was seized one day with the desire to go to the United States for a period of study. A scholarship to Harvard under the name of a Henry Fellowship, had been advertised on the plastered notice-board at the College entrance. (As this sort of restlessness has seized me all my life, I need not elaborate.) It impelled me to request Eliot, for the first time of more times than I care to remember – as it was a chore which I have been obliged to shoulder often enough myself – to act as a referee. Although he willingly complied, it was not without misgivings. On 14 December, he wrote to me:

> Dear Tomlin,
> I shall certainly be glad to stand as one of your referees when the authorities apply to me for my opinion. I rather hope, however, that this scholarship is to be tenanted after you come down from Oxford, rather than as a break in your work there, but I may be mistaken in this opinion, and would gladly know more of your designs. Anyway, I hope you get it. If you go to Harvard I should like to give you some introductions there.

I look forward to receiving another essay from you, and shall write to you to suggest a date for lunch soon after Christmas.
Yours sincerely,
T.S. Eliot.

Although I duly applied for the Fellowship, I was unsuccessful, no doubt to my lasting benefit, as similar failures have served to prove. And again I saw that in his caveat Eliot was right. What heartened as well as chastened me about the letter was his wish to see more of my writing. I had hinted to him that I had been engaged on a paper to be called 'Enslavement by Capital', a title adapted from one employed by Ezra Pound in a *Criterion* article called more characteristically, 'Murder by Capital'. It was about the difficulties experienced by the writer, especially the major writer, in prevailing economic conditions, and I took as examples Eliot, Pound and Herbert Read. The choice of the latter led Leavis, to whom I sent the paper later, to expostulate, but at that time I thought that Read was heading for an eminence which, at least as a creative writer, he never attained. This I posted to Eliot. I also sent him an article entitled 'Interpretation by Economics'.

Meanwhile, I had intervened in a wrangle which had been going on in the pages of *Time and Tide* over some articles Eliot had written. This was in a series called 'Notes on the Way' (January/February 1935). They had provoked Rebecca West to make more than one violent intervention. Her letters were of mounting stridency and, as I thought, extremely unfair. Bridling, I wrote a long riposte, which was printed in the issue for 2 February 1935. In the same issue, Rebecca West's last salvo appeared after a final one from Eliot. Reading my letter fifty-one years later, I am struck by its vigour, but I deplore a certain over-writing and perhaps a 'one-must-not attack Mr Eliot' tone. I have no wish to reproduce it here. Eliot's own letter contained, besides some telling points, an amusing conclusion in which he invited Miss West, in order to 'talk these matters over quietly', to 'come up and see me some time'. This phrase, the force of which may be lost on the present generation, had been made familiar by another Miss West, the buxom and sultry film-star; the similarity of nomenclature was a coincidence of which Eliot took full advantage. That the grave and devout poet should use these words, and even be aware of them, was a source of much mirth. In my letter to Eliot, enclosing my own article, I had expressed the hope that, in contrast to Rowse, who told me that he considered my letter 'ineffective', might approve of it. In his reply of 21 February 1935, he added a footnote in his own hand which put the matter aptly; but about my second article he had his doubts.

> Dear Tomlin,
> I have read your essay once, but must postpone any serious criticism until I have read it again. I found it by no means easy reading. This is no fault of the style, but it seems to me on first reading that you have packed a great deal into a few pages, and it is not immediately clear what the upshot of it all is. As for the comments on Pound and Douglas, I think there can be no objection to your being as hard on them as you please. The only question in my mind is whether it is desirable to mention them at all, unless you are prepared to deal with them more thoroughly. I will write to you again as soon as I can. The article is certainly interesting and full of meat.
> Yours sincerely,
> T.S. Eliot.
>
> [Handwritten] No! I did not object to your letter! – but I doubt if anything is effective against hysteria.

On 20 March 1935, he wrote again:

> My Dear Tomlin,
> I have taken another chew at *Interpretation by Economics*, and while I think I like it, it seems to me, as it did at first, not quite in a form suitable for general consumption. As it stands, I feel it is more fitted to appear in *Mind* or some other philosophical journal than in a general periodical. At the same time, it is handling a problem which I want to see handled, and I think that so far as I can understand it, you have the right end of the stick, but the ordinary reader would not, I think, be quite clear either where you start or where you are going. One would like to have stated somewhere, perfectly simply:
> a. What the problem is
> b. What your conclusion about it is
> c. What are the alternative theories which you reject.
> There is a great deal which is rather in the abstract form of Greats philosophizing, so that one is somewhat distracted from the point

by the brilliance of the gymnastics. I am returning it to you for the moment so that you may collate my comments with your text, and let me know whether you think I am entirely missing the point.
Yours sincerely,
T.S. Eliot.

As Eliot was very sparing of exclamation marks, and must rarely have employed two in juxtaposition, it was clear to me that, with the particular reservation he made, he was far from thinking my letter ineffective. I recall that I had written another broadside in reply to an article in *The Student Vanguard* by Rayner Heppenstall, then a communist, called 'T. S. Eliot: sign of the times'. He had attacked Eliot for worshipping culture, which I considered about as false an imputation as could be imagined. I also wrote to Waldo Frank, who, in an article to which Harold Mason drew my attention, had attacked Eliot. Although this might suggest otherwise, I was all the time working hard for Schools, as I knew that Eliot, now my mentor in most things, would have strongly urged me to do. Indeed, he might have been perturbed to think that I was diverting so much energy towards his defence; but, so far as I know, he was ignorant of these interventions of mine, as I never showed him the letters or alluded to them.

His reaction to my essay, on the other hand, brought me up with a jolt; and although what I had written is of no interest – I seem to have lost the manuscript, so that is the end of the matter – I came to value his negative appraisals. I knew that they were sincere and above all that they were meant to be helpful. When Eliot had spoken well of me in the reply to John Garrett, to which I have referred, the latter was slightly miffed, I could tell; for although he showed it me with some pride as being a favourable reply to his request, he countered the praise it contained by saying that Eliot was being far too kind to an absolute novice. He was indeed kind, exceptionally so; but he never indulged in insincerity for the sake of pleasing, and he could be downright enough when he deemed it necessary. That is why I willingly sent him anything I thought might be of sufficient merit to justify him, as a publisher, pronouncing upon it. In the whole course of our friendship, what I never ventured to do was to send him any poetry. At that time I was turning it out with some facility, and I had had two poems published in *The Isis* in my first year. But the bulk of it, now that I have re-read it in connection with this memoir, I have quietly made away with.

In fact, the next paper I sent him was called, if I remember rightly, 'The Poet – the Public – the Faith', and I had dispatched it to a review called *The Green Quarterly*, the only recollection of which I have is that it was quarterly and that it was green. I had come upon it in thumbing through *The Writers and Artists Yearbook*; it seems to have been an Anglo-Catholic journal. I suppose that Kenneth Ingram, the editor, had not quite made up his mind about what I had written, which is the reason why I had forwarded it to Eliot. On 27 August 1935, he wrote to me at my Purley address about it as follows:

Dear Tomlin,

I find that I have failed to answer your letter of the 18th July, and I hope that the delay has not seriously inconvenienced you. I meant to tell you that I liked your article, and should be glad to use it, though I am not quite certain whether I can get it in by the end of the year or not. So if you would like to get it printed soon, and Ingram has asked for it for his next number, I do not want to stand in your way at all. I see no reason for cutting it down except its being too long for particular requirements.

With many apologies,
    Yours sincerely,
    T.S. Eliot.

If the invitation to the Phoenix Club came to nothing, as it did, an invitation from the English Club, in which I enjoyed no official status, though I was a member, bore fruit. I forget how we learnt that he was coming under its auspices, but I do remember that our wish – that is to say, the wish of myself and Michael Cullis, by then an established friend – to entertain him during the visit, produced a minor clash with the English Club secretariat. We did not want to be the cause of friction; but as we were unable to ascertain what the Club had in mind by way of arrangements, we proposed tea or dinner, or, if he were not being entertained in the evening, both. Eliot's letter of 22 October confirmed that he still had not received details from the Club; but he understandably felt that while he could accept our invitation to tea, he ought to reserve his position about dinner. So we agreed about tea, and invited Father D'Arcy to join us.

On 22 October 1935 Eliot wrote:

THE CRITERION
A Quarterly Review
edited by T.S. Eliot

Walter Tomlin, Esq.,
Brasenose College,
Oxford.

24 Russell Square
London, W.C.1.
22nd October 1935.

Dear Tomlin,
    Thank you for your kind invitation. I believe that I shall be put up at Magdalen on the night on which I speak to the English Club. If I can afford the time I have promised D'Arcy to stay over and spend a night with him at Campion Hall. I see no reason why I should not have tea with you and Cullis, on one or other of these days. Let us make it the Tuesday to be on the safe side. I should like very much to dine with you also, but I feel that unless you can arrange the matter at your end – I don't know whether you are a member of the English Club or not – I ought to hold myself at the disposal of the officers of the club. I have not heard from them what they expect to do with me before the meeting.
               Yours sincerely,
               T.S. Eliot.

What happened, however, was that Eliot caught a cold, and on the 2 November we received a telegram from him:

SLIGHT INFLUENZA DOCTOR FORBIDS COMING OXFORD DEEPLY REGRET
                                    ELIOT

We naturally renewed our invitation as soon as we learnt of the new arrangements proposed by the English Club, and he wrote to me on 25 November 1935 on *Criterion* writing paper:

Dear Tomlin,
    Thank you for renewing your invitation to tea for December 3rd, and I shall be glad to come. If you will be so good as to meet the train, I shall take the 1.45 arriving at 3.4 as I had intended before.
    Yes, I should be very glad if you would do a shorter notice of Collingwood's Inaugural Lecture. I did not even

know that he had been made Waynflete Professor. That will be for the March number.
>   Yours sincerely,
>   T.S. Eliot.

Please let me know the publisher of *The Historical Imagination* so that I may send for it.

For some reason the 'Poet-Public-Faith' article did not get used; but meanwhile Collingwood, whose acquaintance I had made, had received the advancement he amply deserved, and I wanted to write in *The Criterion* about his first lecture as Professor. The short notice I did write was my first appearance in that journal, and I recall that Rowse did not much like it; but then he did not like Collingwood either. Meanwhile, I was looking forward to Eliot's Oxford visit.

Having met him at the station on 3 December, a Tuesday, we walked back to the Old Parsonage, in St Giles's (now a hotel), where Michael Cullis had pleasant lodgings. My place was not suitable, as I was living rather far out beyond Magdalen in more cramped conditions. Wearing a large Stetson sort of hat and a thick brown overcoat, Eliot progressed fairly slowly, wielding a rather formidable sword-stick. We happened to pass a woman pushing a pram, who for some reason produced a torch, no doubt in order to locate something, and directed it straight at the baby's face. This seemed to disturb Eliot, as anything afflicting the eye did – for he had a dread of blindness – and he murmured his concern that the woman had shone the light 'in the child's eye'. For some reason the subject of Marianne Moore came up, and he expressed disappointment that the edition of her poems which Faber's had recently published had sold less well than expected. I was to see her years later, and talk much of Eliot, they were fellow-citizens of St Louis, Missouri, and almost of the same age.

Not long after we had reached the Old Parsonage and climbed the stairs to Michael's rooms, Father D'Arcy arrived. We noticed with what great deference he treated Eliot, though they were obviously on close and confidential terms. As for Eliot himself, he seemed to make himself absolutely at home, as he usually did in a small gathering, and he swung his leg over the arm of the comfortable chair, where it reposed throughout the visit. Father D'Arcy sat on his right. I remember thinking at the time that the two men were father-figures in more than one sense, and that it might as well have been Father Eliot as Father D'Arcy.

It was D'Arcy who raised the subject of *The Criterion*, because he had heard that it was in difficulties. I weighed in by saying that for some reason it no longer appeared in the Radcliffe Camera, as I gathered the library had ceased to subscribe to it. This caused Eliot some surprise. He said that the magazine was in good health and that they had not even had to obtain a 'medical opinion' on the subject (it was of course supported partly by a subsidy from Lady Rothermere), but that he would look into the Radcliffe Camera question. We went on to talk about the articles in *Time and Tide* that had so provoked Rebecca West, and Father D'Arcy observed how, in dealing with 'difficult' correspondents, it was important to strike the right note in replying. 'Never write an angry letter!' he exclaimed decisively and by way of offering advice to us all. He had no doubt come to this decision as a result of bitter experience; for he went on to remark how difficult it was to keep one's equanimity when people deliberately distorted one's views – about Catholic teaching, for example. Eliot concurred; but he still felt that sometimes it was necessary to write a fairly sharp rejoinder. I called to mind his letters in *Time and Tide* (January/February 1935) about A. A. Milne's views on war and peace. This included one of the most severe letters I had seen from his pen. For on the whole he kept to D'Arcy's rule.

He had just published in the *New English Weekly* (28 November) a poem called 'Lines for an Old Man' (to which he added a couplet when it was included in *Collected Poems*). In order to test my reaction, and before I had received my copy, Michael had typed it out and sent it to me, almost as if it might be one of his own efforts, and I had reacted with some reserve. It did not seem to me, in that incomplete version, quite to come off, and I still do not regard it among the successful poems. We questioned Eliot about it. First, what was the exact meaning of the title? Was it 'Lines *in the mouth of* an old man'? 'Yes'. Secondly, what did 'writhing in the *essential* blood mean?' What Eliot said in reply to that question has survived in two versions. Michael recalls him as saying that the notion was suggested by a detective story by R. Austin Freeman, which concerned a negro knocking his brow against a bar, so that the blood issuing forth was 'essential'. Michael: 'A Homeric epithet, in other words'. Eliot (with some deliberation and slowly crumbling his cake): 'Yes, you could say that.'

My recollection was that the detective story was one of E. Phillips

Oppenheim's, and that it concerned a horrific murder whereby the victim was, so to speak, liquefied and poured down the sink, so that the 'essence' of him was thus disposed of. I still feel that this story, if I have retold it right, would have appealed to Eliot more than the tamer one about the negro. In any case, I believe Eliot admired the thrillers of the prolific E. Phillips Oppenheim, who was published in the yellow-backed series to which he more than once referred as a possible source of inspiration. It is true that a form of haematuria is called 'essential', but I cannot believe Eliot was referring to that, though I would not put it past him. Our last question concerned 'inaccessible *by* the young'; And Eliot replied that, according to the OED, 'by' was a permissible use with 'inaccessible' as well as 'to', and in his opinion its presence in the last line sounded better.

Not long before there had been a lively correspondence in *The Times* about cheese, and somewhat to the surprise of certain devotees, Eliot had intervened in it. He had asked to be 'put in the way' of a certain variety, and it was Father D'Arcy who enquired whether his request had met with success. This set Eliot on to a technical disquisition which I at least was unable to follow; but it included the fact that, in order to preserve a certain particularly rare cheese or at least to promote its further maturity, the owners had 'buried it'. The solemn and deep tones in which these words were delivered have remained fixed in my memory. As with so many of Eliot's apparently portentous remarks, I fancy that they were uttered partly in a quizzical manner, and that the mock solemnity was intended to convey the idea of a conspiratorial ritual.

Any conversation at that period was bound to touch on the state of the world, and the question of social reform at home; and the allusion to the *New English Weekly*, which to some extent we regarded as 'our' paper, led to some talk of similar minority reviews, including *G.K.'s Weekly*. Father D'Arcy said that he did not think Distributism was the happiest of terms for a politico-economic movement; but he vouched for Chesterton's total sincerity in propounding it, and he hinted that the review was a regular drain on his pocket. Somehow we then got on to the theme of French poetry, and Eliot expressed surprise at one of Herbert Read's recent pronouncements on Laforgue and another nineteenth-century poet I cannot recall and about whom at the time I knew too little to be able to arrive at an opinion. Even at Oxford, I doubted whether there were many people who could adjudicate on a matter of this kind. Yet again, looking at this urbane relaxed figure seated opposite me and comparing him with the romantic figures of

Spender and others or with the scruffy Auden, I found it difficult to believe that he was a poet and not rather some worldly and successful company director. I sometimes thought that he would enjoy being mistaken for the one rather than the other, because he disliked the idea of poetry as a 'profession': an attitude which some lesser figures found puzzling.

His association with the *New English Weekly* was of great value, and lent considerable prestige, to that minority journal, because some of those connected with it were decidedly eccentric, unpractical and in need of guidance. Eliot, who was tolerant of eccentrics as long as he was not expected to join their ranks, sometimes deplored the degree of ascetic zeal that was expected of the supporters. He referred to a dinner given in honour of A. R. Orage, the retiring editor whom Philip Mairet was to replace, which was of inordinate length and at which there were interminable speeches, and where – this was represented as the ultimate horror, uttered in the tones of a *cri de coeur* – 'you couldn't even get a drink!' D'Arcy, who did not despise the good life, seemed to find this display of hedonism a little extreme. At another *NEW* party, there had been present one of the journal's current gurus, Midrinovic, probably taken up first by Orage, who collected such people (at one time he was a disciple of Gurdjieff). Eliot was plain-spoken about this man. He said he was one of the most unpleasant people he had ever met. Apparently, the guru had played little part in the proceedings, confining himself to putting records on the gramophone; and this, for Eliot, seemed to render him the more sinister.

The subject of modern poetry coming up, which it might have been expected to do, D'Arcy put forward the view that the best of the younger poets was Louis MacNeice, because he had had a classical education. Eliot weighed in by saying that he had great hopes of a young man – 'rather a spotty youth' – called Rayner Heppenstall. This heartened D'Arcy, because he had just converted this former communist to Catholicism. (He left the Roman Church not long after, like D'Arcy's Jesuit protégé Henry John, son of Augustus, and wrote a somewhat snarky account of D'Arcy's efforts at proselytizing.) Eliot added that he had written a rather interesting poem about, here he turned to D'Arcy and asked: 'Who was the saint that had arrows stuck all over him?' 'St Sebastian', D'Arcy put in promptly. 'Ah yes: and the poem', resumed Eliot, 'continued four or five good lines in succession, which is pretty rare these days'.

This was a momentary memory-lapse, as Eliot himself had written a poem on the saint, entitled 'The Love Song of St Sebastian', the text of which was in the notebook given to John Quinn and now in the Berg Collection, New York.

He then reminisced about a house-party at which someone had suggested that Mr Eliot (who did not go to many such parties) should be invited to read some of his poems. 'I'm afraid we haven't got any of Mr Eliot's poems', the host answered ruefully. Eliot relayed this in such a manner as to imply grave delinquency on the host's part, and made the anecdote sound very funny. Indeed, he had a remarkable gift for extracting from even the most commonplace remarks or situations some latent humour, which otherwise might never have been suspected. Even the written word, by conjuring up the Eliot tone of voice, could express this kind of humorous gravity, for example, his remark in the 'Dialogue on Dramatic Poetry' that 'we cannot spend all our time reading large philosophical works'. (I have often tried to analyse what makes this statement so amusing, and I have come to the conclusion that it is due to the words 'all' and 'large', so that the *idea* becomes a preposterous one.) Much of his conversation, uttered in the flat voice which set off the originality of the content, conveyed in this way infinite nuances of banter and irony.

We had referred to the rather disturbing politics of *The Times*, which under Geoffrey Dawson favoured appeasement of the dictators. Eliot remarked that as far as he was concerned he took that paper chiefly for the crossword and the company reports. Later, as I know, he took great interest in the law reports, and he always read the letters.

The party broke up when Father D'Arcy, whose life was organized round the liturgy, rose saying that he had to attend an obligatory office at Campion Hall. Eliot asked to be shown the lavatory. Michael, indicating the stairs and implying that he had to go straight on, then directed him to the left, upon which he said quietly, if a trifle reproachfully: 'You said straight on'. As he was moving down, he whipped out an orange stick and began hastily manicuring his nails. This scrupulous attention to neatness, linked with the possession of the necessary equipment, was typical, and explained in part the number of pockets in his suits of which he was to boast.

While he was in the lavatory, Michael tells me that, observing the large hat reposing by the overcoat, I reverently picked it up and placed it on my head. While most of the events of the afternoon have remained firmly in my memory, I had totally forgotten this piece of mischief.

I delivered Eliot to Magdalen, and was one of the first to arrive for the English Club meeting, accompanied by a Somerville girl to whom I had become attached. Although not so thronged as any assembly addressed by Eliot would later have been, the room was full. He was due to read his own poems, but he prefaced the performance with remarking how extraordinary he found it that students obliged to attend lectures should want to turn up for more such talk after hours. He also made some modest remark about his achievement, such as it was, and hazarded the opinion that he might best be remembered by his devotion to cheese. This did not evoke much response from the audience, because *The Times* was not widely read by university students. They either assumed that what appeared in such a paper was nonsense or establishment propaganda, or they read such papers as the *Manchester Guardian*, as it was then called. These preparatory remarks were rather hesitant and repetitive; I did not feel that extempore public speaking came easily to him; but his readings were good, because they totally lacked affectation. Perhaps the most successful rendering was that of the fifth poem of 'Landscapes', entitled 'Cape Ann', which he read with great gusto and of which the last line 'The palaver is finished' produced a ripple of pleasure. So did his explanatory remark that he had written it 'to show that I know something about birds'. He also made a comment on one of his early poems that it belonged to his 'Imagist period', adding almost *sotto voce* and in a typical Eliot way – 'if there was an Imagist period'. He concluded by referring to some work he had been doing on Tennyson. This was the Preface to a selection of the poems, which Leavis was to handle roughly, as he felt that Eliot had no business to be praising Tennyson, any more than later he had any business to be endorsing Kipling.

When the votes of thanks and other formalities were over, I was able to have a brief word with him as he emerged into the vestibule. I said I wanted him to meet my Somerville friend, who, with a fellow-student, was by pre-arrangement sitting on an inner windowsill, from which with an air of spontaneity I was able to summon them down. I can see them perched up there now, swinging their legs. In particular I recall how the fellow-student, in that breathless voice of teenage girls, strangled in this case with awe, asked him whether he knew some Italian poet whose name I could not catch. Eliot could not at first hear it either and bending down with a friendly expression, asked her to repeat the name. He then answered her gently, saying that he did not know that particular poet but that he knew so-and-so and so-and-so from Italy. And he concluded with a half-smile that put the girl in a condition of partial ecstasy. If she should by chance ever read these words, I think she would confirm not merely that this was how he spoke but that I have not misrepresented her reactions. Having delivered Eliot to those who were looking after him for the night, we walked back to our colleges discussing the evening, with the ardour of youth which included that most interesting of contests, the comparison of recollections. This produced the usual tangle of discrepancy.

Soon after this I embarked on another essay, under what stimulus I do not now remember; but I had formed the habit, not of revising or tinkering with an unsatisfactory piece, but of writing something else instead. This was a politico-literary piece, and it brought the following response, dated 5 May 1936.

Dear Tomlin,

I am thinking of using your article *Poetry and Propaganda* in the September number of *The Criterion*, but I have had it on hand for a considerable time, and am therefore writing to you well ahead of that date in case you now want to alter it in any way, or even have something else which you would prefer to see printed.

It is a long time since I have seen you, and I hope you will let me know whenever you are in London long enough to have lunch or tea with me one day.
                Yours sincerely,
                T.S. Eliot.

I replied at once to say that I should be in London shortly and suggested a meeting on Thursday, 14 May. This elicited a reply from his secretary, Brigid O'Donovan, on 12 May, confirming this date. Years later this lady of character was to write a rather moving piece entitled 'The Love Song of T. S. Eliots' secretary' (*Confrontation*, Long Island University, Winter 1975); and from what Eliot said once, though half-jocularly, when he and his wife and I were having a meal together, there was more than one secretary who could have composed such a Love Song, or at least who had the necessary incentive or excuse. I vaguely recall the lady as of ample build and very cheerful, so she was able to put good face on her sad plight.

As tea had been decided upon, I arrived as planned at 3.30 p.m. This was to involve a procedure familiar to many who arrived in the afternoon at Russell Square. Seated at his desk in the corner by the window, Eliot would switch his chair round, and the guest would be settled down opposite. The tea was brought in usually by what seemed a Faber handyman, with whom Eliot would often exchange some kind of *badinage*. It was a simple refreshment ('jam is too much trouble', to quote Stephen Spender's account), and one remembered things like the steady pouring from the teapot, held slightly aloft and repeatedly ritualistically, and no doubt with intent, half-way through the conversation.

On this occasion, we got straight down to business. I think I must have expressed dissatisfaction with the 'Poetry and Propaganda' article, because, like others that I had submitted to him up to that point, it was never to appear. In those days there seemed so many vistas ahead that I did not mind when I began to go public: it was sufficiently gratifying to feel that Eliot wanted to print some of my work in his good time and in mine. I had already made my debut in *Scrutiny*, however, and he may have felt that this made it appropriate that I should have something equivalent in *The Criterion*. These were after all the two leading literary journals. He expressed interest in the article for Leavis, which had been called 'Scrutiny of Modern Greats', and he questioned me closely about the general intellectual *mood* at Oxford. It was clear to me that his own personal preoccupations, such as had been conveyed to me by Father D'Arcy and hinted at by others, had cut him off from the workings of certain institutions – his unawareness of Collingwood's preferment was a case in point – and again he wanted to be informed what the young were thinking. He was particularly interested in the condition of British philosophy. There had been a moment in his career, as he declared in the interesting preface he wrote to Josef Pieper's *Leisure the Basis of Culture* and as Brand Blanshard has retailed in the Eliot Anniversary Issue of *The Southern Review* (1985), ('Eliot at Oxford'), when, after a good deal of philosophical study, he had decided to renounce the subject as such. With one of those insights which showed a mind much subtler than that of many of his contemporaries, he had drawn an analogy between logical positivism and surrealism; but he told me on this occasion that he had once asked A. J. Ayer, as he then was, what political beliefs were compatible with logical positivism : to which the reply had been, not altogether to his surprise, that they would be decidedly left-wing. From some remarks in Sir Alfred Ayer's autobiography (*Part of my Life* Vol. 1, 1978), it seems that the two met infrequently and perhaps did not altogether get on. Naturally, Eliot was pleased about my enthusiasm for Collingwood, for whom he had considerable regard; but although he told me he liked the *Essay on Philosophical Method*, which had appeared in 1933 and concerning which I had attended Collingwood's lecture-course in my first year, I could see that he was more interested in such works as A. E. Taylor's *Faith of a Moralist*, or more directly theological works, such as those of Jacques Maritain. He spoke about the need for an 'exact' theology, and Maritain, with his handbooks on logic, gave the impression of exactitude which most English theologians, brought up in the Hegelian tradition, failed to do. At the same time, although he much liked Maritain as a person (as who could not?), he felt that the French post-Bergsonian intellectual approach, even if called 'Neo-scholastique', differed markedly from that of St Thomas himself: it was the difference between a hovering darting kestrel and a 'dumb ox' pawing the ground.

Another function in London which I was able to attend was a lecture by Eliot at that same Group Theatre at which I had seen *Sweeney Agonistes*. He had not long declared that poetry was a 'mug's game'; and Rupert Doone, not the most accomplished of public speakers, got rather tied up by trying to say that Eliot was not himself a mug and yet somehow implying that, for saying such a thing he must be. Eliot produced a single page of notes from his pocket which he placed before him on the small table and brooded over for a while; but when he started, he managed to pack in, during 45 minutes or so, a great deal of sound sense on the subject of drama and especially on the relation of drama to religion. He had a habit of beginning each section with some arresting phrase such as 'Savages and churchmen . . .', which made the audience sit up. By stating that he rarely went to the theatre, and needed to be forcibly taken there if he went at all, he managed to lay bare the inadequacies of modern drama and defined the conditions of a new sort of drama altogether. One point he made which I have rarely seen put forward so well: that the audience cannot be expected to follow any profound drama at all levels at once, and that there may be certain aspects which remain beyond the audience's comprehension altogether. Every play should leave a question-mark. And like the performance of the liturgy, the audience may not actually *hear* everything that is being declaimed.

He gave in that connection some instances from *The Rock*, which he described not so much as a play as a revue, a word he pronounced in the French manner. Then, after a longer pause than usual, he affirmed: 'And that is as far as my thought has reached'. It lent to his words an air of impressive finality, as if he had been thinking out each point for the first time and had come to a halt. I had only a brief opportunity of shaking his hand at the end, as I was obliged to rush back to Oxford before I was 'gated'.

Routine played an important part in Eliot's life. Without it, I doubt if he could have undertaken such work as he did. There was a moment, particularly at tea, when I would sense that our conversation was, so far as he was concerned, due to come to an end. I would therefore display a becoming restiveness, or look round for the usual dispatch-case, so that when he started slowly rising to his feet, which he did as if by some inner mechanism, I could, like an adjoining lift, follow him slightly behindhand. There was only one occasion when, either preoccupied or through sheer inattentiveness, I found him rising before I had made preparations to follow. I remember feeling a good deal embarrassed, which he imperturbably pretended not to notice, thereby perhaps further teaching me a lesson in Eliot-etiquette, though he was the last person deliberately to make anyone feel uneasy.

Before I left, I expressed the hope that he could pay another visit to Oxford, though this time a purely private one, and I see that I wrote to him repeating this towards the end of term – the final term – because on 17 June he replied to my home address:

> Dear Tomlin,
> I have your letter of June 12th, and I am afraid that there is no prospect of my getting down to Oxford – except Friday next on business – during the present term. In fact, I see from your letter that the term is over to-day. I am very sorry, but June is apt to be a very full month. I hope I shall see you before long in London.
> Yours sincerely,
> T.S. Eliot.

Back home, I wrote to him on 4 July, enclosing a shortish essay which the comparative leisure afforded by leaving Oxford had made possible. This produced a reply which I am sure was wholly deserved (though I cannot remember the essay), as were his comments on an earlier submission. As will be seen, I had not quite expelled from my system the preoccupation with Rowse's views; and while one barrier to their expression had been removed, the other – that the book was no longer the target it had once been – had just been erected. But true to his plan not to do anything to interrupt, or to deflect me from, my studies, while I was up at Oxford, he took the first opportunity, now that I had gone down, to enlist my services with *The Criterion*. On 14 July, he wrote:

Dear Tomlin,
   I have your letter of the 4th July, and have read your short article once, but must read it again. My first impression is that it is somewhat too concentrated and abstract to be successful, and that it needs, as aesthetics frequently does, continual imersion [*sic*] in the concrete instance. Meanwhile I return your earlier essay *Slaves to the Future*, which I imagine you might want now to revise before you publish it. The objection I raised at the time that it was unwise and perhaps unsuitable to criticise a don in print in this way while you were an undergraduate, no longer exists, and I should like to do something with this article. Only I feel that Rowse's book itself has become a little out of date, and that it is a disadvantage to your article to give it primary place.
   I notice that you have nothing to review for the nex [*sic*] number of *The Criterion*. Would it interest you to tackle a number of volumes of poetry to gether [*sic*] as the man I expected to do it is taking a holiday and would hardly be able to get it done by the 29th of July, when I must have the review? It might make an interesting change for once from philosophy. The most important is probably Michael Roberts's, but there are also Frederick Prokosch, Dorothy Wellesley, and a small book of new poems by Marianne Moore. Also there is a translation of Eluard's Surrealist poems, which might give you the opportunity for generalizations about the nature of poetry. Only please let me know at once.
       Yours ever,
       T.S. Eliot.

The statement 'I notice that you have nothing to review for the next number' could only have been written by him. I had noticed it too, and I was all the more pleased with the prospect of doing something in what was coming to be my other sphere of interest, namely, literature and especially poetry. Moreover, a change from philosophy was in many ways to be desired, as it so often is. I had found myself reacting more and more against the linguistic/logical positivist approach; and, shortly after its appearance in 1936, I had written a sustained diatribe against A. J. Ayer's *Language, Truth and Logic* (1936). This appeared in *Scrutiny*, and attracted some notice, not least from Ayer himself, with whom I was later to form a warm friendship. But I looked to a philosophical point of view more comprehensive even than that of the early Collingwood, and I thought I had found the germ of it in the lectures he delivered in my last year on 'Nature and Mind'. This I still consider the most brilliant *course* of lectures I have ever heard anywhere, and I have heard a great many. (The lectures were posthumously published in 1945 under the title of *The Idea of Nature*.) I turn aside to record this judgment, because it is relevant to a later stage of this memoir. Another reason why I needed a change, or something else by way of reaction, was an increasing interest in current politics.

I had been given a very short time to assimilate the books of poetry and to write the review: a time-limit that would have been almost impossible for me to meet today, so much more sluggish has my mind become; but I felt that if Eliot thought I could do the job, it was doubtless within my capacity. The typescript was delivered on time, perhaps a little early. Indeed, I much enjoyed the work; and, in view of my interest in aesthetics (stimulated by a study of a man almost considered unmentionable in these days, Benedetto Croce), I relished the opportunity of discussing the nature of poetry.

Eliot printed the review in the issue of *The Criterion* for 1936. It was not as good as I should have wished, partly because I was in a hurry, but also partly because I had not yet learnt – if I was ever to master – the technique of literary criticism. In fact, George Every, then a lay brother at Kelham, with whom I had started a correspondence, told me later that Eliot, while praising some individual points, had said that the general impression it gave was of material being put through a machine and coming out the other side more or less as it was before. The simile was so striking and no doubt so apt, and one that was so delightfully Eliotish, that I could not take offence, though a critical word from that quarter could deal a heavy blow to one's morale. Apart from this stricture, I think I overestimated Dorothy Wellesley and perhaps underrated Marianne Moore. Years later, when I met, through Eliot's sister-in-law, that charming, modest, retiring lady in Brooklyn, I was relieved to find that she had liked what I had written about her.

1 The author as a schoolboy.

2 A passport photograph of T.S. Eliot in 1932.

3 T.S. Eliot in his office at Faber & Faber in the early years.

material. But this is a delusion. Religious values are cumulative; the Origins are important because they are the springs of a living tradition. And just as no one would place any considerable value upon a foundation stone which supported no structure, so the Origins of a religion, vitally important and indispensable though they must obviously be, will have no meaning without the tradition to which they have given rise. Indeed, it is quite impossible to imagine these Origins <u>apart</u> from an accompanying tradition; that is to say, it is impossible to conceive of the Origin of Nothing-at-all.

No wonder Lawrence lost himself in a cabbalistic miasma; for he was essentially a modern man — so modern, in fact, that he realised that most of his contemporaries were living upon obsolete ideas. But the curse of his upbringing prevented him from perceiving certain facts that, had he known them, might have reorientated his outlook. To take one example, I quote again from Mr Carter's essay :—

"He was mostly taken by the symbolism of the figure of the Great Man in the stars — the macrocosm. He declared it gave him a feeling of that sense of liberation and freedom which had disappeared with the coming of the belief in a salvation which must be attained in another world. To his opinion, this soteriological scheme had followed on, and usurped, the place of the previous theory of rebirth, a resurrifying descent within oneself. Such a regenerative ceremonial was not otherworldly but was close knit into this life. It meant more and fuller life here. The ritual brought release from This — our prison within the bonds of old habit."

At the risk of provoking a storm of denunciations from both young and old, I do not hesitate to say that the feeling expressed in these lines is one that can only find complete satisfaction in the dogmas and ritual of a traditional Church. For a ritualistic religion has the peculiar nature of being both "otherworldly" (and, in spite of his denial of

4 Extract from the author's early essay on 'The Younger Generation and Politics', submitted to Faber & Faber when at school, inscribed with T.S. Eliot's notes.

5 T.S. Eliot in his office at Faber & Faber. His room was always crowded with books.

ELIOT HOUSE,
CAMBRIDGE MASS.
   Mr. T. S. Eliot.
                  U.S.A
98 Clarence Gate Gardens.
   Regents Park. N.W.1.

6 T.S. Eliot's visiting card with the address at Harvard given to the author at their second meeting, 1931.

7 T.S. Eliot in the grounds at Kelham, headquarters of the Society of Sacred Mission, taken in the mid-1930s.

8 The chapel at Kelham. T.S. Eliot was a frequent visitor to the monastery.

Best wishes for a vS↑fne Convalescence. Mr. T.S. Eliot

9 T.S. Eliot's visiting card accompanying flowers sent to the author in Guy's Hospital.

10 Drawing of T.S. Eliot by the author based on a photograph in *The Green Quarterly*, and from observation, 1937.

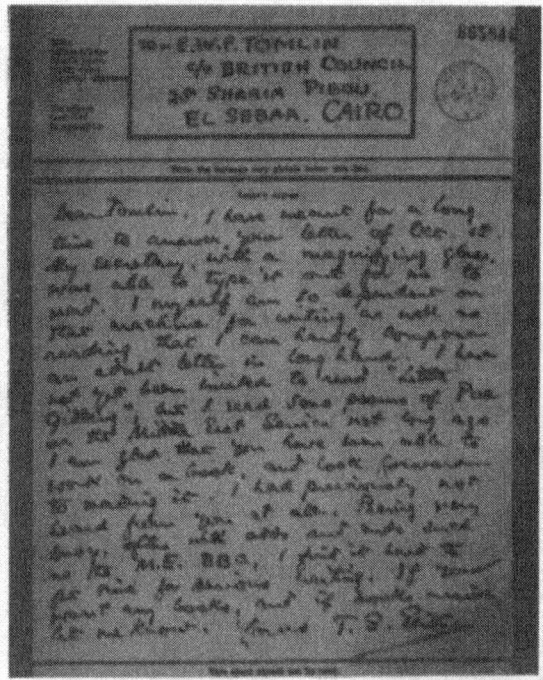

11 A wartime airgraph to the author from T.S. Eliot.

12 Photograph of the author, taken in Paris, 1947.

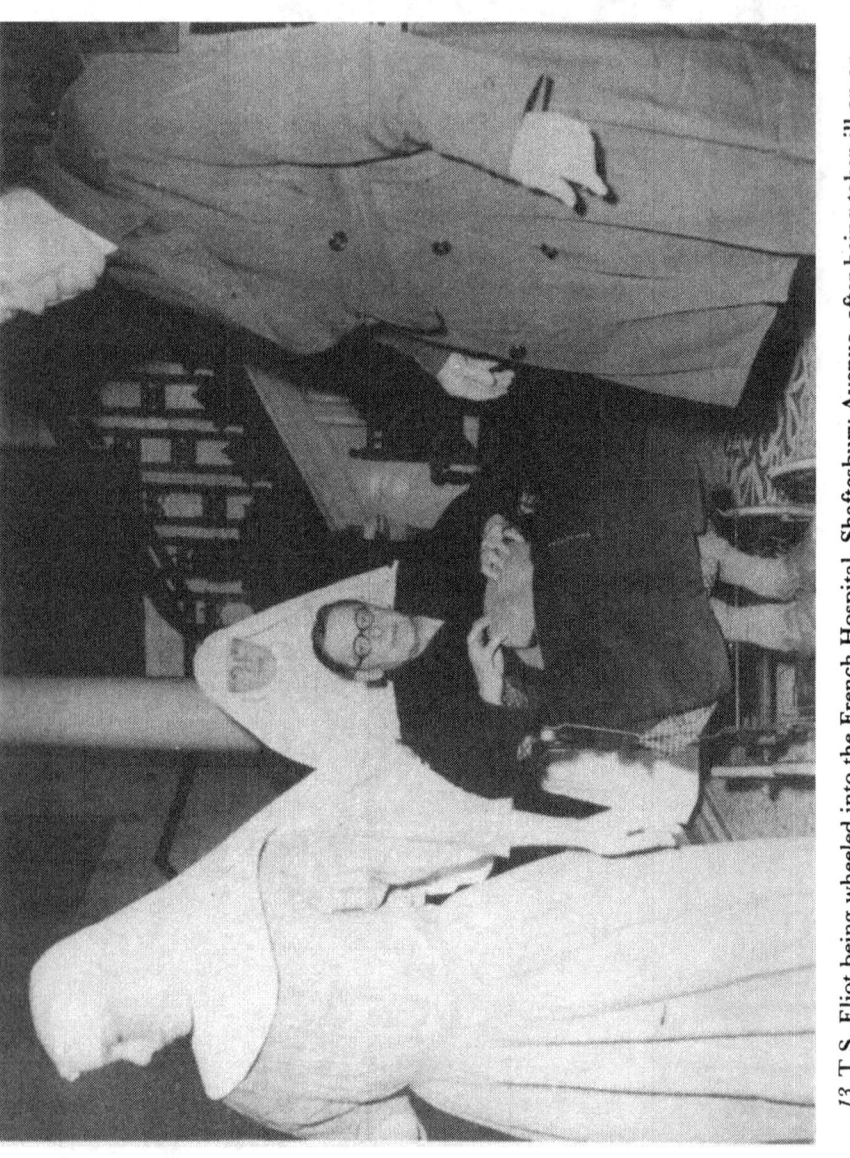

13 T.S. Eliot being wheeled into the French Hospital, Shaftesbury Avenue, after being taken ill on an Atlantic crossing. The photograph appeared in the *Evening Standard*, 12 June, 1956.

14 Drawing of T.S. Eliot asleep, Cambridge, Mass., by his sister-in-law, Theresa Eliot.

15 T.S. Eliot in relaxed mood in his office at Faber & Faber.

16 T.S. Eliot and his wife photographed in the early morning, following a celebration of the opening of *The Elder Statesman*, 26 September, 1958.

Sir Geoffrey Faber, Chairman. Richard de la Mare, Vice-Chairman
T. S. Eliot, W. J. Crawley, Morley Kennerley, (U.S.A.), P. F. du Sautoy,
Alan Pringle, David Bland, Charles Monteith

FABER AND FABER LTD

PUBLISHERS
24 Russell Square London WC1
Fabbaf Westcent London   Museum 9543

TSE/AM   17th June, 1959.

Frederick Tomlin, Esq.,
c/o The British Embassy,
Ankara,
Turkey.

My dear Tomlin,

    I am delighted to see your name in the Honours List, but having some information of all that you have done in the service of the British Council and thinking of your other merits and achievements, of which officialdom is perhaps ignorant, I wish that it might have been a higher honour.

                    Yours ever,

                            T. S. Eliot

17 T.S. Eliot's congratulatory letter to the author, 17 June, 1959.

18 The T.S. Eliot memorial tablet in the south transept of St Stephen's, Gloucester Road.

CHAPTER FOUR

The year 1936 was an eventful one. The threat of unemployment, even for apparently 'qualified' people, was such that I had to cast round desperately for a job. Teaching was the only practical possibility though one of the few other options was acting as an agent for Tootals ties. Finally, I secured a post as an assistant master at Sloane School, Chelsea, the headmaster of which, Guy Boas, himself a writer, was the son of the Shakespeare scholar who had taken the chair at Eliot's King's College lecture. As Eliot had allowed me to give his name as a reference, my appointment, in the face of a number of other young men hungry for employment and no doubt better qualified (for I had neither teaching experience nor teaching qualifications), may well have owed much to him. As to the teaching profession, he said that he could have wished me to have obtained a less demanding post, if I wanted to write, because his experience at Highgate School had led him to believe that teaching, if conscientiously undertaken, was one of the most exhausting of occupations; and, though I do not regret the experience, I was to discover that regarding its rigours he was right.

At the beginning of the year George V died and Edward VIII acceded to the throne. By the end of the year he had abdicated. In my small way, because I felt that the whole business had been handled most unsatisfactorily by Baldwin and exploited by others, including the Archbishop of Canterbury, I plunged into the resulting controversy. It seemed to me that the matrimonial question could have been dealt with more sympathetically and with greater understanding, as perhaps Winston Churchill could have handled it. (In fact, his conduct in the crisis nearly ruined his career.) So I wrote a strong article on the subject in the *New English Weekly*. This was critical of a piece written by Maurice Reckitt. Philip Mairet, the editor, who was sympathetic to my views, tried to persuade Eliot to contribute his, and he eventually agreed to do so. The developments that occurred : the extraordinary behaviour of certain sections of the press; and the later career of the Duke of Windsor, provoked in me both short-term and long-term disillusionment; but I do not intend to go into any further detail here, though I cannot repudiate what I said. My growing interest in politics, however, was reflected in Eliot's letter to me of 4 January 1937:

> Dear Tomlin,
> Would you be willing to look at Stephen Spender's book ('Forward from Liberalism' or some such title) to consider whether you could review it together with Strachey's? I cannot think of anyone who could do it better. There is plenty of time, as it is for the April or June number: if April, review by January 29th.
>   In haste,
>   Yours,
>   T.S. Eliot.

He had already sent me the Strachey book, *The Theory and Practice of Marxism*, and Spender's, the original title of which was *The Approach to Communism*, seemed to me to go with it very well. Again, I am amazed that I accomplished the job so quickly seeing that most of the work was done at weekends. I am no less interested to observe that, for Eliot, who always seemed unhurried, 'there is plenty of time' could mean a period of not much more than three weeks for reading (the Strachey book being pretty long), writing, typing and dispatching: which, given the fact that Spender's book had not arrived, that I was teaching all day and conducting some evening classes, I still consider a tight fit. As his next letter, dated 11 January showed, the Spender book could not have reached me before 12 January at the earliest, and I wanted to keep to the length of an article.

Dear Tomlin,

Thank you for your letter which I should have answered before but have been rather mixed up this week. I am having Spender's book sent to you. I think you can afford to make the review fairly long because I don't think the reviews this quarter will be overcrowded. I should much have preferred to accept your suggestion for turning the review into an article, but, unfortunately, a review by Philip Mairet has already become an article and somebody else wants to convert his review into an article for the following number. So it would really suit me better this time if you would let me print it in review form. I should like to publish something by you in the body of the following number, either that essay on poetry or something else.

        Yours ever,
        T.S. Eliot.

By the middle of January 1937, he had spoken to Mairet, and he gave the impression that anything he might write about the crisis in the *New English Weekly* would be done with some reluctance, not least because he was extremely busy. The church and state broadcasts to which he referred in his next letter were noteworthy as containing one of his own, of which I thought highly. On 15 January 1937 he had written:

Dear Tomlin,

Thank you for your note. It is true that I have talked to Mairet about a note on the crisis for the NEW, but I simply haven't had the time even to get my ideas in order. I have been very busy ever since, partly with a talk in the Church, Community and State series, of which you may have seen the first, a pretty mediocre production too, by Sir Walter Moberley in the current LISTENER. I should be glad if you could hear or read these talks in the successive five weeks, and I should very much like to have your opinion later about the whole affair. It might even provide an article by you for the N.E.W. [*sic*]. The fact of my participation rather precludes any discussion for the CRITERION.

        Yours sincerely,
        T.S. Eliot.

As for his suggestion that I should comment or write on the series, I did not follow this up. Save for his own contribution and not out of slavish concurrence with his views, I found the talks even duller to read than to hear. Meanwhile, to my surprise and gratification – given his heavy schedule – he wrote an article for the *New English Weekly* (25 February 1937) entitled 'Mr Reckitt, Mr Tomlin and the Crisis'. This began with some flattering words about us both, and implied that he had for long been unable to make up his mind about the abdication. Indeed he had changed it several times a day while the crucial events were occurring. But the points he made were chiefly concerned with moral questions affecting the status of divorce, on which he had strong views: whereas I had been occupied more with the Baldwin government and its apparent wish to stifle certain political views, especially concerning unemployment, to which the King had given expression. These had boiled down to the supposed constitutionally irregular remark that 'something must be done'. I also found certain sections of the press grossly biased; and when a representative of the *Daily Express* called at the *New English Weekly* office and asked for a copy of the relevant issue, I thought I might be involved in a libel action.

Today, when even Catholic priests are prepared to advocate radical departures from conventional morality, Eliot's views may appear nostalgically old-fashioned. But that did not perturb me. What caused me concern was, as I say, the slightly uncomfortable feeling that Eliot had been bounced into writing an article which he did not particularly relish doing and to which he would in any case have wished to devote much more reflection. Philip Mairet had written to me on 14 February 1937 saying that Eliot had 'promised' an article. I therefore wrote to express the hope that I had not appeared to expect him to intervene; that I did not necessarily disagree with what he said; and that my underlying feeling was that the Baldwin government, though apparently trying to get rid of a bad king, might damage the monarchy at a time when a great international crisis seemed to be upon us. In this I was happily to be proved wrong, but who could have known that at the time? (For those interested in the whole question, I consider John Grigg's account of the Duke of Windsor in the *DNB* to be the fairest assessment I know.) To this letter I received a reply dated 1 March which contained some of the most interesting remarks he ever communicated to me, and which is of permanent value in reflecting his opinions on much wider issues:

THE CRITERION
A Quarterly Review
edited by T.S.Eliot

24 Russell Square
London, W.C.1.
1 March, 1937.

E.W.F. Tomlin, Esq.,
Wychwood House,
Merstham,
Surrey.

Dear Tomlin,

Thank you for your letter of the 27th. I had feared that I might find you in total disagreement with the position which I took up, and I am gratified that you are not. It seemed to me that to a superficial examination I might be appearing as what I am not particularly anxious to be – an apologist for the Baldwin Government.

You must not think that you had any responsibility for driving me to write. I think that Mairet will be quite willing to shoulder the whole of that burden.

Please understand that I am as apprehensive as you are about the mendacity of the Press: not that I attach great importance to *that* incident in itself, but that I think it one piece of evidence amongst many, of something which you justly suggest is more dangerous than 'corruption'. I had rather also consider my general dissatisfaction with the attitude of the Church in a larger frame of reference than that of the NEW discussion.

What are you doing at Merstham? Do you come up daily to the Sloane School? If so, what days of the week are possible for you for lunch, or if lunch is impossible, could you stay up and dine?

I told you that I should like to have a contribution for the June number, but now it looks as if I would much rather have it for October. Owing to certain complications and misunderstandings I am printing three whole cantos of Ezra Pound's in the April number, and that has meant shoving forward into June several things which I had hoped to print sooner. In that event, is there anything you would like to review for June? I have, by the way, a small book on the Crown by Erskine of Marr, but it looks popular

and rubbishy, and merely part of the expected Coronation litter.
              Yours ever sincerely,
                  T.S. Eliot.

It was a relief to read those lines, especially the third paragraph. They are worth a great deal even today, because of the familiar insinuations that Eliot was as much a political reactionary as a religious bigot. He was neither. He once called liberalism a form of bigotry, but he did not particularly mind being called a bigot himself. Whenever he spoke of these matters it was with a flexibility and charity such as those holding views less firm did not always display. With regard to the Church, however, one wonders how far today such flexibility would have been exercised.

His enquiry about my whereabouts was due to our having moved house. Merstham was in a slightly more rural area of Surrey, and one upon which we had always looked with favour. This meant a slightly longer, but more pleasant, train journey to London; and it presented no problems about staying up in the evening, whereas with my school duties lunch was out of the question.

I wrote to tell him this, and also referring to another book he had sent me, and I received a reply dated 19 March 1937:

E.W.F. Tomlin Esq.,
Wychwood House,
Merstham,
Surrey.

Dear Tomlin,
   I have been waiting to answer your letter until I could suggest a meeting. The next week is not a very good occasion for dinner, but if you would care to dine early with me on Wednesday evening, the 24th, and come to Tenebrae at Saint Stephen's, I should be delighted. I do not know whether you are familiar with that service, which I think is a peculiarly beautiful and moving one, and has always been done extremely well at Saint Stephen's.
   If not, I am afraid our meeting must be postponed until after the 6th of April, as I have to go to Scotland directly after Easter.
   I hope that you found Madariaga as satisfying as you hoped.
              Yours sincerely,
                  T.S. Eliot.

[Handwritten] But perhaps vacation will have started. In that (*sic*)

I imagine you will prefer dinner in April.

The attendance at St Stephen's did not happen for reasons which he would explain, and I was sorry to have missed it. It would have thrown light on Eliot's attitude to the liturgy and to the drama, which in his view were indissolubly linked, though he realized the temptation to enjoy the emotions of the Mass for their own sake; a point he had made in his 'Dialogue on Poetic Drama'. One of the merits of Father Cheetham as Vicar – a man who played an important role in Eliot's life – was that he was, if the expression is not irreverent, a fine ecclesiastical showman. I was not to attend St Stephen's until years later, when I lived in the parish; but meanwhile I had attended Tenebrae more than once, and had indeed found it beautiful and moving, with the abrupt *strepitacula* somehow reinforcing the effect. In this instance, there had been a mix-up, and for once Eliot's memory had played him tricks. In a letter which has disappeared, he said that he could not manage 24 March after all, and he explained why in a letter dated that same day.

24 March, 1937.

E.W.F. Tomlin Esq.,
Wychwood House,
Merstham,
Surrey.

Dear Tomlin,
    Thank you for your letter of the 22nd. What happened was that I had previously asked Mr and Mrs Martin Browne for the same occasion, and as they had been rather long in answering I had forgotten about it. Then of course after I wrote to you I heard from them that they would like to come. I am very sorry indeed, because I think you would have found the occasion very interesting. Perhaps we can manage it next year. However, we must now wait until after the 6th, when I will write to you again.
    With sincere regrets and apologies,
        Yours,
        T.S. Eliot.

The visit to Scotland, which reinforced both his affection for the beauty of that country and his interest in her history (for he was always attached to small countries or communities which had clung to their traditions) had produced the poem 'Rannoch, by Glencoe', published in the *New English Weekly*, 17 October 1935. In the next letter he wrote me, dated 7 May, he announced that he was to have a holiday; and this I knew to be much overdue.

7 May 1937.

E.W.F. Tomlin Esq.,
Wychwood House,
Merstham,
Surrey.

My dear Tomlin,

I am very regretful that I have been rather pushed this week, and unable to suggest an evening for dinner. I am going abroad for a fortnight's holiday on Monday, but would like if possible to fix an evening now. Would either Tuesday or Thursday, the 25th and 27th, suit you to dine at the Oxford and Cambridge Club, and choose your own time?

I read your last article in the N.E.W. with much interest and a good deal of sympathy, though I must wait for an opportunity to discuss it with you. I did not find that it shook my own previous views, because there are several issues involved.

I hear from Reckitt that you have been working at a political book, and I hope very much that you will be letting me see it. Incidentally, would a text-book of Marxist philosophy (Gollancz interest you for October?

Hoping to see you within three weeks,
        Yours ever sincerely,
        T.S. Eliot.

The *New English Weekly* article was a follow-up to one I wrote about the abdication crisis. It would probably read very stale now, if I could bring myself to look at it. I did not wonder that it failed to 'shake' Eliot. All I can say is that this excursion into public affairs further encouraged me in a project I had already formed: namely to write a book on political theory, to be entitled *Liberal and Servile Society*. I intended the word liberal to mean 'free', not as identifying me with the almost defunct Liberal Party of that epoch. As this turns up later in the memoir, I need only report that, out of dissatisfaction, I scrapped the manuscript more than once, and therefore I did not show it to Eliot just then. I forget how it was that I told Maurice

Reckitt about it before Eliot, who usually received prior intelligence about my activities in this sphere. The Marxist book I reviewed with several others in *The Criterion* for October 1937.

On 25 May I dined with Eliot at the Oxford and Cambridge Club. On meeting him again, I at once noticed that he was looking unusually well and bronzed. He told me he had been in Austria and he mentioned how 'handsome' he had found the people. Altogether he struck me as being in better spirits than usual; and I learnt later, though not from him and I cannot vouch for its veracity, that he had had himself psychoanalysed. I doubt whether this implied anything lurid; it may have been just a consultation.

Years earlier he had resided briefly at a clinic with Vivien, where Robert Sencourt claimed to have first met them both: and earlier still he had spoken of a mental condition of 'long-standing'. Concerning this there has been much speculation. I believe that it was, or had some connection with, a species of agoraphobia, which in his case manifested itself as an acute fear of heights. He told me about this condition quite openly, including the impulse to throw himself over cliffs etc. At the Canterbury Eliot Symposium in 1983, Tom Faber mentioned the attacks of vertigo Eliot suffered while on holiday in Wales. What the psychiatrists or psychoanalysts make of this condition I do not know. If in order to get to the root of it Eliot consulted a Viennese expert, the result was not evidently a cure, because I believe he suffered from it all his life: but the consultation, if that was what it was, may have benefited him by disclosure – 'the luxury of an intimate disclosure to a stranger'.

Seated opposite each other, we naturally began by discussing the 'crisis'. Next to that of Suez in 1956, it had divided more families than any I can remember. He began by saying: 'Well, we both agree it's a bad business' – an indication that the subject was still alive months after the accession of a new king. I found him sympathetic, though still in principle opposed to the line I had taken. Indeed he agreed that a great deal of hypocrisy had been involved in what Macaulay had called one of the 'fits of morality' to which the British nation was periodically subject. I also think he had been slightly influenced by Father D'Arcy, with whom he had apparently been in recent touch. The Catholic intelligentsia had been highly critical of the way the government had conducted itself: *Blackfriars*, the Oxford Dominican journal, had taken a line which I found especially sympathetic; and D'Arcy, to whom I had sent my article, wrote to me expressing approval of my stand. He was a staunch monarchist, and possibly even more of a king's man that Eliot.

Our conversation moved cautiously round the subject of corruption in public life, and I quoted Burke, whose *Thoughts on the Present Discontents* I had been studying, to the effect that wisdom consisted in part in deciding how much evil to tolerate. I suppose I was defending a monarchy that had in the past seen some unsuitable sovereigns, while he somewhat deftly applied the same argument to unsatisfactory prime ministers. Looking back, I find one point interesting: the chief actors in the drama, Baldwin and the Duke of Windsor, were both to fall in public esteem, and the reputation of neither seems likely to recover. Although Eliot expressed some liking for Edward VIII as a man, he felt he lacked character. He also referred to some presumed sexual oddity, which had made the unfortunate Prince lean more heavily on the one woman, out of a number, who seemed able to cope with it. That Eliot tended to be curious in such matters, others have noted, and they have sometimes inferred some oddity in his own make-up. I rather felt it testified to the contrary. At any rate, in those days such matters were rarely discussed in detail, let alone in a London Club, and we did not pursue the subject.

We moved to a discussion of events at home. From 10 to 23 of the month there had been a bus-strike, which had naturally caused a great deal of inconvenience. The busmen's case had been that their strict schedules made the satisfactory operation of physical functions difficult. At that time, strikes were regarded by most members of the middle class as conspiracies against the established order, as sometimes they may have been; but this particular stoppage, concerning itself chiefly with man's natural being and constitution, seemed to Eliot to be quite different from the normal down-tools affair. 'I'm all for the busmen', he remarked decisively. And he meant it. He was a very radical conservative, more genuinely radical than many of the rabble-rousers who had monopolized the term, and even than the members of the intelligentsia who claimed to have the 'workers' interests at heart. When I told my friends Bill Page and Bill Adams, both of whom were bus inspectors and the first of whom had been at Whitgift with me, they were astounded. They had assumed without question that Eliot, the royalist and high churchman, would have sided automatically with the establishment or what was then called the ruling class.

Except to say that it was scrupulously chosen, as was usual with Eliot, I forget what we ate on the occasion: we had so much to talk about. What I do recall is that we drank beer which Eliot, like George Saintsbury, regarded as having certain virtues, especially at lunch-time, which wine did not possess. It also enabled him to wrap his hand round the glass, even if it had a handle, in a manner peculiarly his own.

When we adjourned to the lounge, he glanced down at a newspaper that had been cast aside, commenting in a murmur: 'the usual half-finished crossword!' No doubt the sight afforded him quiet amusement, because he was a crossword expert himself, being renowned for finishing *The Times* daily puzzle in record time. But I think it also reflected his sense of the inherent fragmentary nature of life. Once settled in an armchair, he took out a shortish but fairly carbonized pipe and began smoking. Noticing that I was not provided for, he slapped his right-side coat pocket and, diving in, produced an opened packet of Gauloise Bleu, from which loose container he took out a cigarette. Then, as now, the smell of Gauloises would immediately evoke Paris, and to one accustomed, as I then was, to Players or Craven A, a French cigarette was still a novelty. But what struck me then was the idea of his habitually alternating with pipe and cigarette-smoking. Over the years this must have harmed his chest, as it had already badly discoloured his teeth. Yet I could see, sitting next to him, that it brought him contentment which at other levels he lacked. He also enjoyed luxuriating a little after a meal, and at such moments he seemed all the more benign and at peace even with himself.

Having by then disposed of public affairs, he asked me about my work at the LCC school. As stated, he understood only too well the problems and burdens of schoolmastering. He reiterated one of the problems that dogged him throughout life, which was fatigue; for although he had on the whole a 'tough' constitution – at least he liked to think so – and tremendous will-power, he had driven himself very hard over the past twenty years. This and his personal worries, which must have seemed without issue, were perhaps responsible for a certain reliance, though by no means dependence, on alcohol. True I never saw him the worse for drink, but often the better. He was perhaps one of those people, myself included, who, to quote a character in a Compton Mackenzie novel, were born two whiskies below par. Except in a reference to the composition of *Sweeney*

Agonistes, he wrote little about the place of alcohol, or any other narcotic, in literary creation. But he mentioned in an essay the degree to which certain forms of anaemia were conducive to such creation; and, in our conversation that day, he described how, when he was working on *The Waste Land* in Switzerland in 1921 ('by the waters of Leman'), he felt at one moment that his brain was going to burst. That is perhaps the reason for his saying, in an interview late in life, that at that moment, he 'did not know what he was writing'. Indeed, the poem has all the inevitability of subconscious control.

He more than once declared that, compared with schoolmastering, work at the bank was almost a rest cure. But it had its problems, even so. One of them was his habitual slowness, especially in handling and totting up cash; for, before he took up duties in the foreign exchange department of Lloyds in the semi-basement room at the branch at 20 King William Street (no wonder that the eyes and back, at the end of the day, turned 'upward' from the desk), he worked for a period behind the counter. He seems to have pleased certain customers; he was once, as he told me, presented over the grille with some game, which, before accepting, he was naturally obliged to take to the manager's office. The sight of the slim, prim, young American moving towards the managerial door carrying a brace of partridges, or whatever it was, must have been diverting. I think he enjoyed the bank, not merely because it was a change from teaching, but because the City exerted so great a fascination over him. With the river, the hemmed-in churches, and certain pubs, it provided much of the raw material of *The Waste Land*. Moreover, as he made clear, he found the measured pace and rhythm of the work especially congenial, coinciding as it did with a period of remarkable creative gestation. He was always against the Poet's Pub idea. To him, the poetry of taverns resided in their authentic atmosphere, not one rendered bogus by the intrusion of 'art'. Like all office work, as I myself knew only too well, the bank was not invariably plain-sailing. A letter I came across in the Houghton Library at Harvard bemoans to his father an incident in which, for some reason, he had offended a women clerk to whom he had consigned some typing. The incident, which has parallels in most people' experience, irked him evidently a good deal; for he could not leave the subject alone.

I must have said something about being in reasonably good health despite a rather dismal daily round of commuting to Charing Cross and a crawl by bus up the King's Road to the appropriately named

World's End pub, but that I was more tormented at that time with a clash of affections with two young ladies. For the purpose of this memoir, the details are irrelevant, and my experience was commonplace to that time of life; but I needed to talk to someone. What struck me was the way in which he seemed to have little difficulty not merely in coming down to my level but in entering into my feelings, as if I were telling him about the most natural matter in the world. Later, I reflected that to be in receipt of confidences of this kind, if my own experience was anything to go by, could be insufferably taxing to the patience. If this were so in the present case, he concealed the fact with remarkable aplomb; but my impression was that he rather welcomed this degree of personal contact, as if it provided some sort of relief from the heavy intellectual conversation repeatedly forced upon him. If 'we hear the key turn each in his prison', it may be a satisfaction to find occasionally that entry rather than closure is being sought; for while he had a great many acquaintants and, as his fame increased, hundreds who wanted to meet him if only in order to say they had done so, he lacked relationships which were simple, straightforward, and stable.

At any rate, whenever I abandoned the usual literary-cum-public-affairs talk, I would observe him, as in this instance, perceptibly to relax. In fact, I felt he was more than ready to discuss male-female relations. Looking back he said he realised how clumsily he had behaved in certain situations, and indeed what an 'unpleasant' person (that was the adjective he used) he knew he had sometimes been. Whether this referred to the monocle-and-green-face-powder period (though the latter can, I believe, be explained by a skin rash), I have no idea. A possible clue to this unusual verbal spate of self-revelation, which caused me some surprise, was, as we now know, that he was at that time engaged in writing *The Family Reunion*.

Writing the play brought back a whole period of his early life: not merely the marriage to Vivien but the friendship with Emily Hale. That companion of his undergraduate years, who obviously hoped that one day she would replace Vivien, was visiting England during the school vacation. Her visit, which had been repeated since 1935, was, I learnt later, not an unmixed pleasure for him. Nevertheless, in speaking of the different 'rhythms' of which any relationship needed to take account, he showed a pretty shrewd understanding of the female character; an understanding which has sometimes been denied.

He brought our conversation to an end by alluding once more to the past; and in comparing the difference between his present achievements and the tribulations that had led up to it (though he did not put it quite like that), he appeared to coin on the spot an epigram which, so far as I know, he never committed to print but of which there are echoes in *The Family Reunion*. 'Success', he propounded, 'is what a man does with his failure'. He then gave me a slight shock by lapsing into a brief sort of reverie, and saying that if one had ever felt like 'murdering someone', one could never do anything about it. Something had been registered in the past and in one's own being, and that was that. I recalled the lines from *Sweeney Agonistes*:

Any man might do a girl in,
Any man has to, needs to, wants to
Once in a lifetime, do a girl in,

This was to be echoed later by Harry's impression in *The Family Reunion* of having killed his wife. In view of the evasive comments he later made on this latter episode (Canon Demant tells of his being pressed by some German students and saying that he was the last person to be able to answer them), I believe that he had experienced a *moment* of horrifying self-revelation 'of all that he had done and been' and *thought*, which had opened up a wound that could not heal. This, it seems to me, and not some homosexual fantasy, was what *The Waste Land*, with its afflicted Fisher King, was basically about.

I could not help feeling that this particular meeting of ours proved a milestone, at least for me; and thereafter I found it easier to get through to him, as in after years I sometimes needed to do, on that wavelength. In view of the remarks about the hypersensitivity of a man 'who could be extremely shy and nervous in the company of other people' (to quote Ackroyd's paraphrase of his own words to Djuna Barnes in 1951), I should like to record that, save in respect of sensitivity, I never found him like that.

It was a privilege for me to be invited to one of the *Criterion* Evenings which were held at irregular intervals at 24 Russell Square. This was what today would be described as a prestigious event. I recall that on this occasion there were present – besides Geoffrey Faber and other members of his staff – Dylan Thomas, William Empson, A. L. Rowse, Charles Madge, Babette Deutsch (who had just published a book called *This Modern Poetry*), and some Faber and *Criterion* authors.

Eliot, the most commanding figure there, dominated the assembly in the quietest way possible. He never seemed to raise his voice, whereas Empson, who rapidly got tight, would end every other sentence with a 'whoop', accompanied by a lunge endangering the wine glasses of anyone who happened to be near. Dylan Thomas arrived drunk and, as I gathered, was particularly foul-mouthed. In contrast to the parties given in his honour, from which Eliot would contrive to slip away after a token attendance, these functions, never too large, were the kind he most enjoyed. He could preside without being too much the centre of attention. He once told me that he found a company of not more than eleven people the most congenial. And although his name will always be associated with a Cocktail Party he found such uproarious assemblies, at which no one could have a satisfactory conversation, increasingly insupportable.

The *Criterion* Evenings, at which there was food as well as drink in quantity, used to continue until fairly late. Towards the end of the soirée, Eliot stood for a while by himself in a seemingly abstracted state, and, looking at him across the room, I could not decide whether he was looking in my direction or not. I felt he had been struck by some arresting thought. On departure, many of the younger guests, deeming themselves insufficiently primed, were about to 'go on' somewhere, and in the end I found myself alone on the pavement with Eliot. It was a clear but rather chilly night. As usual, I felt that, on taking leave, I ought to proceed in a direction opposite to that which he was taking, because there was a mystery as to where Eliot lived, and I did not want to appear inquisitive. He glanced up at the sky and remarked: 'There's nowhere to go at this time of night', at which I said that I would be going home, and moved off to the right. This proved the correct thing to do, as he turned to the left at a brisk pace. Later I heard from more than one person how, landed with him outside Faber's, they had been conscious that he was waiting from them to take their leave first, as he was reluctant to provide any clue as to the whereabouts of his home.

About this time Wyndham Lewis expressed the wish to paint the Somerville friend of mine, and the 'Portrait of Miss Close' appears in Walter Michel's compendium (No. 5). As a result of the controversy over the rejection by the Royal Academy of his portrait of T. S. Eliot, Lewis had resumed the kind of fame he had attained before the First World War. During the sittings, he was always in good spirits; and as long as you did not try to glimpse what he was putting up on the canvas, he would dilate on any subject that took his fancy. He spoke often of Eliot, trying from time to time to poke gentle fun at him. As Lewis was very fond of champagne, he had offered Eliot some during a sitting in the spring of 1937. Eliot had apparently declined it on the plea that it was Lent. He murmured that he would have some whisky instead. This had greatly tickled Lewis. The truth was, I suppose, that by renouncing champagne, of which he was as fond as Lewis, Eliot felt that he was exercising a measure of self-denial. Lewis several times commented on Eliot's capacity for alcohol, which, as I have mentioned, seemed never visibly to affect him. In fact, Lewis was in no position to reproach his friend on that score, because he would drink far too heavily himself, which in his case was against doctor's orders.

Eliot was worried that I should have money troubles with Lewis, and in this he was right. But Miss Close's father was a man of substance, and he finally bought the picture for a rather large sum.

It was in the late summer of 1937 that I took the train to Newark, in Nottinghamshire, and paid a visit to Kelham, centre of the Community of the Resurrection. I had been invited there by George Every, and he chose a time when Eliot would be coming up too. It was the first occasion, but by no means the last, on which I stayed in a monastery. As a particularly honoured guest, Eliot sat at High Table, whereas others like myself were placed among the students or 'novices', and I preferred it that way. Eliot had arranged with me beforehand that we should have a private meeting, and meanwhile I sank myself into the communal life of the place. The weather was perfect : the memory of such a 'distant summer' endows it with possibly exaggerated serenity.

Apart from offices, we spent most of the time outside. In those days before Vatican II and *Honest to God*, there were few – and those scarcely noticeable – upheavals in theology or morals; and behaviour tolerated today not merely in students but in their religious instructors (see *Some Day I'll Find You* by Harry Williams), would have been unthinkable then. If anything, there was a kind of competitive emulation of piety. When the young men, released from silence, were not talking about 'shows' in London – which, as their only excursion into permissiveness held out vistas of slightly forbidden enjoyments – they commented with a kind of awe on the ardour of devotion which Eliot was seen to display at Mass. It is true that Eliot went through all the ritual gestures with almost perfect precision; and his impeccably-dressed figure stood out among the rather battered brethren stationed in front of us. I noticed as he moved forwards, that he swung his head slightly from side to side. But I always felt that, despite his liking for ritual and pageantry, his religious life was something very personal – indeed, intensely so. To quote his own words,

> Most people suppose that some people, because they enjoy the luxury of Christian sentiments and the excitement of Christian ritual, swallow or pretend to swallow incredible dogma. For some the process is the exact opposite . . . . To put the sentiments in order is a later and immensely difficult task ('Second Thoughts on Humanism').

One felt that he regarded this task, the task of gaining 'spiritual freedom', as the supreme, and never quite realizable, end of the religious life, with which no form of humanism could compete. And this was necessarily an inward thing, not a matter of hieratic gestures. But the ritual was nevertheless a way of protecting the devotional intimacy, whereas the non-liturgical denominations exposed it in a way he would have found offensive. Of the devotional intimacy, I suspect that few people, including even some priest confessors, were afforded any glimpse.

My private meeting with Eliot was in the afternoon. I was to go up to his room and tap on the door. This I did, and, on hearing a rather sleepy 'Come in', entered. Eliot was stretched the length of his iron bedstead. Theresa Eliot's sketch of him (see plate 14) recalls what he looked like. On the bedside table, he was in the act of placing a Bible, so that he may have dropped off into a doze while reading it. Sitting up, he was overcome with one of those slow yawns that seem like a prolonged agony, which he stopped with his hand, murmuring, when sufficient oxygen had been inhaled, that he was not yet properly awake.

In view of the warm weather, he suggested that we should take a walk, for which purpose he would change into lighter things. In a moment, he was off the bed, whipping off his belt and slipping down his trousers. Although I remember him stepping out of them and the sight of his white pants, I felt it was not seemly to observe too closely: otherwise I should have been able to verify the assertion that his underclothes were American but the rest very English. With the prudishness of the day, I glanced aside until he had pulled on a pair of greyers. The whole operation was performed with such straightforward openness that I believe, had he observed my slight embarrassment – which stemmed chiefly from the unexpectedness of the action – he would have been a trifle put out. He then ripped off his tie. At any rate, I can say that I am one of the few people who saw T. S. Eliot with his trousers down.

He was a great strider. There was no greater contrast than between his slowness of speech and quickness of pace. We walked for quite a long time and covered a good deal of ground. Now that he was thoroughly awake, he seemed particularly buoyant in spirits, which at that time was rare. We began by talking politics, which he enjoyed doing with someone not out to convert him to socialism – then, as now, the established faith of most intellectuals – and, referring to A. L. Rowse's fervent attempts, the first of many, to persuade him to join the Labour Party, he flung wide his arms and said: 'I *refuse* to be tied down to allegiances of this kind.' To him, Labour was not merely a political party; subscription to it entailed embracing the faith, the *doctrine* of socialism, an that was to embrace an *ersatz* religion. One (genuine) religion was enough.

As we approached the river, the Trent, which had a bathing-place in the grounds, he mentioned that he had already had a dip and recommended it. The river was running fast and I learnt later that bathing could be perilous. That he was a good and strong swimmer I assumed, because his American youth had familiarized him with the sea and coastal sailing; but, owing to his agoraphobia, I cannot exactly imagine him enjoying a high dive.

Eventually we made our way back to the terrace and sat down on a bank. We began talking in a general way about modern theologians. All of us young people, even unbelievers, had been taking an interest in Thomism. This was largely as a result of Eliot's own initiative; and what we knew of it was derived from the works of Jacques Maritain, which were largely the source, I suspect, of Eliot's own knowledge. He commented then, what he was to say in print later, that while he found Maritain a most charming man, his philosophical work, though claiming to reflect at every point Thomist orthodoxy, was in spirit quite unlike that of St Thomas: by which I presume he meant that Maritain had converted Thomas Aquinas into a French intellectual. The formidable names of Sertillanges, Garrigue-Lagrange, and Cajetan were like archetypal figures. He then went on to say that, despite this qualification, he still greatly respected Maritain, but that another theologian with whom, after an initial enthusiasm, he had become somewhat disillusioned was Berdyaev. I could well understand why; a 'Christian theosophist' or 'believing free-thinker' was not quite Eliot's cup of tea. I imagine that Eliot's early admiration, if that was not too strong a word, was due to Berdyaev's excellent little book on the Russian Revolution; a movement of which four years' personal experience was enough to dispel early hopes.

I remember that we got round to talking about historical hindsight, or the kind of attitude to which André Maurois (to whom I was to introduce Eliot years later) referred when he imagined a man saying 'Gentlemen, we are about to enter upon the Middle Ages'. It was amazing how much Eliot knew about history, as I, who had just completed a History degree, my second qualification, had reason to know. But just as Eliot remarked that Shakespeare acquired from Plutarch more essential knowledge than most men could from the whole British Museum, so he himself seemed to have acquired from books like F. S. Oliver's *Endless Adventure* an extraordinary grasp of historical movements and tendencies, for example the seventeenth century 'disassociation of sensibility' was a piece of historical perception which no pure historian would have been able to originate. In this conversation he cited the case of Montaigne: here was a man who seemed to understand the kind of world he was living in. At that time I knew very little about Montaigne: but Eliot had come to him through Shakespeare and the influences upon Shakespeare (who must have read the *Apologie de Raymond Sebond*); and, as he said in his essay on Pascal, Montaigne's outlook is the only credible *alternative* to that of belief.

It was an enormous subject upon which we had embarked, and I felt that, as a minor guest of the monastery, I must not monopolize the time of the guest whom everyone wanted to meet. No doubt perceiving my uncertainty (for he had an extraordinary intuitive grasp of people's moods), he said: 'Perhaps we each ought to talk to someone else.' We got up and found ourselves roped in to join a group of Fathers dressed in light gear, as it was a hot day. I found that they were engaged in retailing rather heavy jokes; and there came a point when Eliot, feeling perhaps that he ought to contribute, embarked upon a rather long story about George V. It ran somewhat as follows. Wearing one of his more elaborate uniforms complete with medals, the monarch had been using a soda siphon, which, because of some defect, had backfired and showered him with mineral water. Extremely annoyed, he had been obliged to change his uniform, substitute another set of medals, and order that Schweppes (as I believe it was) should be informed of the royal displeasure. That is why, according to Eliot, soda siphons from that firm – I have never checked this – bear on their labels some phrase to the effect that they had been thoroughly and exhaustively tested. After this narration, delivered at a slow pace, there was just the slightest pause in case the denouement, instead of being reached, was still to come. Then there followed polite, slightly hesitant, expressions of mirth. I believe that that was the only occasion, in both public and private, that I saw Eliot not to his best advantage. However I had perceived that he had been caught in that familiar predicament of being obliged to continue to the end of a story which half-way through he repented of having begun. Otherwise he could be very funny, if always in a quiet way.

It was after this that Brother George (Every) and in his own way Father Gabriel (Herbert), whose book Faber's had published, told me that, on arrival at Kelham (as everybody called the monastic headquarters), Eliot had been extremely, if not painfully, shy: so much so that the Fathers had not known how to deal with him. This applied in particular to the Prior, Father Stephen Bedale, a man of huge stature and extrovert character, and the kind of man who, had he been a layman, might have given the poet a hearty slap on the back in the belief that this would make him feel at home. Of course it would have made him feel anything but that. The truth is, I believe, that, while Eliot might have been fond of clubs, he was not, in the conventional sense, a clubbable man. He was not gregarious. The kind of company he would most have liked would have been that of a family, his own. It is likely, as I have said in another place, that he preferred in general the company of women to men. In my view the idea of his being monkish, or that he could have for a moment dreamt of entering a monastery, is not to be entertained, despite the claim of the Reverend William Levy in his Memoir. At Kelham he seemed to enjoy the company of the lay brothers and the students more than that of the fathers, though I fancy he enjoyed the company of the more lively minded among them, such as Father Gabriel, a shrewd and lively thinker.

After the first day, his manner had thawed, and, no doubt refreshed by his dip in the river, he was in good enough spirits when I had my talk with him. My last recollection of him at Kelham was when he gave a reading of his poetry. Brother George told me that he had persuaded Eliot to include the passage in *The Waste Land* about the seduction of the 'bored and tired' typist by the small house-agent's clerk, because he (George) thought that the young men ought to know a little more about the facts of life. How much enlightenment they obtained I do not know, but the details about 'exploring hands' were, in those days in contrast to the present, unusual. When Eliot had finished an extract, he would pause for a second or two, and then, as if to break the spell, switch his head quickly to the right. Then he would announce the next passage, ending with one from what he called, in a tone lower than usual, 'Murder'. I heard him giving many readings, and now of course they are on record; but I think he was at his best – with every word clearly articulated – among a small group such as that at Kelham. I think also that he liked Kelham – provided it were a short visit, for he was by nature and inclination a townsman – because he felt that such establishments were of great value in carrying on, in addition to theological instruction, the classical tradition. He would have been saddened by the closure of Kelham and by the decline in numbers at similar Anglican institutions. A successor to *Thoughts after Lambeth* would have borne a more sombre message.

Later on, I ventured to express the hope that one day he would perhaps visit my family in Merstham. I was pleased that he at once took to the idea. Naturally, I wanted to see him and to introduce him to my family; but I also felt that he needed to get out of London from time to time, because he seemed to be assuming an increasing load of public work, as well as public lectures and broadcasts. On 17 August he wrote to me suggesting dates.

> Dear Tomlin,
> Thank you for your note. I have to be in the country from Saturday next until the 30th. Would either Wednesday or Thursday the 1st and 2nd September be convenient? Preferably the Thursday. I think you said there were trains to and from Victoria which make it possible to spend the evening and get home; but if either of these dates suits, you will no doubt let me know about routes and timetables. Otherwise, the following week, or will you dine again with me?
> Sincerely,
> T.S. Eliot.

It appears that all this time I too was working flat out, because, in addition to a heavy load of teaching, I was writing articles right and left, as well as tinkering with the political book. I thought of seeking a more congenial job, and, with Eliot as a referee, applied for a post at Winchester. I was unsuccessful, but in due course my brother was to join the staff and the family connection extended with my sister's residence there.

There were also the personal matters, which, as every young person knows, consume an unconscionable amount of time. In those days before the National Health Service, one did not run off to the doctor except in real emergencies; but, at this juncture, my mother, noticing that I showed unusual signs of debility, urged me to seek medical advice. The counsel given was probably the best in the circumstances, which was that I should go abroad for a break. A group of friends was going to St Servan near St Malo and they asked me to join them. I must have recognized that I needed a change; for no reason short of extreme exhaustion would have induced me to alter my plans with Eliot. Replying to my explanatory letter, he wrote on 15 September 1937, with typical solicitude:

> THE CRITERION
> A Quarterly Review
> edited by T.S. Eliot
>
> 24 Russell Square,
> London, W.C.1.
> 15th September 1937.
>
> E.W.F. Tomlin Esq.,
> Wychwood House,
> Merstham,
> Surrey.
>
> My dear Tomlin,
> Thank you for your letter. I am very sorry indeed to hear of the reason for your having to go abroad at such short notice, and hope that you will take care to be well restored by the beginning of the Autumn term. If the writing of an article for the *Criterion* is likely to be a tax on your energies, I would not for the world have you try to do it for this number, but remember that it will be welcome whenever it comes. On the other hand, if you find work of this sort a help go ahead with it.
>
> I shall be glad if we can meet as soon as possible, though I doubt if I shall be able, in the near future, to take as much time as the timetable you gave me suggested. I find myself engaged

for several weekends ahead so that my Saturdays are not free, and I am doubtful whether I can afford a whole afternoon and evening. I could come out to you if there were a train at the end of the afternoon which would get me to you shortly before dinner, and, alternatively, I should be delighted if you would dine with me in Town any evening next week; but perhaps you do not care to come up to London until you have to. Please suggest whichever is easiest for you.
With best wishes.
               Yours ever sincerely,
                    T.S. Eliot.

He had wanted to publish a full-length article from me in *The Criterion*; and in expressing the hope that this sort of work would be 'a help', he was, with his knowledge of the therapeutic value of work, perfectly right. I regret only that the article entitled 'Philosophy and Politics' and published in *The Criterion* for January 1938, is not better. It formed one more effort, renewed over the next decade, to produce a book which in the end turned into another book altogether, and which Eliot published. As to the visit to Merstham, I had hoped that if he were to come all that way, he ought to see something of the country, as it was then still of an unspoilt rural character and in autumn especially beautiful. He was so tied to London, and had been especially so during his increasingly unhappy marriage, that his knowledge of the country, even the Home Counties, was patchy. This ignorance could be exaggerated, of course; there were several anecdotes in circulation to suggest as much. For instance, before the war, it was reported that he was heard to say over the telephone, in reply to an invitation from a leading London hostess, 'I should especially like to come, as I have not been to Hampstead since 1916'. But, as with most of the Eliot jokes (of which there were an increasing number and an accumulating apocrypha), the humour in the retailing depended to a large extent on reproducing the low-pitched Eliot drawl, a last relic no doubt of his southern accent. In this way, he made the commonplace appear of great import. He could also reduce the solemn to the apparently trivial ('nothing in this life is wholly serious'), lending often to his ordinary conversation, as to his poetry, that element of surprise which Elgar Allan Poe held to be an essential ingredient of art itself.

Given his many commitments and the preparations for the new play, his second, *The Family Reunion*, on which he probably worked harder than on any other – it was understandable that he could not consider sparing more than an evening away. In his letter of 30 December, he wrote to me about fixing a day and about the timing of the production of the play. The reference to the 'friend' had to do with my association with the Speech Institute, where I was giving a course of lectures on what the Directress, Miss Marjorie Gullan, liked to call 'Modernist Poetry' (for it was still considered that 'poetry' ended with the Georgians, whom we had all studied at school, and that Pound and Eliot were advanced experimenters). The Speech Institute group was similar and perhaps a rival to the band directed by Miss Elsie Fogarty, who had done the choruses in *Murder in the Cathedral*, and I believe that one of them had asked me what were the chances of taking part in its successor. As the two plays could not have been more different, there were very few. On 30 December he wrote:

Dear Tomlin,
    I am glad to hear from you. I am trying to keep myself free from engagements as much as possible for the next three months, but I should be very glad to come down and spend an evening with you, say the week after next, if that is convenient. Will you suggest an evening. Will we be travelling down together?
    You probably are imagining that the production of the new play is very much nearer at hand than it actually is. I think the production will probably be early next autumn. Martin Browne has to be in America during the first part of this year, and I am sure that nothing will be done about the casting until the summer. I can let you know when the time approaches. There is no reason to assume that any of the performers will be the same, as the play is of a totally different character. It would probably do no harm if your friend were to write to E. Martin Browne, at the Mercury Theatre, 2 Ladbroke Road, W.11, though he will certainly be able to do nothing about the matter for five or six months.
    With best wishes for the new year,
        Yours sincerely,
        T.S. Eliot.

In fact, the country visit had to be postponed for some time, because, although he had promised himself some months' freedom from engagements, he found himself, as usual, saddled with responsibilities.

I had a number of telephone conversations with him, and an interim letter dated 7 January in which he suggested, or asked me to suggest several possible dates. Finally, it was towards the end of January 1938 that the visit took place. I called for him at Faber's – which meant waiting downstairs either *du côté de chez Swan* or in the small waiting-room crowded with Faber books ready for dispatch – and we caught a train to Merstham from Victoria. On the way to the station we heard a kerbstone musician playing the concertina, and Eliot, struck by the tune, asked me if I knew what it was. I happened to know – 'Is it true what they say about Dixie?'. It seemed to fascinate him, as the South in general did. Trains were so frequent on this line that there was no need to aim for a particular one. We travelled first class, still something of a treat, and had the carriage to ourselves. Although very much a townsman, Eliot was, like G. K. Chesterton, a great advocate of country life, and he shared the attitude of many townsmen that most other people ought to live in the country. Indeed, in one of the *Criterion* Commentaries he maintained that a rural existence was 'the best life' for most people – a view which 'most people' have not shared. Yet as the view became increasingly rural past East Croydon Station, he grew more elated. Now London suburbia has almost merged with the encroachments of Brighton.

On the journey, between lapses into contented silence, we spoke a good deal about *The Criterion*, the prospects of which were now less rosy. He referred, perhaps a little ironically, to the respect in which it was held, and he remarked how each issue was spoken of as containing besides a noteworthy article or two, 'the usual brilliant batch of reviews'. That was intended to be a pat on the back – as one of several others – for me. We somehow got on to the subject of detective stories, for it had been with some surprise that I learnt at the Old Parsonage meeting that at one time he had read them with avidity. The 1930s were the era of the detective story, and it had reached its maximum popularity with Edgar Wallace. At Oxford and Cambridge, dons were reputed to spend much of their time reading a slightly higher 'body in the library' sort of book. At a lower level, there were not any libraries for bodies to be found in. Eliot seemed to have sampled the genre at every level; he mentioned in one of his essays that even poetic inspiration might come from reading a 'yellow back' novel (a series published by Hodder & Stoughton).

But he agreed that the genre was degenerating. That was why he relied chiefly on Simenon, an author for whom he preserved a high opinion all his life. Sordid occasionally, yes; but the man had 'pity' – that was what Eliot most valued in him. Needless to say, whenever he could, he read the books in the original French.

Merstham was then very much of a village, an appendage of the Colman Estate. It was almost a model village, with its Quality Street, where a future head of the Secret Service lived for many years. It has now greatly changed. On leaving the little station there was always a sense of freshness and freedom. My brother, then on the staff at Eton, met us in the car. The house, Wychwood, from which I like to think that Eliot derived the name in *The Family Reunion*, was easily within walking distance; but we felt some responsibility for getting the great man from London without subjecting him to too much fatigue; and if my brother reached home by a circuitous route, it was partly in order to show off the beauty of the place.

In contrast to Wyndham Lewis, who when I invited him home expressed apprehension that he might have to meet my family (a prospect which seemed slightly to unnerve him), Eliot showed no such anxiety about my people. I had told him that I had a brother and sister and that my mother was a widow. Consequently, when I introduced him, he seemed completely at his ease with us all, and most appreciative of the meal we gave him. He was, as usual, quietly spoken, but not, like Herbert Read, inclined to whisper, as if to lend his utterances an added confidentiality. On the contrary, he spoke very clearly. And he gave the impression, by bowing his head and turning rather gravely towards his interlocutor, that he was ready to treat every communication with the utmost seriousness, and would be reluctant to miss a syllable. He thought hard before he spoke, and the parchment brow would slightly corrugate while he deliberated his answer.

Neither my sister nor I can remember exactly what we had for dinner, but we chose not merely a good cheese but a claret of which we hoped he would approve. What we as a family were unanimous about was that he adopted no pose of being the distinguished writer, and even gave the impression that he much preferred not to be treated as such. The occasion was one which he seemed to wish to enjoy, and to make his enjoyment evident. Nevertheless, as my sister records: 'I recall vividly sitting next to him at table and the feeling of awe at actually passing things to my hero as he had then become.' He was so naturally modest (some have described his so-called humility – 'the most difficult of Christian virtues', as he put it – as an irritating pose) that had he been aware of this silent hero-worship, he would no doubt have felt uneasy. Among snatches of conversation, both of us remember his referring to the underground as being rather like hell. Indeed, some of his most effective imagery in *The Four Quartets* was based on the underground, which he patronized for reasons of speed, economy, and no doubt of experiencing the *frisson* of imagining himself consigned to perdition. Then, to quote my sister again, 'I took my little black kitten in my arms up to the poet to introduce it, and tall Mr Eliot bending forward to look at it remarked "That's a nice little catlet" '. *Old Possum's Book of Practical Cats* having become well known, I think we had called our specimen Leviticus.

After dinner we listened to some music on records, which included Mozart's 'Oboe Quartet'; and when we asked him if he would like to hear some more, he replied quietly that he was 'insatiable'. So far as I am aware, Eliot was not a concert-goer, but chamber music in the home – which in his case meant somebody else's home - and above all the last Quartets of Beethoven, were to him a source of more than aesthetic pleasure. Before he had fully conceived the idea of *The Four Quartets*, he had remarked that what drew him to Beethoven was that in these last works the composer did what he himself had sought to do in poetry – and may have actually done in 'forty or fifty lines' – namely to 'get beyond' that art.

My family then left me alone with Eliot. We sat together on the settee oblique to the fireplace, and talked about work, which meant writing. I said that literary work often left me with a depressed feeling. This remark, slightly sententious in a young man and in one whose production was pretty slender, was proffered in the belief that Eliot would immediately endorse it. But, as it happened, he didn't. I cannot quite recall what he said; it may be that he said nothing, which, rather than utter anything trite, he sometimes preferred to do. But I realized afterwards that, for him, writing, though no doubt excruciatingly difficult, was the form of therapy most satisfactory to one who was subject to doubts, misgivings and self-inquisition. For all he said about poetry being a 'mug's game', he must have felt an interior exultation at knowing that he possessed outstanding gifts. For, as Leavis remarked, a great writer knows he is great and cares little what others think: whereas a minor writer, one might add, cares very much indeed.

We saw Eliot off that evening, not too late, because we knew he was an early riser who went to morning Mass. He had said goodbye quietly, making a lasting impression on my mother. Quiet men with graceful manners were the ideal of her generation, and he seemed to embody it. We very much wanted him to come down to Merstham again when the weather was better, so that we could drive him round the country. Among other things, I was anxious to show him Chaldon Church, with its medieval wall painting of the Last Judgment. References to another visit recur in later letters, but events precluded it.

Meanwhile, he was anxious for me to contribute further to *The Criterion*, and he remained hopeful that I would write something more substantial. This was reflected in a letter dated 7 March 1938:

> Dear Tomlin,
> The book on Cornish Crosses looks a very interesting work. It hardly seems to me the type of book to justify a long review in the CRITERION, but as it has been sent, I think it ought to have a short notice. I don't know whether I ought to ask *you* to review it or not in the circumstances, and I think I ought to try first to find somebody else who may know something about the subject.
> Meanwhile I am sending you Maurice Dobb's book, which I mentioned in conversation. I have not given the time to it to find out whether the essays make a coherent book, or whether they are merely collected, so I will leave it to you to let me know whether you want to review it at length or briefly. There is another book which I think ought to be reviewed, but I don't think could be reviewed with it, called A PHILOSOPHY FOR A MODERN MAN, by Professor H. Levy, published by Gollancz, and looks as if it deserves a thorough cutting up. Would you care for that or not?
> And how are you getting on with your work?
> Yours ever,
> T.S. Eliot.

The book on Cornish Crosses was the work of my archaeologist uncle, T. F. G. Dexter, completed by his brother, and seen through the press by his widow. I had suggested that Longman's should send it to *The Criterion*, but obviously I was not the right person to review it. I need not go into detail about my long connection with Cornwall and my interest in Celtic history, which had this family origin. Since Eliot's family was of West Country provenance, he retained all the more interest in that region and in minority cultures, as I have mentioned. The two leftish books to which he referred were duly reviewed, and I admit to have rather enjoyed undertaking the 'thorough cutting up' which he declared the Levy book to deserve (it did).

Eliot's enquiry about my work recurred in a letter dated 17 June 1938, sent to Wychwood, Merstham:

>THE CRITERION
>A Quarterly Review
>edited by T.S. Eliot
>
>24 Russell Square,
>London, W.C.1.
>
>Dear Tomlin,
>I must apologize for my delay in replying to your letter of the 7th, but I had to go to Cambridge that week, and also had to be out of London for the week-end. I am very interested to know what plans you are trying to make for the future, and should like to see you soon. June is rather a busy month for me – I mean in the way of odds and ends of distractions from serious work – and I see no prospect of being able to get down to you at Merstham. I know that lunchtime is inconvenient for you, but we might have an hour's talk soon at the end of the afternoon before you catch your train. If that is possible please let me know of any days when we could arrange it.
>
>Yours sincerely,
>T.S. Eliot.

I had been forming some plans, which included writing a book on modern philosophy. It was not that I had abandoned the political book : it was that the mounting gravity of current events had turned my interests from theory to practice. The two countries on which I had set my eyes were France and Italy. I had visited Paris once or twice, but now I was fortunate enough to secure a grant from the LCC – £15, but princely for those days – which permitted me to spend a week or two there for the purpose of study, my subject being modern French philosophy. On 19 July 1938 Eliot wrote me:

> Dear Tomlin,
> Thank you for your note. I am afraid I shall not have time to come down to Merstham before you leave, but I should like to see you if possible. Would a glass of sherry on Friday afternoon, at the same time and place, be convenient?
> Yours sincerely,
> T.S. Eliot.

It was duly arranged that we should meet after work, and it was then that I gave him further details about my 'sponsored' trip to Paris and about my much more ambitious idea of a trip to Libya. He had been keenly interested in the first: about the second he was much intrigued. What particularly touched me was that, practical as always and among the most financially-shrewd of men he said that perhaps he could be of material help over the longer tour. That is to say, he was prepared to commission an article for *The Criterion* and to pay for it in advance. This was one of the kindest of his gestures. Although the cost of living was very much less than it is now, schoolteachers' salaries were modest. Our conversation concentrated on the international situation. It was gratifying to me that he approved the political and economic articles I was writing for the *New English Weekly*.

Events were moving rapidly: in March, Hitler had annexed Austria. The Sudeten Germans had begun their contrived agitation in April. A meeting between Hitler and Mussolini in May was especially ominous. No less ominous was the visit to Prague by Walter Runciman, one of Chamberlain's appeasing colleagues, who, to the consternation of many, reported in favour of acquiescing in Hitler's ruthless demands on the Czechoslovak government. Although the idea of a general war was still 'unthinkable', the upsurge of Nazi power was in the forefront of everyone's minds. Eliot reiterated his view that, as between a Communist world and a world dominated by the Nazis (which would mean a world dominated by Germany in the West and Japan in the East), the latter would be the more horrible immediately to contemplate. In this judgment he never varied. Accusations that he was a 'fascist' (revived or fuelled in the play *Tom and Viv* by Michael Hastings) are little short of preposterous. What particularly shocked him, from then until the outbreak of war, was the repeated humiliations heaped on Czechslovakia, especially at the Munich conference in September. For although Britain, France, Germany and Italy had guaranteed the frontiers of that country (minus the Sudetenland) at that same conference, the Czech Republic was fragmented a few weeks later, and by the following March Germany had completed her design by totally absorbing an independent state. Eliot felt that at Munich there had been a betrayal which seemed to demand an act of almost personal contrition. It was in this mood that he decided to bring *The Criterion* to an end. The last number, in which there was no room for my long article (which in any case formed part of a backlog) appeared in January 1939. No journal comparable to it in scope and direction has appeared since.

CHAPTER FIVE

Of his contemporaries Eliot was one of the few who not merely looked to a culturally united Europe but knew personally many of the writers and intellectual leaders on the Continent. That was why when I told him about my LCC-subsidized visit to Paris, he insisted that I should pay calls on friends of his like Paul Valéry, Jacques Maritain and Charles du Bos; and he set about providing me with letters of introduction. Wyndham Lewis kindly provided me with a similar introduction to James Joyce. Never did I embark on a foreign visit with more keenness; for I felt that time was short, and that such an opportunity might never recur.

To take the trip to Meudon and to visit Jacques and Raissa Maritain, and also her sister – a visit which turned into two visits – was most rewarding. This was not least because of the respect and affection in which, as I found, Eliot was so clearly held as both a writer and a man. Details must await another memoir. This respect for Eliot and the desire to do something of which he would approve, was further manifested in the Maritains' wish that I should visit Bergson. Alas, he was lying ill and semi-paralysed and not expected to recover, though that great man, whose reputation today has regrettably fallen, survived to die a more noble death in the Occupied Paris of 1941. Charles du Bos, the literary critic, another figure who is scarcely known to the younger generation even in his own country, was equally devoted to Eliot. He would have given me an introduction to Paul Valéry as well, except that *he* was out of Paris. No less devoted was Joyce, who was anxious to talk about Eliot as about the Enemy. Despite the fact that I succumbed to a mild form of food-poisoning through eating at the cheapest restaurants – a meal could be obtained for ten (old) francs or less, but less meant the more chance of prostration – I have never known Paris so surpassingly beautiful as that year. Through my mind there reverberated the words from *Portrait of a Lady*, 'Memories of my dead life, and Paris in the Spring', the meaning of which every lover of Paris can echo, even if he had no dead life in either George Moore's or Eliot's sense, or even if his most memorable visit to Paris took place, as mine did, at another season.

It was for a number of reasons, apart from a wish to escape from teaching, that I set out some weeks later for Libya, then a country almost entirely unknown. I had sought to interest some of the more enterprising newspapers, especially as I hoped to be able, if possible, to push on to Abyssinia; but, in the end, I went in independence, as I have undertaken most excursions, both terrestrial and mental. What I had in mind all along, however, and possibly Eliot did too, was the eventual production of a book. This was to be not just a travel book but one which should be of use if, as seemed increasingly likely, we should be involved in hostilities with Italy: a circumstance which I nevertheless felt could, with diplomatic skill, be avoided.

The mention that I was journeying via Marseilles prompted him to warn me, somewhat to my surprise, not to let the street-girls of the special quarter (since abolished) commandeer my hat – a favourite play of theirs to enveigle one inside – which suggested that he had experienced such an approach.

When I returned from Libya via Egypt, just after the Munich crisis I at once got in touch with Eliot, and put my proposal before him. It seemed to me that, in this way and with some fresh views to submit, and possessed with a totally new interest in the Orient, I might contribute something, however modest, to the Italian 'problem'. It was impossible to imagine a people – I do not say a government – with less relish for war, if my contacts with the Italian colonists and equally with the Italian army were any guide. Eliot saw the point, and asked me to sit down forthwith and draft a synopsis. From then on I did a great deal of telephoning to him; but, as usual, he preferred contact *de vive voix*. On 10 October, having arranged a meeting, he wrote to me about the earlier essay for which he had already arranged generous advanced payment:

Dear Tomlin,

Did I give you back your article, or keep it here? I remember that it was too late to use before you went away, and that it was of such length that it would have to be cut, and I don't remember whether I gave it back to you or held it here, pending your return. I have had a search for it, but if you tell me that I have it, I will search again more thoroughly. I hope to see you on Thursday.
    Yours ever,
    T.S. Eliot.

Having compared notes with some others, I have the impression that this was a rather typical letter to receive from Faber & Faber at that time. Eliot was the most orderly of men, and Anne Bradby (who became Mrs Ridler shortly after) was, I am sure, a methodical young lady; but typescripts did get lost or mislaid, though other people suffered more than I did. What I liked about this letter was the phrase 'if you tell me that I have it'. This conveyed almost the speaking tone of the writer, as he might glance up impishly from one of his colloquies with the carpet. Whether or not he had sent the article back (if it had been rejected) did not in the least matter. It was sufficiently damned to rule out any offer of reprieve elsewhere.

We duly met, and I was as before, astonished to find how much interest he could take, by clearing his mind of more pressing matters, in a subject not obviously familiar to him. But, as he pointed out in *The Use of Poetry and the Use of Criticism* (1933) with reference to abstract philosophizing, his mind was a 'heavy' one. He had that sense of fact which he considered to be more useful 'than nine-tenths of the most pretentious critical journalism'. Within a short while he was on to the subject of Libya's exports. When I told him that one of the most important was esparto grass, his grave face lit up, because Faber's, it appeared, purchased consignments of it to meet their paper needs. He was no less curious about the life of the newly-arrived colonists; for this Italian experiment, though short-lived, had few precedents. Whole communities were being, so to speak, lifted out of the mother country and planted down in villages already prepared for them, even down to food in the larder. As some of his remarks in the *Criterion* commentaries made clear, he was not hostile to the idea of Empire, 'whatever the Daily Express may say'; and if this should rouse the indignation of anti-imperialists, it should be realized that I am talking about a bygone era, since which the world-scene has been transformed, and the term colonialism is now employed usually in the service of invective.

He urged on me the need to embark on a full-sized book, and to send him a synopsis as soon as possible. We had a few concluding words about the literary scene in London, which he thought to have reached a pretty low ebb. For me, and to some extent for him, the liveliest literary intellectual circle, though small enough, was still that associated with the *New English Weekly*. Eliot, who lent the circle considerable prestige, found himself in congenial assorted, and in some cases strange, company. He commented on 'the excitable XY', a female author who later achieved considerable fame. In fact, he was often quite outspoken about people, though usually with reference to their harmless foibles. I never heard so much as a malicious word or imputation. Some of the NEW group had opinions which were slightly dotty, though on the whole, in comparison with today's weirdies, they were a conventional lot. If, on the other hand, he felt that someone was a really harmful influence, he did not hesitate to say so. If he had no wrath, he had a kind of steely ire.

I did my best to produce an attractive synopsis, embellishing it with some of the sketches I had made on the spot. In those days I had been doing a good deal of drawing; and, having come under Wyndham Lewis's influence, I took my Vorticist efforts round to the Master, and, to my surprise, I found that he thought quite well of them. I also bound up with my brochure, a number of photographs; for I had taken two cameras abroad. Obviously I should have provided more text than I did, but I suppose I was in rather a hurry. I delivered the stitched brochure (which it had become) to Eliot, and he went through it, sitting with it on his knees and brooding over each page. At the end, he looked up and said: 'This looks very promising.'

On 26 October, having submitted it to his colleagues, he wrote to me:

Dear Tomlin,

My committee is keenly interested in your proposed book on Libya, with two qualifications. The first is that they would like to have something more on which to decide than merely the summary outline. A chapter or preferably two chapters would be a great help. It is rather more important, I feel, to have such specimens to offer them as this is to be quite a different type of writing for you than your work with which we are familiar.

The second point is that they do not feel quite satisfied with the photographs as a whole, and hope that some better photography can be obtained from the Italian travel bureau or elsewhere. I imagine that the Italians would be pleased to have a book written about their colony though it is, of course, possible that they may not be altogether pleased with everything you say. But in advance they ought to be quite ready to provide the best photographs obtainable. I expect you would like to have your admirably arranged outline back for reference meanwhile. I am, therefore, sending it herewith.

    Yours ever,
    T.S. Eliot.

Not only did I draw a blank about the pictures, but political events were moving so fast that the book I had begun to write had ceased, after the completion of the amount of text Faber's required, to be the one that needed to be written. I therefore decided to abandon what I had planned, because I felt that Faber's too, despite their initial keenness, would now want another sort of book, if they wanted one at all. I did submit what I had written, and, not altogether to my surprise, I received not long after a letter from Eliot beginning 'I am sorry to tell you. . .'.

This rejection at least served the purpose of bringing me face to face with the uncomfortable fact that I was now without a job and almost without an occupation. In those days, it never occurred to me but to employ my time as best I could, without any thought of 'going on the dole', which was for the underprivileged. So I set to work learning Italian intensively, because I continued to feel, and increasingly felt, that anything that could help to keep Italy out of any war that might take place, ought to be done. I therefore managed to get myself accredited as a journalist to cover the visit to Rome by Neville Chamberlain and Lord Halifax in early January 1939 for talks with Mussolini. On my return, in order to earn a living, I engaged in intensive writing, including a detailed report to the War Office covering Libya as well. Then, quite out of the blue, there had come the offer of a job at Marlborough; for although I had resolved to abandon teaching, I had found, like so many others, that of all the means of earning one's bread, freelance authorship was among the most precarious.

I told Eliot of my new post, but when I next heard from him, in a letter dated 31 January 1939, the day after my twenty-sixth birthday, it was with a slight hint of reproach.

Dear Tomlin,
    I have not written to you before, because I thought that I might be hearing from you on your return from Italy. I hope that you had a satisfactory visit, and shall be interested to hear your impressions of Marlborough in due course.
    The immediate occasion of this letter is a letter which I have just received from Ronald Duncan, asking us to send you as many back numbers of the CRITERION as possible, so that you may, apparently, review the whole 16 years. This is rather a large order for you, and incidentally is a large order for us. We cannot undertake to supply the whole 16 volumes to anybody, or anything like it, and indeed of some of the early volumes there are only the file copies in existence. Were you to be in London, it would be simplest for me to give you the run of my bookcase for an afternoon, because all that you really have time to do for a survey of this sort is to glance over the title-pages of the early numbers, but if there are any particular numbers, or samples of the CRITERION at different periods, I could supply a few from one year or another. From your point of view, I think it would be more satisfactory if you could postpone the article until you are next in town, and spend a couple of hours or so looking at the file.
  I want to say, in any case, that I should be very pleased indeed to have you do such a review, and extremely interested to have your judgment.
    Incidentally, I am returning at last the article, which can no longer be published in the CRITERION.
        Yours ever,
        T.S. Eliot.

When I look back on the long friendship, I realize that I need not have had certain misgivings about troubling Eliot or taking up his time – misgivings due to temperamental diffidence rather than to genuine modesty, I am afraid – because he was both generous of his time and solicitous about the welfare of those in whom he took an interest. But once or twice in a while I would despair of producing the kind of thing that seemed likely to win approval from one whose standards were so high – impossibly high, I felt, so far as emulation on my part was concerned – and therefore I had moods in which I would feel unworthy of his attention. Naturally, once the first paragraph of his letter met my eyes, I sat down with reassurance to say how sorry I was not to have written earlier and to have delayed giving him an account of the Italian visit. By this time I was settled in one of the staff residences in Marlborough (Hillside) to begin what proved to be one of the happiest interludes of my life.

In alluding to Ronald Duncan and *The Criterion*, he was referring to a proposal by Duncan – with whom I had been in correspondence, though I did not meet him until after the war – that I should write for *The Townsman* (a magazine which he edited from an ancient mill situated in a valley on the Devon/Cornish border, where I was later to live and write about), an article analysing the reasons why *The Criterion*, after flourishing for seventeen years, had so suddenly come to an end. The request that I should receive a consignment of most, if not all, of the issues was obviously impossible to meet; and although I should much like to have had the 'run' of Eliot's bookcase for an afternoon, I felt I could not seek permission, so soon after my arrival at the school, to go to London for that purpose, so I told Eliot that half a dozen well-spaced numbers would suffice for me.

Meanwhile, the Consul-General at Florence, Mr Wakefield-Harrey, whom I had first met in Tripoli, stayed with in Florence and met once more in Rome for the Chamberlain-Mussolini talks, had sent me a long Miltonic poem (for these slightly underemployed officials in remote places often took to authorship as an alternative to the bottle) about which he begged me to seek Eliot's opinion. I felt I had to comply, out of gratitude to one who, with his wife, had been most hospitable; and, no doubt detecting merits which were not there, I forwarded it to Eliot. At this distance in time, I cannot pretend that I had my doubts about its merits: what I did dwell on was a certain psychological subtlety in retailing the author's love-life, though in terms which today would be considered ludicrously niminy-piminy. Back came a snorter the like of which I was never again to receive from Eliot, though I am sure it was thoroughly well-deserved. Although I realized

that my faulty literary judgment was the occasion for his reaction
– for he must have been well-accustomed to reading manuscripts of
surpassing dullness – because when he wrote to Wakefield-Harrey
it was in firm but polite terms, which, since they were from Eliot,
were to him the next best thing to commendation. To me, he
wrote on 10 February as follows, the invective being tempered by
the desire expressed at the beginning that we should have in due
course a prolonged *tête-à-tête*:

My dear Tomlin,

I was glad to get your letter of the 2nd instant, and look forward
to hearing more from you about your visit to Italy. But I suppose
that can wait until the Easter vacation, when I shall look forward
to a long talk with you.

I have read Mr. Harrey's poem twice, and propose to give it a
third test, but I confess myself so far completely baffled by what to
say about it. The versification seems to me of a mediocrity which
is excelled by half a dozen writers of the eighteenth century, the
most conspicuous of whom might be Mallet. There may be a
good deal in the stuff as psychological analysis, but when I read
poetry I have to be satisfied by the author's technical ability
before what he has to say can make any impression upon me,
and so far Mr. Harrey seems to me, as a poet, to exhibit nothing
but industrious dullness.

       Yours ever,
       T.S. Eliot.

P.S. I will look out some of the back number of the CRITERION
and let you have them as soon as I can find time.

When I had sufficiently recovered from this onslaught, two
points remained fixed in my mind. The first was the industry which
Eliot was prepared to devote to such poor material, even to the
extent of giving this particular piece three readings: whereas most
publishers or critics might not have had the patience to complete
one. The second was his insistence, not so common in his day,
that any poetry worthy of serious attention had to display high
technical competence. Indeed, some of his contemporaries were
highly critical of his preoccupation with the technical side of
verse; even friends like Herbert Read placed emphasis on the
Wordsworthian 'spontaneous overflowing of powerful feelings'. But

to Eliot the power lay in the letter rather than in the spirit – hence his famous remark that 'the spirit killeth while the letter giveth life' – and all his memorable lines of verse exemplified that. But I think there was a third reason why Eliot took exception to this particular effusion. This *was* the nature of the content. A long and laborious analysis of *affaires de coeur*, though not of the explicitness we should expect today, was not to his taste. When reviewing some essays by A. R. Orage, he singled out the one, 'On Love', as being a piece with which he was 'not qualified' to deal. There was a note of irony in that reservation. To him, *The Waste Land* was primarily the desert of extinct emotion, which symbolized his own failure. He could be warmly understanding and sympathetic, as I knew, when dealing with a friend's problems; but, for that very reason, a catalogue in mediocre verse of a stranger's supposed *education sentimentale* was something he found thoroughly distasteful. The repeated readings must have been in the nature of a penance, which, because of his awareness of his own prejudices, was deliberately self-imposed.

I duly completed the essay on the rise and fall of *The Criterion*, and I sent Eliot the relevant copy of *The Townsman*. Looking at it today, I consider it neither profound nor convincing. I tried to argue that the *Criterion* had neglected to pay enough attention to certain lines of contemporary thought, above all that represented by Collingwood. Just Collingwood: for he had no disciples. I see now the inadequacy of this explanation; but, apart from the fact that at that age one's loyalties are defended with more than usual zeal, my conviction, in the Oxford of that time, was that Collingwood was the only alternative to linguistic philosophy. The latter was to become the orthodoxy of the next few decades, whereas Collingwood died in 1943 virtually in the shadows, for more reasons than one. But, in any case, I should have realized that a review of high seriousness like *The Criterion*, the circulation of which never reached 1,000 copies and I suspect hardly more than 500, was supported by an intellectual minority whose allegiance did not wane on account of the neglect of a man of whom many may not have heard. (After the war, when Collingwood was discovered by the younger generation, and found to be highly readable and stimulating, the situation was totally different, and the aging linguistic philosophers were obliged to start reading him in self-defence.)

As a letter to me at Merstham dated 1 May 1939 indicated, Eliot was polite about the article in question:

Dear Tomlin,
   Thank you for your letter. Don't bother to send back the copies of THE CRITERION. I must thank you for the article in TOWNSMAN, and only wish that you might have had the space to say more. I feel that there are other more obvious reasons for the decay of THE CRITERION than merely the neglect of Collingwood, though I think you put that forward merely as a symptom. Are you free for lunch most days now? If so, I will suggest a meeting in the near future.
         Yours ever,
         T.S. Eliot.

That was the last, as I thought, of my *Criterion* obituary; but because of some slightly disparaging remarks I made in it of Montgomery Belgion, a *Criterion* contributor, I incurred the bitter enmity of that enigmatic figure, which exploded years later when he reviewed my book on Simone Weil. But Eliot, of whom he made some absurd insinuations, imputing plagiarism, told me later on that he found Belgion an exceedingly tiresome man to deal with. Nor was he the only one to do so.

Over the next few days I was in touch by letter and by phone with Eliot, and finally it was arranged, in a note dated 9 May, that I should lunch with him on Thursday 18 May, which, as he carefully specified, was Ascension Day.

As usual, we met at the Oxford and Cambridge. We had much to talk about. The international situation was growing increasingly gloomy. The day before, Norway had declined Germany's offer of a non-aggression pact, which no doubt weakened her position some months later, though even had she signed one, it would probably have made little difference. Eliot, as was to be expected, was particularly interested in the kind of propaganda we were putting out to Germany and Italy: for the propaganda war had already begun and was intensifying. He raised a point, which had never occurred to me, like not a few of his *aperçus*, that, in the case of radio broadcasts, it was a mistake invariably to employ German refugees or perfect German speakers to warn the German public of the evils of Nazism. Far more effective, he considered (and there was no anti-Semitism involved, though inevitably most of the recent refugees were Jews), would be to put on the air people who, while speaking intelligible German, would be identified as representative British people. When William Joyce ('Lord Haw-Haw') began his revulsion felt by the British public, if the reaction was not mirthful, was due to the fact that he was, in a sense, a stranger to them by reason of his apostasy and unnatural situation and therefore he carried far less conviction than a less articulate but sincere German would have done. Propaganda could be effective – this was what Eliot was getting at – only by ceasing to be mere propaganda.

I see that an article I wrote at the time entitled 'What should we say to Germany?' reflected this point of view, though with less explicitness. Altogether Eliot, who later offered his services to the Ministry of Information, which was founded on 5 September, two days after the outbreak of war, believed that a great deal could meanwhile be done by way of the spoken and written word. He hoped that I could undertake something in that line, especially in relation to Italy: for I had been giving him my impressions of the visit to Rome, which included encountering at close quarters, Mussolini, Count Ciano, and Edda his wife, and the by comparison rather puny Neville Chamberlain. I told him again how I had been reinforced in my belief that, whereas Germany seemed intent on war, Italy, while verbally identifying herself with the Axis, would clutch at any straw to evade participation, and that our policy should be to keep her out of it with every means in our power. I could see that he was sceptical of our diplomatic capacity to do so; and when, later, Chamberlain despatched a female relation to 'negotiate' with Mussolini, it became clear that his misgivings were justified. In fact, Hitler and Mussolini signed a ten-year Pact on 22 May 1939.

At that lunch in the Oxford and Cambridge he was in the sombre mood that had descended on him with the signing of the Munich Agreement. Never one to believe in quick or facile solutions, he cared very much about the national welfare; and as he was one of the few British writers whose word carried any weight with the authorities – in contrast to such authors as Priestley who carried more weight with the public through his remarkable war-time broadcasts – he gave the impression of a certain helplessness in face of government policy which appeared to lack resolution.

As Peter Ackroyd has pointed out in his biography, Eliot was apprehensive about the approach of war: which was not the same as being faint-hearted. He was of course not the only one: the idea of a nation roused to righteous anger and determined to crush Nazism in the most resolute manner, applied – and then chiefly because of the fire and resolution of one man, Churchill – not to that period but to a year later. Eliot did not doubt the resilience or resolve of the British people; but he remarked to me that he could not see a man like Neville Chamberlain coping with a major conflict. He classed Chamberlain the 'Conservative' with Baldwin as a representative of that mercantile tradition, descending from Adam Smith, Ricardo, Cobden and Bright and from which the Fabians were themselves derived, as being the official receivers of the capitalist system. He therefore considered them of a tradition quite different from that form of conservatism – so admirably defined by Russell Kirk in his study *Eliot and his Age* (1971, 1984) – which, as Eliot said to me more than once, was the best and perhaps the only defence against the extremes of Communism and Fascism.

There was, however, another reason for Eliot's mood of dejection. *The Family Reunion*, about which he had spoken in his letter of 30 December had opened in March and lasted only five weeks. He felt that the play upon which he had bestowed such care had been a failure.

When I told him about Marlborough, he cheered up a little. In view of his experience at Highgate School, he had always been interested in the life and tribulations of schools teachers; and in any case he held strong views about education, about which he lacked an opportunity to state his ideas at length until he gave some lectures in Chicago in 1950. As I had been enjoying Marlborough, which in atmosphere, personnel, and not least location, was in total contrast to the Sloane School, Chelsea, I no doubt gave him a slightly rose-tinted account of the life there. I did tell him, however, that the older boys – and I was form-master of the modern sixth – were keenly interested in what was going on in modern literature, but that they seemed to some extent cushioned against modern life in their ignorance, which was almost total, of such currents of thought as Marxism. Eliot picked on this. He was quick to point out that when they went up to Oxford – as most of my pupils would be likely to do – the impact of Marx, the one reputation which most politically-conscious dons revered, was likely to sweep them off their feet. (I have since called to mind G. K. Chesterton's remark in *Heretics* that ideas are dangerous and most dangerous to the man of no ideas: 'the man of no ideas will find the first idea fly to his head like wine to the head of a teetotaller.')

Of modern poets, I had of course spoken to the boys – and to the masters for that matter, for most had ventured no further than Hardy and Houseman, like the Brasenose dons – of Eliot, Pound and the later Yeats; and I discovered that they lapped this up as if slaking a mental thirst. In fact, I perceived once again, as I have repeatedly done since, that young people – and this applies to girls just as much as to boys – need, almost to the point of desperation, writers, inevitably older, who speak to *their* generation and in *their* language, or at least in language which, once they hear it, they perceive to be theirs. This proved true above all at the time of which I write, or up to that time, because adolescence is as much a mental as a biological experience, and the arts meant much at that epoch, the last before the advent of Pop Culture, which has since taken over the adolescent mind rendering present that 'future' which Eliot dreaded.

Eliot once said that all poets would like their work to be said or sung by the common people (which was realized in his case by *Cats*). He also said that he would prefer an audience that could neither read nor write. I noticed that he never put on an air of diffidence when, as here, his own work was being cited. In fact, contrary to what has sometimes been said about his modesty, he enjoyed talking about his work, even when it was no more than work in progress. The thought of the Marlborough boys 'discovering' him gave him obvious pleasure; and whether or not he believed that the curriculum should include modern literature (as Auden was later to say that it should not), he certainly believed, with his own youthful experience in mind, that the young should be enabled to explore new fields in the arts for themselves. Where otherwise was the public for new art to come from?

It was when we had settled down to talk in comfortable armchairs that I told him that the man for whom I had substituted at Marlborough, in the hope of replacing him altogether, now planned to return, so that once more I should be out of a job. It happened, however, that while I was at the College I had been approached by the Bristol University Board of Extra-Mural Studies, where a post was for the moment vacant organizing adult education work chiefly in Wiltshire. I would be employed also by the WEA and as a Trade Union lecturer (which, as far as I know, I still am). As the work was being reorganized to promote the war effort, I was to be given a National Service driving licence and other facilities – Conscription having been introduced on 27 April, this seemed the ideal transitional job to undertake pending the call-up. I therefore asked Eliot if I might quote his name as a reference. As good-luck would have it, he was in a stronger position than usual, because, as he mentioned with one of his quick smiles, the University of Bristol was about to give him an honorary degree, one of the fourteen that he was to accumulate. The formalities took some weeks, but by the end of July 1939, I learnt that I had got the job. On 31 July, Eliot wrote to Merstham:

> Dear Tomlin,
> I was glad to get your letter of the 28th and to hear that your application at Bristol had been successful. I hope that you will have a very satisfactory winter. I should like to come down and see you again soon, but I am afraid that engagements with relatives and American friends and a visit to Wales will not leave me the time until after the middle of September. If you do not have to start your work in the west until October, I hope that we can arrange a time then.
> Yours ever sincerely,
> T.S. Eliot

Ever since the happy visit of the year before, I had been trying to persuade him to pay a second and, if possible, longer visit. Apart from the worry over *The Family Reunion*, I perceived that he was under considerable strain. This manifested itself partly in his waxy parchment-like complexion and a habit of sitting in an increasingly hunched posture. He was, I recognized, one of those people – Dickens was another, and Eliot was very much a Dickensian – who needed the stimulus of London streets for the maintenance of his mental vitality. He also needed the London underground, for which he had a love/dread relationship, and the London theatre, not of the new kind, but, when available, of the old music hall tradition and, when in season, the pantomime. He told me that he made a point of seeing one pantomime a year. But I felt strongly that, like Dickens again, though not to the same extent, he needed occasionally to get out into the open: which is why he made his way down to Cornwall once or twice to see Ronald Duncan. Just at this time he was thinking about and drafting his meditation about home, namely the West Country, in the poem which became *East Coker*. But the outbreak of war on 3

September 1939 made a second Merstham visit impossible, though I always regretted that it could not be managed.

The assignment in Wiltshire proved for me an extremely full and busy one. Never before had I covered a number of villages and country towns, with the added novelty of intensive driving in the blackout, with dimmed lights in anti-camouflage of white striping. Until I moved in to the Rectory at Seend, I lived briefly at the Bell Inn, St Edith's Marsh, Bromham, near Devizes. I must have delivered hundreds of lectures, pep-talks, addresses, speeches, and organized many others. As was found throughout the war, there was an increased interest in private reading (partly due to blackout conditions), and, as I found early on, an increasing public for current affairs as well as for music and poetry. I was much encouraged to find that the most unlikely audiences appreciated modern poetry, and Eliot's perhaps most, though that was perhaps due to my own advocacy. With service audiences – Wiltshire was dotted with army camps – I had less success. Yet although my addresses were chiefly in the nature of pep-talks, I usually contrived to work in what today would be called 'culture', and sometimes the pub scene in *The Waste Land* or parts of *Portrait of a Lady* would go down with a wow. In the many visits I paid in the course of promoting these activities I again found the kind of awareness of what was new in literature in places I had least expected; and when in the autumn of that year *The Idea of a Christian Society* was published, it was much more successful than Eliot hoped. The rectories and vicarages I visited played a more important part in the rural community than they have done since or are likely ever to do again. It was significant that, when the war took a grave turn the following year, it was to every Anglican incumbent in the land (and no doubt to many others, though I can speak only for the parish clergy) that Duff Cooper, the Home Secretary, sent letters expressing apprehension of the state of public morale and urging the incumbents to do their utmost to help raise it.

It was obvious to me my projected work on Italy would have to be either abandoned or drastically modified. A travel book would not be enough: anything I wrote on that country would need to be designed to assist, in however small a way, the war effort, even though Italy was still uninvolved. I thought that the best thing that I could do, anticipating the worst, would be to start on one entitled *Italy's Betrayal*. Although Eliot considered this idea a good one, especially in view of the articles I had been writing for the

New English Weekly (for example, 'Italy must Choose; and 'An Open Letter to Ansaldo', which Mairet had forwarded to the spokesman in question and also to the Vatican), he felt that such a book, issued in time of war, would need official backing. He therefore recommended me to get in touch with the Ministry of Information. That institution, peopled by a number of well-known figures, but from which a number of others had been turned away – so much so that one of them, C. E. M. Joad, wrote that 'the corridors of the Ministry were hissing with the sound of deflated reputations' – proved extremely difficult to approach, still more to negotiate with and most of all to extract money from. But it enabled me to see how tough a negotiator Eliot himself could be.

I had lunch with Eliot just after Christmas 1939. By then he had been encouraged by the success of *The Idea of a Christian Society* (1940) though it is sobering to reflect that the sales, so he told me, were not much more than 6,000 copies. Although the 'phoney war' was still continuing, the outlook was sombre: bacon, butter and sugar rationing was introduced that month, and people were not yet adjusted to the blackout. But I found Eliot quieter and calmer than I had done recently, when he had begun to sign letters 'in haste'. This may well have been due to the satisfaction he had been deriving from the composition of *East Coker*, though he made no mention to me of the new poem. Probably creative work was all the real satisfaction he obtained in those stressful years. As in the past, he was anxious to know what my new job was like, and it was reassuring for me to learn that he thought that such work was very much needed. He was also sure that I ought to mug up as much as I could about Italy. He mentioned his own abortive approach to the Ministry of Information. Wartime controls, though necessary, might, he thought, give rise to a whole new set of abuses, because it was always his view that the more you imposed restrictions, the more people would think up ingenious ways of eluding them. As an example of corruption, I cited the case of a châtelaine in my part of the world who had applied for, and received, a number of supplementary petrol coupons (which were by no means easy to obtain) for attending a committee-meeting held in her own drawing-room. To which he uttered the classic comment, in the more than usually low drawl he employed for such deliverances: 'There's always bound ... to be a certain amount of iniquity .. in these matters'. 'Iniquity' was Eliot all over: the slight archaism, the slight hyperbole, exactly fitted.

As I had come to know a number of rectors and vicars in the course of my journeys, for reasons which I have mentioned, Eliot questioned me about what he felt might be a mounting danger, namely that the Church might seek to increase by chauvinism what it appeared to be losing in spirituality: and indeed the vicar of my own village had been upbraided by a group of parishioners for not preaching sermons directly furthering the war effort, which Eliot said was tantamount to making him into an unpaid official of the MOI. I also spoke of my difficulty in giving talks to the armed forces; for nothing remotely intellectual was acceptable, and the only use which I felt I could be was in taking along a few maps and indicating the whereabouts of places increasingly mentioned on the wireless or the press (though they read only the 'picture' papers).

It is difficult for the present generation of comparable age to realize what a change, in this respect, has been brought about by television. Eliot was at this time increasingly preoccupied with the question of 'public knowledge'. As he had stressed in *The Rock* this was not in the sense of information, but rather in the sense of consciousness of values; and he deplored a situation where the term society implied simply a group of 'well connected' and affluent people, which had almost no relation to that other group or society which maintained moral and intellectual standards, which for him was the church. Of the composition of the 'bench of bishops' (again the exact expression) he shook his head a little sadly, though he knew some of them well: I felt he was not so enthusiastic about William Temple, now Archbishop of Canterbury, as many of his fellow-writers were, however, grudgingly. The latter seemed to hold the view that, if there had to be an Archbishop of Canterbury at all, it were best that he should be a socialist. Indeed, most of the intelligentsia assumed outright that the post-war society would be a socialist society, and that one of the chief justifications for fighting the war was that socialism should be its outcome.

It was on this occasion that I drew Eliot's attention to the remarkable tribute to the English church contained in Thomas Hardy's Preface to the volume *Late Lyrics and Earlier*. When I had first read *The Idea of a Christian Society*, I was at once struck by the compatibility of some of Hardy's remarks on the role and function of the Anglican Church with Eliot's own views. No doubt because of his strictures on Hardy in *After Strange Gods*, and because he found Hardy's view of life personally antipathetic – and when Eliot disliked a writer, as he disliked Aldous Huxley (i.e. the work, not the man), and as he disliked Addison, and above all Goethe, his antipathy was intense and difficult to budge – he reacted in rather a lukewarm manner. Indeed, I saw that he was not convinced. Possibly this was because he distrusted the enthusiasm, sometimes pushed to excessive lengths, which some agnostics felt for the church (for example their defence of *Cranmer's Prayer Book*), and Hardy's enthusiasm amounted almost to love. It was almost, I ventured to suggest as if the agnostic were declaring 'Lord, I want to believe, but please cosset my unbelief, because the resulting tension is so delicious'. The real point of this story is that, so far as I know, Eliot never read the Hardy Preface, because when I referred to it again about twenty-five years later, he gave the impression of not knowing about it. It was for that reason that I never showed him my poem '*To Thomas Hardy in 1940*'.

He brought this part of our conversation to an end with some remarks about the kind of world that might exist after the war. That this Second World War would not last so long as the First, and even that it might not be a war on such a world-scale, were legitimate presumptions at the time, and Eliot was firmly of the opinion that we should be thinking then and there of the world which would finally emerge. In fact, the struggle was longer, on a greater scale, and with an outcome very different from that anticipated; so that, as far as Eliot was concerned, the task, as his *Notes towards the Definition of Culture* (1948) made clear, was not merely that of rescuing the Christian religion but of salvaging culture itself.

CHAPTER SIX

In February 1940, at the Labour Exchange at Devizes, I duly registered for military service. It was then a question of waiting to be called up, and none of us had any idea how long this would be. Meanwhile, I had formed one of a group of Local Defence Volunteers, an emergency organization set up in May 1940, later to be transformed into the Home Guard. With no uniform but an armband and all but no weapons, we kept watch in rotation through the warm nights of that early summer, with German planes passing overhead and all of a sudden the ground shuddering from bombs dropped on Southampton or Bristol. One night I was joined by a visitor to Seend, anxious to be of help, Colonel Faithorne, who was some relation of the Bishop of Bath and Wells, and who showed intellectual interests, including a knowledge of Eliot, which I was not to meet again in a soldier until I made the acquaintance in 1974 of my late father-in-law.

The intensification of the war increased when on 10 June 1940, Mussolini, making one of his last balcony performances, declared war, so that my newly-projected book on Italy seemed of immediate relevance, though whether I should complete it was another matter. I was thereafter in frequent communication with Eliot about the synopsis and concerning my negotiations with the Ministry. One of the officials with whom I had dealings was John Hampden, who years later was to become a colleague; but although he did his best to be co-operative, it was the men who held the purse-strings that counted, and, going between the MOI and Faber's, I could not extract from officialdom any commitment and Eliot naturally need certain specific undertakings regarding finance before Faber's could think of commissioning a book, which also needed the Ministry's imprimatur. For the first time, but by no means the last, I became involved in that Kafkaesque bureaucratic fog which, more than any aspect of public life, serves to drain one of psychic energy. I was at that time calling on and off at Faber's, sometimes seeing Eliot and sometimes missing him. A typical letter was that which he wrote on 8 July 1940:

> Dear Tomlin,
> I am sorry I didn't see you but I have read your synopsis and it seems to be all right. The synopsis of course is more a matter for the Ministry of Information. The chief point that interests us at this stage is the length, 50,000 words, but I have to remind you that we shall still want to know the number of illustrations, probably half-tones and maps, and what material the Ministry can provide. If you can let me have this information by Wednesday morning, it will be helpful. We can only base our estimate on the retail price which we think such a book would bear at this time and if the Ministry should want it to be produced at a lower price, they would have to increase their support accordingly.
>   Yours, in haste,
>   T.S.E.

This letter induced me to pay him an urgent visit, as I was doubtful of getting anything out of the Ministry so soon as that, if at all. Eliot's comment was: 'They should do business.' He was right. What he suggested was that I should then and there telephone my contact with the object of tying him down. Accordingly he vacated his desk and, inviting me to occupy it, he shifted the guest chair towards the door and there seated himself. As I was obtaining the number, I remember squinting at the view of Russell Square to my left. At the same time I thought how few people, apart from Eliot, could have sat and telephoned from that desk: meanwhile, reflecting that it were more proper to appear to be contemplating the exterior than to be glancing at Eliot's papers scattered in front of me.

My conversation with the Ministry seemed to take ages, and, as I had already anticipated, it proved abortive. But I was far from being depressed. Although he seemed to be oblivious of what had happened, because he was concentrating on some letter or other, Eliot looked up resignedly and with a smile of one all too accustomed to the lack of business acumen in other people; but I could see that he was also relieved to find me not too cast down. Fifteen years were to pass before I had a book published by Faber's, but by then I had been launched by other publishing houses.

Since the fall of France in May, the possibility of invasion increased. Such a thing not having happened for many centuries, the idea, even though the smell of cordite had spread across the Channel and could be picked up in the Charing Cross Road, seemed difficult to envisage. My brother had enlisted in the Grenadier Guards, and was at Camberley, but my mother and sister were still in Merstham; and it seemed to me that, in the event of a German landing, for which Churchill had alerted the public, a place as safe as any would be my Wiltshire village of Seend, where there was a delightful little Guest House, kept by a Mrs Earle. Here I would provisionally assemble the family. I had a Morris 10 which went like a bird, and I thereupon conceived the wild idea of rescuing Eliot from London if the danger should seem acute – and assuming that I were still available – and settling him, however temporarily, in the village. Admittedly at this distance the idea appears fanciful and even ludicrous; and no doubt if an enemy landing or landings had taken place, the roads out of London would have been jammed. On the other hand, my journeys in Wiltshire had made me a familiar figure to the police, and I consulted them about evacuating from London a distinguished man, of whose name, I need hardly say, they had never heard. That there would be evacuations, they thought very likely and if I could leave Wiltshire and get back again, there would be no problem.

I duly put this plan to Eliot, who, to my mild surprise, did not seem to regard it as so fanciful an idea as I had anticipated. I had chosen the right moment, because I found him, not so much irresolute as musing on the possibility of being wiped out by 'a stray bomb'. He also expressed regret that, so far as taking up arms was concerned, he was 'no good' as a shot. He even seemed slightly grateful that I had raised the matter. Nor did he dismiss it outright, though he said that my first duty should be to my family, with which of course I concurred. From his manner and general reaction, however, I realized how lonely a figure he was. Years later, his sister-in-law Theresa told me that her husband, Henry Ware Eliot, had written to some department of the British government, presumably the Home Office, requesting them to give Eliot some sort of protection at this critical moment. There had been no reply. I suppose it is not impossible that, if I had needed to make application to the authorities to undertake a dash to and from London for the purpose I had in mind, the brother-in-law's request might by some happy chance have 'married up' with my own application. It is an interesting thought. Whether Henry Eliot's letter is still on some Home Office file or other among the seventeen miles of paper which Toynbee (if I remember right) calculated to comprise the total government documentation of the war, I do not know; but some research worker may conceivably yet come upon it, and it would be interesting to learn whether it contained any apt comments. Possibly it was dismissed as the work of an eccentric; and just as Henry Eliot received no reply, I have no doubt that Eliot himself remained in ignorance of its existence, unless Theresa later mentioned it to him. He would certainly not have approved of being singled out for special treatment.

That was my last meeting with Eliot until the end of hostilities. I remember his tall spare figure, filling the door of his office. He looked slightly abstracted; and I noticed for the first time that his habit of addressing remarks with head bowed – often appearing to contemplate the floor or the 'figure in the carpet' – had begun to bring about that slight spinal curvature which became accentuated later in life though not without adding to his dignity of bearing. At such a time, with his formal dress, he looked like a diplomat of the old school.

While waiting for the call-up, various opportunities or openings of an official nature came my way, and I was summoned for interview, usually at extremely short notice, in connection with some of them. In more than one case, I never heard another word. This applied to a possible opening which Eliot mentioned in a letter of 2 April 1940. He had gone to great trouble to ascertain ways in which my knowledge of Italy and especially Libya might be put to use:

Dear Tomlin,
  My enquiry has only elicited the advice that you should attempt to get into Military Intelligence, with special reference to the affairs of Italy and Libya. My informant suggests that you should apply to a mutual acquaintance, Professor F. C. Green, who is now in the War Office, but I won't write to him without hearing from you first.
    Yours ever,
    T.S. Eliot.

As I was once again unemployed and earning no money, I needed to obtain some work. The *New English Weekly* could not afford to pay contributors. A post in Italy, the nature of which I never fully learnt, save that it would be of sufficient importance to take me out of uniform if I were in it, fell through with Italy's declaration of war. This was a disappointment, since I had been striving even more to acquire expertise in Italian affairs, and I was doing some propaganda work for the BBC, some of which was 'beamed' to the Arab population of Libya. Then a communication reached me from a newly-formed organization called the British Council, which no one, including some of its officials, seemed to know much about. The general aim was to counter Axis influences and propaganda. The Chairman, however, was Lord Lloyd, a fiery patriot and Anglo-Catholic, with whom Eliot was quite well acquainted. With his usual pertinacity, he pursued this new line, and on 8 April 1940, he wrote to me:

Dear Tomlin,

Some remarks I made, without mentioning your name, in writing to the British Council, have elicited a reply from someone there named T. P. Tunnard-Moore, whom I have never met, and whose name is not on the letterhead, so I don't quite know what his position is. But the point is that he says the British Council has now received permission to send out men down to 25, and, he adds, 'even to extract them from the army if their qualifications are sufficiently outstanding. So send your man along, or let him write, but don't let him construe this as a promise'.

If you want to write to him, mention that this came through correspondence with me, and also that I should be glad to be one of the people to speak for you if necessary.

Yours ever,
T.S. Eliot.

I was at length summoned for interview, during which I was told that the War Office wished to fill a post of Instructor-cum-British Adviser at the Staff College and Royal Military College, Baghdad, Iraq, and that in order to reassure the Iraqi High Command that they were not sending a British 'plant' (for relations between the two countries were strained), they asked the British Council to fill it. Lord Lloyd interviewed me, and explained that I was to report to the Military Attaché at the Baghdad Embassy, though I was to be attached to the British Institute. My task was to identify myself as much as possible with the personnel of the College and their activities in order to mitigate their hostility and pro-Axis leanings. One of the qualifications, according to Lord Lloyd, was polo, but he considered that this was not essential, but that my Cert A, my apparent taste for adventure, and, I suspect, Eliot's backing, were enough to justify his appointing me. A few weeks later I was on a troopship, the converted *Andes*, with 3,000 men, bound for the Middle East via the Cape.

At Glasgow on 8 August 1940, I wrote last-minute notes to friends for the recent weeks had been hectic, but the one intended for Eliot never arrived. Communications were no doubt temporarily dislocated: our jam-packed train had been halted during the night owing to an air raid in the region. My mother fortunately wrote to Eliot on 20 August 1940, and he answered:

FABER & FABER
Publishers

24 Russell Square,
London, W.C.1.

Mrs. Tomlin,
Woodside,
Dean Lane,
Merstham, Surrey.   23rd August 1940.

Dear Mrs. Tomlin,

Thank you very much for your letter of the 20th. I had not heard from your son for several weeks and the news you tell me of comes as a surprise. I am, however, very glad to hear of it as this sounds as if it might prove the kind of job for which he had been looking, and I know that with his interest in the East he will both be of great value in Baghdad and will acquire experience which he will be able to turn to further account later.

Thanking you very much for writing and with best wishes,
I am,
Yours very sincerely,
T.S. Eliot.

In embarking on this section of my reminiscences, I need to stress once more that I am not writing my own memoirs. On the other hand, I have needed from time to time to provide a certain amount of background, because the progress of a friendship cannot be traced otherwise than by describing attendant circumstances. For us two the war meant, as for so many others, a break in physical contact: but if, as Simone Weil said, 'every separation is a link', such a break is not a breaking off, but a period in which, at least in my case, that ties of friendship continued in another form.

If you held the kind of philosophy that I do, you would realize that, in friendship, presence and absence, propinquity and distance, do not make quite the difference that they do in mere acquaintanceship. There is a crucial and fundamental difference, not always appreciated, between acquaintances and friends. Acquaintanceship imposes its own discipline and obligation. If I am in the habit of greeting my neighbour or a regular passer-by in the morning, I must not omit to do so, or I shall cause immediate pain and offence. A similar lapse in the case of friendship, provided it were inadvertent, would be better and more charitably understood. Therefore, while absence may spell the end of acquaintanceship, it will not in itself destroy friendship; and while Dr Johnson was right to say that we should keep our friendships in good repair, the perpetual shoring up of friendship might suggest that it were less enduring than we had supposed.

I am not implying that there is communication between friends on a supernormal, still less a supernatural, plane, though I would not exclude it: there is just enough evidence for telepathy to explain certain experiences that most of us have had, or are convinced that we have had, once or twice. I am thinking of a feeling of confidence which has been built up and which it would take some drastic change to break down.

For my part, there can hardly have been a day when I did not think of Eliot, when his growing prestige was not a source of immense satisfaction and pride to me, and when personal news about him, however brief, was more than welcome at such distance than propinquity without meeting would have been. The course of my life during the period from the end of 1940 until the autumn of 1945 is one of which I intend to write an account; but this is not the place for it. Here I need mention only that my work at the Staff College and the Royal Military College in Baghdad put me under suspicion of espionage, and that had the pro-Nazi rebellion of Raschid Ali of May 1941 (during which I was given protection in the American Embassy) been successful, I should have fared badly, as it was surmissed much later that I was on the rebels' hit list. The new order after the collapse of the rebellion brought Iraq, if somewhat reluctantly, into the war on the Allied side. For some months I worked in the Information Department of the British Embassy, where I was engaged in propaganda, which included writing leaders for the *Iraq Times*. With Iraq in the war, it was most desirable to endeavour to bring in Turkey too, and I was therefore transferred there by the British Council in the autumn of 1941. An enormous effort, directed by Michael Grant, who had been taken out of the army for that purpose, was being sustained. From that time dated my devotion to Turkey and the Turkish people.

Unfortunately, many of my letters home miscarried, because, Turkey being neutral until towards the end of the war, the post went through enemy-occupied Europe: I do not know what the Nazi censors made of some of my missives. To ensure passage by way of Egypt it was necessary to mark the envelope 'Mısır yolu'. Only one letter from Eliot survived the war, written on 24 February 1943. My sister, however, kindly kept him informed of my whereabouts, and he replied in two letters, the first of which was dated 30 November 1940:

Dear Miss Tomlin,
    Thank you very much for sending me your brother's address. I shall write to him, but I know that letters to and from the Middle East take an extraordinarily long time; and if you hear from him meanwhile I shall be very glad of any news of his well-being.
        Yours sincerely,
        T.S. Eliot.

The second was dated 27 May 1942:

Dear Miss Tomlin,
    Thank you very much for your letter which I find on my return from Sweden where I have been doing some work for the local British Council. I have heard nothing from your brother for a very long time but I am glad to have his new address and will write to him. I am afraid that letters to Ankara take many weeks and that knowledge always inclines one to postpone writing to people, but I shall try to write to him as soon as I get my affairs straight.
        Yours sincerely,
        T.S. Eliot.

Meanwhile, during journeys to Palestine and to Egypt, I picked up copies of *The Dry Salvages* and *Little Gidding*. There was also no lack of contacts, who, starved of literature, were exhilarated to be able to talk about Eliot: a Captain Richardson, whom I met in Eritrea, engaged to a charming Italian, proved one of those contacts whom the war brought together and separated, reminding me in some ways of the young Eliot and Jean Verdenal. If he survived the war and should ever read these words, I hope he may resume contact after nearly fifty years. The same applied to a Polish officer, one of the most cultivated men I have ever met, whom I encountered in Khartoum. Nor must I omit a dozen or so Turkish friends, whose friendship I was able to resume years later, above all Aziz and Ülviye Isvar and my closest Turkish friend – indeed one of my closest friends – Naci Ortaç, whose wife was the daughter of a Grand Vizier. Alas, he died in 1987. Then there was the politician Bulent Ecerit, who had translated Eliot. Otherwise, the war meant much loneliness, which was assuaged in my case by writing, reading, learning languages, and studying such countries of the Middle East as I was able to visit. But one was never off duty.

A further family link with Eliot was momentarily established in 1941 by the fact that my sister attended a poetry reading by him under the auspices of the English Association. He read – and this helps to fix the date – the beginning of what he announced to be 'a new poem'. This was *Little Gidding*, and, as she wrote, 'I shall never forget the experience of hearing the words new-minted as it were from the poet's own lips'. Afterwards, she ventured to go up to him and say that she was my sister: to which he replied kindly – 'I can see that you are'.

Of the letters I wrote to Eliot and kept copies I reproduce one, which might perhaps have some more permanent interest than the ephemera. I believe that my account of events is a good deal nearer the truth than some that have since been published: but then I was perhaps in a better position than some other observers to know what was going on.

> The Black Sea Coast,
> near Samsun,
> Turkey.
> July 18th 1944.

Dear Mr. Eliot,

I am returning from a short trip to Trebizond, where I have spent the last fortnight. This is the first time that I have visited the Black Sea coast, and I find it most interesting as well as a great deal less bleak than I had been given to expect. Although I spent most of the time in Trebizond itself, I managed to fit in a trip to Rizé, where the countryside resembles that of Switzerland, and also, by great good luck, to Hopa, which is not far away from the Russian frontier. I say 'by great good luck', because the Turkish authorities do not like foreigners wandering about in the neighbourhood of frontiers, particularly the Russian frontier. I was fortunate enough to obtain permission to go, but I had waited until arriving at Rizé before applying for it. When I returned to Trebizond, I was told that the authorities at Rizé were exceeding their rights in allowing me to proceed. This was no doubt very wicked of them, but I bear them no animosity at all: I had done what I wanted to do, which was to obtain a glimpse of the Caucasus from the most easternly town of any size in Turkey.

This concern over the movements of foreigners is far from being an isolated example of its kind. As the danger to Turkey recedes, the number of restrictions seem to multiply: the country's nerves grow daily more touchy. There are several possible explanations for this increasing nervousness. My own view is that the Turks do not interpret the course of the war in the same sense that we do. To them, the danger is not so much receding as increasing: but that is because their definition of what constitutes danger is very different from ours. The danger which they believe to be increasing is precisely the danger of the war ending too soon. For the Turks have always hoped that the war would be prolonged until both sides were too exhausted to remain a menace to anybody. Decisive victory for either side: that is what Turkish policy, in so far as it has any power, has been striving to prevent. And if anything, they regard the coming victory of the United Nations with more apprehension at the moment than they did the possibility of a German victory two or three years ago: the reason being that, in achieving decisive victory, the United Nations will leave Europe with no nation sufficiently strong to shield Turkey against possible Russian demands in the post-war period. I date the present coldness of Turkey towards us from the expulsion of the Axis from North Africa. That victory of ours was the first to which they gave less than their usual measure of approval. The truth is that, while they want us to win, they do not want Germany to lose.

Coupled with her hope that the war may end in a stalemate goes the hope that she may never be obliged to become a belligerent nation. Turkey does not want to fight (her people

are at the moment almost frantically pacifist): and, if she can
help it, she does not intend to fight. The Cairo Conference was
a near thing for her. Her obligations stared her in the face, but
she did not flinch! And on the return of the President from that
journey, the whole country gave a sigh of profound, if somewhat
complacent, relief. This was followed by an interview between
the President and Von Papen: and I cannot help thinking that,
during their conversation together, the former must have assured
the latter that, so long as she could hold out against Allied
demands, Turkey would abstain from hostile action towards
Germany. She has had to give in over the question of chrome:
and the Foreign Minister, who never struck me as being too
friendly towards us, failed to get away (as he apparently hoped)
with letting armed German ships through the Straits. But, more
recently, the opening of the Second Front, together with its initial
success, has sent a faint thrill of alarm through the country: and
the latest utterance of Cordell Hull, which came over the wireless
yesterday, is not going to cheer things up, nor is it likely to be the
last exhortation of its kind.

To say that this sums up Turkey's attitude as a whole would
nevertheless be untrue. Combined with their reluctance to enter
the war, the Turks entertain great hopes of their army, upon
which a major portion of the budget is spent: and they cannot
fail to recognise something ludicrous in an attitude which, at one
moment, abhors the idea of fighting and at another lauds it as the
noblest activity of man. Consequently, I think we may legitimately
expect to see an attempt, though not before the Nazis are observed
to be definitely on the point of throwing in their hand, to undertake
some minor military venture independent, if at all possible, of the
general strategy of the Allies. It will probably be directed against
Bulgaria, but there is also the possibility of an attack upon the
Dodecanese, if such an expedition could be undertaken with the
small fleet that Turkey possesses. And it may be that the warning
of Cordell Hull was designed, among other things, to make it
clear that, should Turkey finally decide to become a belligerent,
she must do so in conformity with plans already agreed upon by
the Allies themselves.

I intended this to be a letter, but I see that it has turned into
a political commentary. Having caught the fever of the country,
which induces inflammation of the political speculative faculties,

I am inclined to imagine that everyone else is so addicted. But I fancy that England is content to get on with the war, and that things take a more practical turn at home.

I occasionally receive a copy of the NEW, most numbers of which evidently get lost on the way. In this matter, I seem to miss those issues to which you contribute articles: I have not seen one for many months now. For the last year, I have had little time for writing, though I get something down on paper when I can. Something may emerge from it later. In a few weeks time, I hope to get a short spell of leave, and I mean to devote it exclusively to literary work. The major difficulty is to find somewhere in the Middle East in which seclusion and moderate comfort can be combined. Last year I set out on the same quest, but met with little success. My wanderings took me first to Beyrout, which I found much too crowded and hilarious. After that, I went on to Cairo, where the heat was insupportable. Finally, resolved to find at least a change of heat, I went on to Khartoum, which had the merit at least of being dry in contrast to the swelter up north. But this did not satisfy me either, so I ended up in Eritrea, having passed through Keren, Agordat, and Asmara. And by that time I was due to return to my work in Turkey. I must not make the same mistake this time. I have my eye at the moment on the little-visited town of Amman, capital of Transjordan, which I am told is charming. I have also been recommended Zanzibar, but that is going to cost a great deal of money, and likewise the journey there and back will occupy much valuable time. The trouble with having lived in the Middle East for a year or two is that, wherever one goes, one is bound to run into acquaintances; and that means drinks at the nearest bar, and more acquaintances, and finally the complete derangement of one's intended programme, and great loss of time.

In spite of much travelling and various kinds of work, I have been able to get through some interesting books. One that I enjoyed very much recently was H. J. Massingham's autobiography 'Remembrance', which, if you have not read, I am sure you would like. I have also just finished 'The Well of Loneliness', which I had not read previously. I presume that it was banned because, instead of treating its subject frivolously, it treated it seriously, even solemnly. Solemnity is perhaps its greatest defect. 'Nightwood' is, I think, a better book.

I ought to have mentioned, in my remarks about writing, that I have just completed an essay, written chiefly for my own amusement, entitled 'The Claims of Basic English', in which I treat the subject from a somewhat new angle (or so I believe). When I have revised it thoroughly, I will send you a copy.

I shall be delighted to hear from you when you can spare a moment. There are three addresses to which letters can be sent: (1) The British Council, I/IO, Kazim Özalp Caddesi, Ankara: (2) c/o The British Consulate, Mersin: (3) The British Council, 25, Sharia Abou el Sebaa, Cairo (for airgraphs also).

Yours sincerely,

With the surrender of Germany and Turkey's entry into the war, it was felt that one phase of our work was done, and that at last we could go home. In my case, 'we' was the right word, because in 1944 I had married. Once back in London, one of the first people I wanted to meet was Eliot. I wrote to him and he asked me to ring him, so that a date for a meeting could be arranged. On the telephone, I was greeted with a very friendly and hearty 'Well . . . well . . . well!' and we chatted for a few minutes as if there had been no break in our contact. I found always this to be the case: resumption of acquaintance was so natural that small talk, as mere material for continuity or improvization, was unnecessary.

When I paid my visit, I was surprised to see how comparatively well he looked. He had scarcely changed. Nor had his manner. We resumed conversation almost as if we had never left off. On this occasion he occupied a chair at right angles to his desk, and he leaned much further back than had been his custom, stretching out his legs; and, being denied by this posture the opportunity of studying the floor while collecting his thoughts, he addressed the bulk of his remarks first to his feet. I sat on his left, and had the impression of looking slightly down at him. At that time, Russell Square was showing its scars. From the window I could see that the block on the far side to the right had had most of its front ripped off, and Eliot commented how odd and rather disturbing it was to see a bath on an upper storey sticking out into the void, as in a surrealist picture. He also spoke of lying awake and listening for the flying bombs, and noting the difference in volume between one explosion and another, and then, on hearing one more definite in sound, concluding that, as in the old artillery box-barrage, they had at last 'got the range'.

About his work at Faber's, he remarked – and it is now a somewhat nostalgic thought – that books were being bought as never before; the trouble was that the impressive or 'excess' profits were heavily taxed. These commercial matters were as much as ever in his mind. In contrast to some other material, my essay 'The Claims of Basic English', to which I had referred in my letter of 18 July 1944, had reached him; and I was much cheered by the fact that he expressed unqualified approval for it. He said he would be prepared to place it for me, and he was as good as his word. It appeared in January 1946 in the *Dublin Review* – which was a most lively periodical, and of which, now that it is no more, there is no equivalent. The essay has since been listed in several bibliographies, and has exerted an influence which, when I composed it as a kind of *riposte* to the British Council's purchase of the copyright of that crack-brained idea from its originator, C. K. Ogden, I could not have foreseen. But I owe its initial success to Eliot.

While we talked, I had an opportunity of glancing round the familiar room, which was even more cluttered than usual. I noticed in particular a large placard placed on the floor in a corner, which I assumed to have been presented to him by Montgomery Belgion, who had been a prisoner of war in Germany. It recommended fellow-prisoners to occupy their time to the best advantage, such as attending a talk on 'The Poetry of T. S. Eliot', and there was a sketch of a man studiously reading a book with this title.

Before I left, I told Eliot that I was still toying with the idea of writing the book on politics, which had increasingly been absorbing me, and I described to him something of what it had been like to live under a benevolent dictatorship. We also discussed the next great problem in international affairs, that posed by the Soviet Union, that victorious and self-confident power, with which our politicians, and above all Ernest Bevin, were already grappling. I found him reflecting on this problem with his usual shrewdness. Although he did not underestimate the dangers of insurgent Communism, and considered it pathetic that the Soviet leaders should have as their strict aim the overtaking of the Capitalist states, he still felt that something might come out of Russia from which all might benefit. By that it was clear that he was referring to some sort of spiritual renaissance, and he succeeded, as so often, in implicitly prophesying the emergence of men like Solzhenitsyn.

His preoccupation with Russia was to show itself shortly after with the publication of *The Dark Side of the Moon*, to which he wrote a most interesting Preface.

Although I have said that Eliot had not greatly physically changed, he felt the deprivations of the war as acutely as anyone else. One of the satisfactions, at the secular level, of which he keenly felt the lack was in the gastronomic sphere. He could not endure substitutes. Saccharine, for instance, or the *ersatz* in general, he abominated. I once shocked him by admitting that I sometimes took it in my tea. Except for the occasional food-parcel from the United States, he would never have sought to diverge from the rationing system, which, like many other controls, were maintained long after the war ended. Prices were controlled too, so meals in restaurants, even though dull, were not expensive.

For reasons which I could never grasp, some restaurants seemed in a position to provide much greater variety than others, and my wife and I found one such place in the Hanover Square area, where I worked. As I wanted Eliot to meet us together, I invited him to lunch at this crowded chatter-filled establishment on 22 October 1945. We called for him in a taxi at Faber's, Margaret waiting inside the vehicle. In those days stationary taxis still throbbed a little, like the ones he had compared in *The Waste Land* to the waiting human engine at the day's end. Apart from that, what remains vividly in my memory is the sudden look of extreme melancholy which possessed his face as he was about to climb in. Some memory must have stabbed him at that moment. Otherwise he remained throughout the meal in the best possible spirits; and Margaret, who had not perhaps quite reconciled herself to my admiration for him, surrendered to his spell. As to Eliot, he was interested in her Scottishness, because although his knowledge of that country was limited, he had been captivated by its beauty, and, as I have said, he had a particular *penchant* for small countries, and even for regional 'nationalisms'.

We ventured to ask him what he was writing, and he replied that the trouble with being a publisher was that one was so absorbed in other people's books as to have insufficient time and energy to devote to one's own. He deplored the paper shortage and the fact that books needed to be produced on such poor material. The edition of the *Selected Essays*, which I had picked up in Cairo during the war after my copy had been pinched by someone in the Foreign Service (whose identity is known to me), had a pleasant silk binding, but the paper was of the colour and of the dryness of a tobacco plant.

Another topic on which we touched, because it was one of our preoccupations, was London and the most desirable districts in which to live. After some search, we had been fortunate in finding accommodation, admittedly very cramped, in a mews flat in Kensington Court. The address was, and I think still is, Kensington Court Garage, because the stables had been converted to the needs of the automobile age; and we were perched up in the gallery. Years later Eliot and his second wife were to live a stone's-throw away. He himself had not long left his rooms in Courtfield Gardens, *chez* the Vicar, Father Eric Cheetham, and settled with John Hayward in Carlyle Mansions, Chelsea. One of the attractions of that district, he remarked, was the proximity of the Thames, particularly so for him, for whom rivers had a particular fascination. What he most liked, so he explained, was the feeling that from that proximate stretch, you felt that you could set sail, if the impulse took you, to any part of the world. This was the kind of observation which he was inclined to drop with apparent casualness but which stuck in the mind. Indeed, that was why so many of his remarks have echoed in my mind over the years, because experience has merely served to confirm their aptness.

Of the lunch itself I can remember very little. Being still in the period of Stafford Crippsian austerity, I know it was rather plain and dull. I do recall him saying, not in that connection (which his good manners would have forbidden) but with reference to the system of rationing in general, that it made one obsessively conscious of the working of one's digestive organs. He was often down to earth in that way. As to the restaurant itself, I recall that we had to shuffle and wriggle our way out between the crowded tables, and that the noise had been a little taxing on the nerves. Not that he showed it. Nor do I for a moment suppose that anyone there recognized him, nor was he the sort of author who basked in that kind of admiration. Not long after that meeting I was faced with a problem over my official duties and I urgently sought his advice. To whom else, indeed, would I have turned?

Accordingly, he asked me to lunch, and we went to the Russell Hotel, which was conveniently near his office. I must have poured out my troubles at such length, and he must have put to me a sufficient number of searching questions, that, before we had drawn breath, the afternoon was already far advanced. I remember that we sat opposite each other – the arrangement I most preferred – so that I could observe every modification of his countenance; and I have to say that never in all our acquaintance had I witnessed such patience and sheer kindness. This was further demonstrated by the fact that, when I murmured some apologies that I must leave, he insisted on my staying for some tea. True, this was a meal of which he was very fond; but on the other hand he usually did the bulk of his office work in the afternoon, and I was conscious of having been instrumental in seriously holding this up. All the same, once he appeared to be actually enjoying this extension of our meeting, I felt as reassured as I was grateful.

This was all the more so, since part of the problem with which I was faced was due, as I recognized, to lack of forethought on my side, though it had been complicated by a stroke of ill-luck. Eliot did not beat about the bush. He agreed that a regrettable lack of foresight was at the root of it, but he felt that there were extenuating circumstances, and he seemed resolved to do something about it, in so far as he could. I noted then, what I had noted earlier, that, at such a juncture, he seemed to sink his own personal problems and interests in concentrating on the troubles of the other person. That is why I cannot agree with Stephen Spender's remark, quoted by Ackroyd, that he seemed 'blinded to the existence of people outside himself'. To my mind, he was the very reverse of blind. though he took every precaution, as I felt, to render his own self invisible. Hugh Kenner's title 'The Invisible Poet' was much more to the point. As I have written elsewhere, 'for one who was in perpetual self-inquisition he was remarkably outward-looking, and always showed interest in other people's activities'. If people felt occasionally frustrated in their relationship with Eliot – as Herbert Read told me he did – it was because they could not get behind 'the mask'. But then what is this habit of trying to penetrate to people's inner life? In judging other people, we have to rely on intuition and empathy. The souls *mis a nu*, like the persons who 'tell all' in our popular newspapers and magazines, usually show by the exposure that they have very little to convey. Eliot has said it himself in *After Strange Gods*: it is during those 'bewildering minutes' that 'we are all very much the same'.

The upshot of this long sessions was that Eliot asked me to send him all the relevant documents, which I did in a letter of 20 May. It arrived just before he was leaving for the United States (another example of his self-forgetfulness, as he had not mentioned this to me), and he was not due to return until the end of July. He wrote a longish letter on 23 May ending with the words:

> If I were not leaving immediately I should want to have another talk with you but I hope you will write to me in New York and tell me of any developments, and if I can be of any use from there I shall be glad.

Again, I was touched by his solicitude. A busy man who was prepared for 'another talk' after the prolonged exchange of a few days earlier, was not quite the self-absorbed, withdrawn person he has sometimes been portrayed.

The crisis passed, somewhat to my surprise, and I would not dismiss the possibility that Eliot, acting so as to ensure that the information should not be disclosed to me, had something to do with it. And within a few days of his return from the United States, he wrote to me on 4 August to the Kensington Mews flat:

> Dear Tomlin,
> I have your letter dated 4th July but I expect you meant the 4th August as I only received it this morning. I got back from the United States last Friday. I am very glad to have your news, both good, indifferent and bad, and I hope that I may see you and your wife again before long. This is just to let you know that I am here again and available.
>   Yours ever sincerely,
>   T.S. Eliot.

It was a remark of this kind that I found particularly heartening. In so unequal a friendship – unequal not merely in respect of age but in the extent to which the giving was preponderantly on his side – I would repeatedly wonder whether I had presumed too much. At a time when he had so many claims on his time, what with his normal work, committees, visitors from overseas, particularly from the United States, a growing acquaintanceship and a formidable correspondence, the assurance that he was 'here again and available' was of great moral support to me, especially as I was still uncertain about the future, and as the news, as his letter hinted, was by no means all good. Indeed, the next months were taxing in a different way, culminating in my appointment to a post in Bahrein for which I had little enough relish.

We wanted very much to ask Eliot round before departure, especially as we had now moved to a bigger flat. I was in touch several times by telephone, and I remember noticing for the first time a slight labouring for breath on his part, which was to become increasingly marked. On 15 November, he wrote to me at 41A Roland Gardens:

Dear Tomlin,

As I promised I am writing to suggest an evening when I could come in to see you. I am afraid it cannot be next week which is rather full. I could manage Tuesday the 26th or Friday the 29th if either of these dates were possible. I should be disappointed, certainly, not to see you before you leave for the East.

Yours sincerely,
T.S. Eliot.

The Tuesday was duly fixed up, and we prepared as good a meal as the rationing system, still in operation, made possible. The time appointed, 7.30 p.m., came and went. As we were installed in a sort of penthouse flat, with no lift: and as occasionally a guest had found the front-door bell erratic in its functioning, I hurried down to see what, if anything, had been happening. As I opened the door, a familiar tall figure, swinging a stick, strode past. When I detained him by a greeting, he looked up a little puzzled, saying that he thought that we lived in Cornwall Gardens. What would have happened had I not arrived at the door at precisely that juncture, I cannot imagine. He had a long, brown, American-style overcoat, a woollen scarf against the cold, the usual hat, and the sword-stick, perhaps an imitation, which was no doubt a present. (He was in receipt of numerous walking-sticks and umbrellas, some huge, as admirers translated their support in this literal way. When a French journalist wrote of him carrying *un grand parapluie*, Eliot crossed out '*grand*' and put '*immense*'.)

He quietly made himself at home, and launched upon the usual enquiries about my work and my writing. Nelson's had just issued a short book of mine on Turkey, and he scrutinized it with care, holding it high up and bending back the spine as if to test its durability. When I was out of the room, he told Margaret that he wanted to see me write weightier books than that. We talked about the *Dublin Review*, where my Basic English article had been published, and referred to a characteristically splenetic article by Montgomery

Belgion which had also appeared in that journal. Belgion, a man who seemed to be equipped with a steam-boiler instead of a body, had criticized a remark of Eliot's in *After Strange Gods*, namely that in order to study with thoroughness Hindu and Buddhist thought and the Sanskrit and Pali languages in which they were expounded, he would have been obliged to turn himself into an oriental. For some reason, Belgion had resented this observation, not because he thought it untrue but because he claimed to have said it first. Eliot mentioned that he had written to Belgion, gently protesting against the intemperate way in which this comment had been conveyed. He also remarked that Belgion was something of a mystery man, about whom very little seemed to be known – even whence he acquired his undoubtedly vast store of knowledge. (He did not remark, but I did later, that if anyone truly deserved the title of 'egg-head', it was Belgion, with his huge bald, smooth, oval-shaped head.)

After these preliminaries, including some observations about Kensington, conducted before a rather feeble gas-fire, we moved to the low-ceilinged dining-room. Again, I cannot remember what we had to eat, though we had tried to obtain a suitable cheese; but it was during the meal that Eliot uttered one of the most Eliotic of his remarks. There was a particular dish, in those days something of a delicacy, which needed cutting into sections before serving, and the question was how this was to be done. Eliot pronounced the verdict with great and grave deliberation. 'Each one', he said by way of final adjudication, 'will perform that operation for himself.'

Although we did not attend it, we had visited St Stephen's, Gloucester Road, together, no doubt out of forgivable curiosity, though Eliot might not have thought excusable any curiosity he had been the means of exciting in that sphere. But he seemed disposed on this occasion to discuss St Stephen's, because its problems had lately been much on his mind. The details have escaped me, but he and Sir Andrew Clarke, as churchwardens (their memorial tablets are near to each other in the south transept) had been obliged to take legal action over the advowson – the word which, because of its precision of meaning and its sound, I could see he enjoyed introducing; but they had evidently covered themselves in so doing, because, the Anglican Church being established, their office carried official responsibilities. Although Eliot was privately a most generous man – to an extent that many people, especially the young, may not always have been aware – he exercised a public prudence that sometimes faintly amused his associates. This was no doubt in part due to his Puritan ancestry.

I remember that when he got up at the end of the meal, his head nearly touched the ceiling, and, as usual, the rising to his feet was undertaken by means of the silent swivel-mechanism. As we had referred to Turkey and the fact that Margaret and I had met there, and as we knew he took great interest in genuine peasant culture, we showed him some Turkish embroidery and in particular two typical Turkish saddle-bags, which we had transformed into cushions. He was much struck by the latter, turning them over and myopically examining their patterns. 'That's what I call civilization,' he said decisively and gave one of them a smart pat. The present generation should be informed that in those days we tended to talk about 'civilization' rather than 'culture'. Civilization, or 'civilization as we know it' was what people had fought for. Culture, which later became current with the rise of social anthropology, tended to be associated with what the Germans had believed they had fought for. During the next few years, the subject was increasingly to preoccupy him, and when his thoughts finally appeared in print, they were concerned with 'culture': the word civilization does not feature at all.

We sat for a while in the sitting-room over coffee. The fact that we had met Michael and Janet Roberts came up, and he was moved to explain that, with his growing acquaintanceship with the children of his friends – to several of whom he had become godfather – he had felt the need to adopt some sobriquet less solemn than Uncle. That is why he had suggested that he should be known as Possum. It was already his nickname with fellow-writers such as Ezra Pound; and, in adopting it for use by the youngest generation, he may have again wished to convey, though with slightly less emphasis, the elusive character of that animal, with its instinct for feigning and dissembling.

I saw him to the door and watched him pace away along the streets he knew better than most others in London. Some, like Clarence Gate Gardens, had sad associations for him. The name remained in the telephone-book as his address long after he had left. Some, like Bina Gardens, where he had spent pleasant evenings with Frank Morley and Geoffrey Faber in the 1930s at John Hayward's flat, resulted in the *Noctes Binanianae*, a little private anthology which I came upon later in the Houghton Library at Harvard. There is a book to be written, and almost certainly will be written, on T. S. Eliot's Kensington, as a companion volume to Patricia Hutchings' *Ezra Pound's Kensington*. And three days before these lines were written, English Heritage set the seal on Eliot's Kensington associations by putting a plaque on the block where he spent his last and happiest years.

During the next few weeks my fortunes took a more propitious turn. The posting to Bahrein was cancelled, and I was to stay on in London, at least for the moment. One day, in an elated mood, we thought we would give Eliot a surprise. Just before Christmas, we visited Carlyle Mansions, climbed to the third floor and, ringing the bell, delivered to the housekeeper a rather nice, mature Camembert. Whereas today such a cheese is accessible enough and almost commonplace, in 1946 this was far from being so. Such cheese was, in rationing terminology, on points, and the chances of getting a really good one were fairly rare. *Anything* of quality was exciting in those days, for the usual run of food was of a dullness today hardly comprehensible. The housekeeper, French by origin and known as Madame, was one of those fair Nordic or Norman types whose hair and complexion were of a uniformity to suggest that she had been dipped in custard. She took the packet with some fussy excitement, and she was clearly a little relieved when we made it clear that we had no intention of staying or seeking entrance. We also had to make it plain that the present was for Mr Eliot, though we knew perfectly well that he would share it with John Hayward. Just as we were engaged in these *sotto voce* instructions, Eliot himself was perceived to walk across a passage at the far end of the flat. This was in the neighbourhood of his humble quarters. On realizing that there was someone at the door, he quickened his pace, so that our view of him was a fugitive one. We were able to see, however, that he was formally dressed in a three-piece dark suit. As we were paying our visit at the end of the morning, he may have been dressed ready for the office.

This visit to the flat, the only one I paid, produced a letter which was, as I know, typed with his own hand. It was headed with the address, but not the name, of Faber's, for he had been anxious, especially when he lodged with Father Cheetham, that his private address should not be known. I was glad that we had not troubled him personally, though we confessed that we should like to have set foot in the flat.

He wrote:

> 24 Russell Square, W.C.1.
> 22 December 1946.

Dear Tomlin,

How very kind of you (I am sorry you did not ask for me, as I think I was in when you called) and also how very generous: as I think cheeses need points, so that you and your wife are depriving yourselves of nourishment in feeding me. It is an excellent Camembert, and very welcome. (I had been given one a fortnight before, by someone coming over from France, and our housekeeper had popped it into the refrigerator over night – this time she knew better.)

I do hope that you will find yourselves settled in London after all, as I have been much distressed by the thought of your being exiled to a place like that. And in any case, I hope that I shall see you again in February, when I have recovered from my operation and am again about.

Wish best wishes to you both for Christmas and the New Year.
>   Yours very sincerely,
>   T.S. Eliot.

It was a delightful letter; and the reference to being 'fed' by us and to the heresy of refrigerating a mature Camembert were typical of him. Again, I was moved that he should have perceived how miserable an exile to the Persian Gulf would have been. The fact that he had been 'much distressed' by that prospect proved his genuine regard, which I knew was not contrived. Despite chest trouble and the serious illness of his mother, he was, as the letter provided a small piece of evidence, much happier about his own work. *The Family Reunion*, which we went to see and much enjoyed, had that autumn been put on again, and its success greatly heartened him.

We had also been in touch with him indirectly through learning early in the year that he and John Hayward were needing a housekeeper.

Through family connections, Margaret knew a handsome Greek lady, who seemed suitable. She had not merely been a housekeeper but her qualities of efficiency, cheerfulness and gastronomic expertise seemed to fit her for the task of looking after this unusual pair. I was several times on the phone to John Hayward, who supervised such domestic matters, and I was struck by his almost fierce, perhaps too possessive, loyalty to Eliot. He made frank, often ribald remarks about other people, especially fellow-writers and intellectuals, and he was scathing about the award by Oxford of an honorary doctorate to a minor littérateur, E. V. Lucas, instead of to Eliot, and I don't wonder. Given his distressing complaint (muscular dystrophy), he possessed, apart from a commanding voice, an ebullience which, as I can now see, suited Eliot, though I believe there were moments when the two temperaments were at odds. Moreover there was gossip about the two which disgusted me. Once only was I able to talk to Hayward *de vive voix*, and that was at the Institute of Contemporary Arts, when I referred again to the housekeeper problem; but in the end, for reasons that I do not know, our Greek candidate, who might have been an admirable choice, was not summoned for interview.

The French housekeeper, who triumphed, stayed at Carlyle Mansions for more than ten years. She must have come to know her employers better than many others, and certainly in a quite different and unusual way. Like Miss Swan at Faber's, she had a particular regard for Eliot. This was also the case with the housekeeper, Elizabeth Hinson, who had looked after the Vicarage and who died in a nursing home about a year before these lines were written. A friend of mine, who ministered to her late in life, gained the impression, from one or two things she let drop, that, contrary to what has been stated, Eliot did indeed go to Northumberland House, the nursing home where Vivien was looked after. When I was told this, I recalled hearing it said, back in the 1930s, that these visits had been observed by a young writer or two who, out of rather callous curiosity, would follow Eliot at a discreet distance, and observe him to turn round, as he approached the door, in order to see whether anybody had been spying on him. But this story is definitely false; and it illustrates how myths can grow up, especially concerning the great.

I deeply regret that I was unable to have a word with the housekeeper when she was more collected in mind. So far as I know, she never gave a coherent account to anybody of her recollections, and there is no reason why she should have done; but just as any scrap of information about Shakespeare – from anybody, a servant, amanuensis, ostler, for instance – would be of the greatest interest, so a testimony from one so close as Miss Hinson would have been worth having. Mere tittle-tattle dredged up for purely prurient interest is another matter. In the case of John Hayward, there is plenty of that. When I wrote the entry on Hayward for the *DNB*, I found this made my task difficult.

The operation to which Eliot had referred in his thank-you letter of 22 December was one for hernia, a trouble with which he had been afflicted from birth (in fact he had a double hernia), and for which he was obliged to wear a truss. An operation which he could describe as due to take place some weeks ahead was the second to correct the condition. Had the hernia been strangulated, action would have had to be taken at the first sign of trouble. In fact, intervention of another kind took place on 27 January 1947, with the sudden death of Vivien Eliot. There was every reason, apart from the unexpectedness of the news, why this should have given Eliot the greatest distress. From what I knew of John Hayward, I think that Ackroyd is right in his surmise that at this personal crisis he was able to help Eliot more effectively than some more 'tender' spirits might have done.

Although the operation was deferred until July, Eliot spent a period in hospital on account of an attack of his chest complaint, which may have owed its onset on this occasion to the emotional blow that he had received. Ronald Duncan, whom I came to know about this time (our first meeting took place when I made a bicycle tour of Cornwall in the summer of 1947), spoke of having received a telegram from Eliot cancelling an engagement and saying that he had to 'bury a woman'. He repeated this in his second autobiographical volume *How to make Enemies*. Ackroyd quotes him; but apart from the fact that Eliot, especially in his distressed state, was unlikely to have used those words of Vivien, there is no record of his having sent such a telegram. The correspondence shows that the lunch-date was eighteen months *after* Vivien's death, and makes it clear that he had to attend the funeral of Mrs Mirrlees, a great friend at whose house at Shamley Green, Surrey, he had spent some of the war.

I was at this time that I renewed my acquaintance with Herbert Read, whom I had met first at Oxford in the company of Nevill Coghill. He had known Eliot since the First World War, and at that time and until the poet's death in 1965, he was seeing him frequently. He always spoke of him in the most affectionate terms. As a director of Routledge, he took an interest in what I was writing, and in 1946 he commissioned the first book I was to produce on philosophy, *The Approach to Metaphysics*. I duly sent a copy to Eliot; and although he showed interest, I think it possible that he never read it through, as the following letter shows. Not that he need have done. As he had said in a lecture delivered in Dublin in 1936, 'I have myself no capacity whatever for abstract thought or indeed for any sort of thinking' (the *Southern Review*, October 1985). And although I believe he was referring to a certain kind of abstract thinking – the kind that reduced the English Hegelian tradition to a lyrical hymn to the Absolute, and of which his own thesis on Bradley of 1916 came very near to imitating (which is why he declared, on its publication in 1963, that he did not pretend to understand it), he possessed an outstanding capacity for reasoned argument. This was nevertheless dependent upon his having something concrete to argue about. Although he published much of Herbert Read, he told me that he could not cope with Read's numerous books on Art. This was no doubt because Read had a way of writing about Abstract Art in his own highly abstract manner, so that abstraction was further compounded.

Read had not been particularly interested in my political book (which I had submitted to him in fulfilment of the option clause in my contract with Routledge, so I got together some more representative pieces and sent them to Eliot, no least because he had published my article on 'Philosophy and Politics' in *The Criterion*, and because I had again spoken about my plans at our first meeting after the war. On 24 February 1947, he wrote me an interim letter in which he said he thought I had tended to 'overwhelm the reader by a tendency to say too much at once', and that the material might need some reorganization. On 21 March, he wrote that he had 'thought a good deal' about the book – which, bearing in mind the Spanish use the word 'servile' in contrast to 'liberal', I had called *Liberal and Servile Society* – but that his Board had agreed that in its present form, which was in any case fragmentary, it was insufficiently co-ordinated. He would either need to spend 'a couple of hours' analysing where it was deficient or, preferably, he hoped that we might meet to discuss it over a meal. He concluded: 'Could you dine with me on Thursday, April 10th?' So we did, at the Athenaeum, in the days when that club, like most others in London, was rather livelier in the evenings than, for social reasons, it is now.

As my son had been born on 5 March of that year, we talked at first about children, and he observed somewhat wistfully that the experience of having children must, despite all its responsibilities, be a unique sort of pleasure. It was obvious that he would love to have had a family, and this has been amply confirmed by his second wife. To have asked him to be a godfather had crossed my mind; but I knew that he already held this office in plurality.

It was in the Drawing-Room upstairs that we discussed the book in detail. He pointed out that although my title was an attractive one – since there *was* such a thing as a 'servile' society, namely a totalitarian one – the reader would assume that I was using the word liberal in the modern sense, which was certainly not my intention. He then went meticulously through my argument, and it almost pained me that he should take so much trouble over a work which I cannot think it deserved. At one point, when some pages spilled out on the floor, he remarked, as if it were an integral part of his commentary, that 'some people' did not realize the importance of properly securing a typescript. His quiet reproaches, as I had felt on more than one occasion, were all the more devastating. As I had made some pretty critical remarks about the Soviet Union, at a time the war-time alliance still commanded admiration, especially among the young, he pointed out that if printed, these views would be taken by the Kremlin to be officially inspired. By way of illustration, he cited the case of his Preface to *The Dark Side of the Moon*, which, according to what he had been told by a Foreign Office official, would certainly be so taken; but I felt that there would be infinitely more likelihood of the remarks of T. S. Eliot being heeded than those of E. W. F. Tomlin. He was known and respected in the Soviet Union, if only through the writings on British society by Prince Mirsky and through an anthology published in Leningrad in 1937.

He concluded his examination by turning to me suddenly and saying: 'I feel you are going to write this book one day.' This put heart into me, because in all the years that followed I came increasingly to believe that the genuine radicals were neither the 'philosophical radicals' (much as I admired J. S. Mill, and have even found good in Bentham) nor the Fabian radicals, the socialists or social democrats, but the kind of conservative radicals of whom Cobbett was perhaps the earliest example. But, as fate would have it, my work has lain for years in a field where I was obliged strictly to keep my political convictions to myself. So the book, or one of the books, which Eliot wanted me to write has not yet seen the light of day.

CHAPTER SEVEN

In the autumn of 1947 I was posted to Paris; and once we had settled down and found a flat, I wrote a longish letter to Eliot, who had expressed delight at my appointment, describing the conditions of life in a city still feeling the effects of foreign occupation. In my letter of 31 December I also told him something of the intellectual movements which Paris, true to her own character, was getting excited about. Among them was *Lettrisme*, a new approach to literature devised by a young Rumanian immigrant called Isodore Isou, which I personally considered a load of rubbish, and I told Eliot so. No doubt my references to movements with which he could have little sympathy may have increased his reluctance to cross the Channel.

FABER AND FABER LTD
Publishers

24 Russell Square,
London, W.C.1.
23rd February 1948.

Frederick Tomlin Esq.,
1 Rue Saint James,
Neuilly-sur-Seine,
France.

Dear Tomlin,

    I have been very tardy in thanking you for your letter of the 31st December, but I have been extremely busy and at the same time had deferred acknowledgement in the hope that I might be able to read at least part of your book before writing. So far I have not been able to do so, but I do want very much to read it, and I do not see very many reviews but I seem to remember having seen one of an eulogistic kind, certainly not Joad's. I hope it will be very successful.

I am glad to hear that you have a flat in a healthy part of town, and I trust that your family flourishes in spite of the difficulties of provisionings and high prices. I see no prospect of my visiting Paris in the near future. I am to go to Aix and Marseille after Easter, but I do not want to take the time for a visit to Paris as well. Indeed apart from seeing a few people such as yourselves I have no great curiosity about Paris at present.

With best wishes,
Yours ever,
T.S. Eliot.

The reference to Joad was to do with an unexpectedly hostile review in the *New Statesman*, perhaps because I had criticized *Guides to Philosophy* with which he was himself identified; all I can say is that he made up for it afterwards. With the book's reception in general, I had no reason to be dissatisfied.

His mention of a visit to Aix and Marseilles was to a British Council tour; but he did in the end pay a quick visit to Paris, where he was persuaded – somewhat against his will, I would surmise – to sign some of his books at the La Hune bookshop in Saint Germain-des-Prés. I went to see him there, and I was shocked to observe how jaded and unwell he looked. The first thing that struck me was that he had had most of his teeth removed (this was probably overdue), and that the new set of false ones were putting him to a good deal of inconvenience. The upper set in particular kept snapping down; and when at the signing session he enquired of the purchasers their names so that he could duly inscribe the fly-leaf – a procedure over which he took obvious pains – the effort, involving the use of French and accurate hearing, seemed to exhaust him. Then in the middle of the session, his fountain-pen began to leak (he had forgotten to unscrew it on the plane), and he had to be escorted behind the scenes to wash his hands. It was obvious that he was not enjoying himself. When my turn came, I confined myself to enquiring how long he would be staying and whether there would be a chance of seeing him. He explained that his visit had been entirely unexpected, and that his stay would be a lightning one; but he asked me to jot down my telephone number. I did not hear further, nor was I surprised, as I thought that in his condition he ought to go back home as soon as possible. All in all, it proved to be a critical, though also a triumphant, moment of his life and career. Only a month earlier he had been awarded the Order of Merit, and in November 1948 he was to receive the Nobel Prize for Literature. Yet this was the year in which he seemed first to show signs of decrepitude – his stoop became more pronounced, even though sixty is for many men the beginning of a vigorous decade.

Of course he was world famous. The mail addressed to him as a result of these honours was such as few writers can have received: I was told that the telegrams alone covered the carpet of the sitting-room at Carlyle Mansions. This was the moment, he later told me, when the task of replying to all his letters began to be beyond his powers, even with good secretarial help. Those I wrote him by way of congratulation were not supposed to be answered. But one thing I can say without qualification: fame, and the fact that he soon became accepted as 'the greatest writer in the world' (which he undoubtedly was), made no difference to his character or to his behaviour. There is just one qualification to that remark: he did become a little short with importunate visitors – for every literary figure who visited our shores 'wanted to see T. S. Eliot' – and he was obliged to make elaborate plans to escape from the 'bores', as he called a number of the continental intelligentsia. True, when he was pushing John Hayward about in the wheelchair, he would sometimes be greeted by total strangers. An American girl told me that she had smiled at him in Battersea Park, and that this had seemed to put him in a minor panic, as he immediately accelerated the vehicle, presumably to John Hayward's surprise. On the other hand, to most people in those pre-television days his face was unknown: my own secretary, Mavis Cooper (Day) reported seeing him standing conspicuously in the underground, but nobody, except perhaps herself, showed the slightest sign of recognizing him.

At the Sorbonne at that time there were some very able professors of English, many of whom became friends. The students had a good deal to make up in the way of knowledge of English literature; and, besides, they were a keen lot, and the aversion to attending lectures had not then set in. In fact, lecture-going, either academic or public, was very much of the fashion: public addresses were attended by society ladies dressed up to the nines, whether in search of higher wisdom as with the author of *Pèleringe à la Source*, Lanzo del Vasto, or to learn about distant lands from which the war had cut them off. The passion for *les vacances* had not yet possessed them. In the academic field, one of the most successful lectures I have delivered was at the old *Institut d'Etudes Anglaises*, when I spoke on Eliot as a man and as a writer to a packed and overflowing auditorium. The lecture was followed with a concentrated attention on the part of mostly young people that I found immensely gratifying. Despite the years of European intellectual darkness, it was clear that Eliot had become for them a revered figure. For the French, the early years of the war had brought Charles Morgan to the fore, as he seemed the one English intellectual prepared to stand by them, with his 'Ode to France', etc., but by the end of the war, the figure who had come to stand not merely for France but for the entire civilized order of the West was undoubtedly Eliot.

Life in Paris proved increasingly busy, and currency restrictions prevented travel to other countries: but who would have wanted such excursions when there was France to explore? Accordingly, when we were due for leave, we rented a villa at Bormes-les-Mimosas in the Var. It was so idyllic a spot that we felt that Eliot might like to pay a visit to us there. The following letter, dated 27 February 1950, and addressed to Le Vieux Chateau, Bonnes (*sic*)-les-Mimosas, indicated that, but for his having taken a prolonged holiday, he might have decided to join us for week or two. Also, it was always something of a relief and satisfaction to me whenever he alluded to the fact that I had not written for some little time. In fact, I had written at length from Fiesole, where we had taken leave a year earlier, as guests in another *vieux chateau*, that in which the fifteenth-century humanist Politian, friend of Lorenzo de Medici, had lived; but I rather think that this letter – like some others dispatched from the chaotic Italy of that time – never reached its destination. The book to which he referred was on oriental philosophy, which, with its companion on Western thought, was revised and republished in one volume in 1986. As for the visit to South Africa, undertaken with Geoffrey Faber and his wife, this must have been his first real holiday for many years.

My dear Tomlin,
    I found your letter of the 16th February on my return from a six weeks' holiday in South Africa. I was very glad to hear from you after such a long time, and very pleased by the invitation which I should have been only too happy to accept in other circumstances, but having just had the first long holiday for years, I have no excuse

for going away again, and indeed should throw my affairs into great confusion if I succumbed to the temptation. I do hope that you and your wife are still enjoying living there, and that it is favourable to the completion of your book. I am delighted to hear that the first volume has been successful.

With best wishes,
Yours ever,
T.S. Eliot.

At the beginning of the 1950s, my marriage broke up, and I escaped to the Left Bank and spent the rest of my time in Paris in the Hôtel d'Alsace in the rue des Beaux Arts, where Oscar Wilde had died. Although I wrote to Eliot with news of various kinds, I chose not to refer to the more personal matter: I left that until a brief period of leave made it possible for me to see him. In reply to a letter of mine, he typed out a letter addressed from Minsted House, Midhurst, on 11 August 1951 (this was where Geoffrey Faber lived). He wrote:

My dear Tomlin,
I hope that on this visit to England it will at last be possible for us to meet; but I return to London just before you arrive in Sussex. I shall be in town until then until at least the beginning of September: so I hope you will communicate with me as soon as you are back. Please remember me to your wife: is she with you?
I look forward to seeing you.
Yours ever,
T.S. Eliot.

The letter was addressed to 32 Trinity Church Square, where, having no longer a London home, I had temporarily moved in with my brother. The visit to Sussex was to friends of his. It was to this address that I received a card suggesting tea at Faber's on Thursday 30 August at 4 o'clock. This was the first communication that I received directly from Valerie Fletcher, who had been appointed Eliot's secretary in August 1949.

I remember feeling slightly uneasy as I ascended to the upper room in the familiar uncertain lift: but when I told him what had happened – and the last lines of his letter could be construed as an inkling that something might be wrong – I found, to my surprise but also to my slight relief, that he did not waste time in commiseration or in the more conventional expressions of sympathy. After putting a few questions, he spoke quite bluntly about relations between men and women, and the particular problems of modern marriage. I had half-expected a homily and even an injunction about the wickedness of divorce; but except for another blunt remark about the Catholic teaching about re-marriage (I mean the forbidding of it), the whole drift of his comment was what might be called realistic. At no point did he speak in a derogatory manner of my wife, as I knew he would not do. Nor, I trust, did I. Some of his remarks about the female character, however, would nowadays be labelled sexist; but when talking about a relationship one of the partners to which is female, it is difficult to pronounce any comment which, if remotely critical, must not seem to be sexist as well. The choice is between saying something anodyne or not saying anything at all.

For the first time, apropos of some related matter, he referred to his own marriage, and the fact that his wife had had to be put in an 'asylum' (that was the word he used), as if he thought that I might not know about it. Then, appearing to be talking about wives in general, he remarked of their tendency to say accusingly 'someone has been influencing you': a comment which he delivered with such emphasis and in words I resolved to remember, that it seemed likely that Vivien had reproached him in such terms. He provided no clue to the identity of the person supposedly wielding the influence – perhaps it had been Bertrand Russell, who knew as much about the Eliot marriage as anyone, and may be said to have added to its complications. I had had complications too. I had been involved in a stand-up fight with a half-tipsy man in the Cumberland Hotel, which prompted Eliot, perking up, to comment 'Good for you!' (pronouncing the latter more like 'yew', I noticed).

On this lighter note I sensed that the farewell mechanism was preparing to operate, and I had the feeling of having been in the company of a man who, whatever his reputation for living on the loftiest plane, knew a great deal about those lower down, and that in one fundamental experience of life he had picked up a good deal of down-to-earth know-how. There was also the possibility that, in addition to his sense of guilt, with which he seemed sometimes almost unable to cope, there was a certain amount of emotional debris of which he felt the need, but lacked the occasion, to expel from his system. If I proved to be a catalyst in this respect – and no doubt there were others – I am pleased. He did seem to be getting something off his chest, and to feel the better for it.

In the November of 1951, when I had returned to Paris for my last 'term', the British Council and the Ministry of Foreign Affairs organized a large Book Exhibition at the Bibliothèque Nationale, which Eliot was invited to open. The ceremony was admirably organized in the best French tradition; but the minister who introduced Eliot did not seem over-familiar with the *oeuvre*, and referred to *The Cocktail Party* with an emphasis suggesting that this was not merely Eliot's most recent work of fame (which it was) but that it was the only one he or anyone else had heard of. Eliot, his arms folded, looked up at the speaker now and then and gave a weary assenting smile. He then read a speech in English, which was perhaps shorter and less flamboyant than the French expected; and although he acted his part in his best courtly manner, I felt that he was excessively tired, and it soon became obvious that he had been recovering from one of his heavy colds. As I was not immediately concerned with the exhibition and its organization, Henry Harvey-Wood, Director of the Council in France, Brenda Tripp and Enid McLeod (who had come over from London) had more to do with officially looking after Eliot than I; but I remained, so to speak, in attendance. I gathered from him that, on the night before the opening, he had slept so badly that he had been obliged to change the bedroom in his hotel in the Rue Balzac. He had a moment to tell me that John Hayward, as a member of the organizing committee, had found himself a trifle at odds with some of his colleagues – a remark which, when I learnt the British Council account of the episode, turned out to be a considerable understatement. After the initial ceremony, everyone was obliged to go round the exhibits with the appearance of inspecting them with conscientious approval; and there is a press photograph of Eliot, exactly as I remember him at that time, bending down and peering myopically at the contents of the glass-cases. It was during this peregrination that I introduced him to André Maurois and some others. A rather pathetic figure was cut by John Masefield. He was present as Poet Laureate, but few paid him any attention, chiefly because they did not know who he was, and, if enlightened, would probably have been none the wiser. He had little taste for Eliot's poetry; but after Eliot's death, he addressed him a rather touching, if otherwise undistinguished, piece of verse by way of a threnody.

Eliot and I, and a French professor whom I cannot now remember, had dinner together a day later. On this occasion, Eliot was in a much more light-hearted mood. The subject of Simone Weil came up, because her work was just beginning to attract posthumous attention; and someone - not me, though I was already studying the writings of that remarkable young woman for the purpose of a book – ventured to say that she was very much of a heretic. To which Eliot, with some jocularity, interjected that he was a heretic himself or so a good many people thought. My impression was that our French friend, being unfamiliar with the branches of Anglicanism and puzzled that an Anglican should describe himself as a Catholic, did not quite know how to respond to this levity. Otherwise, but chiefly perhaps because Eliot was not at his best in company unless he knew every member very well, I can remember little about the evening, much as the poet in 'Mr. Apollinax' could remember of the company at the teaparty nothing but 'a slice of lemon and a bitten macaroon'. The reference is appropriate because it was oysters which remain in my mind; for when it was suggested that he might like some, he declined, saying mysteriously 'I have problems'. This set him off on that jerky laugh which repeated itself in four or five implosions.

Enid McLeod, a warm-hearted and clear-headed woman, told me afterwards that she had had a meal by herself with Eliot and that he had spoken very kindly of me and mentioned our long acquaintance. From the way she conveyed this information it was obvious that she had been unaware that I knew him at all and puzzled that, before or during the visit, I had not trumpeted the fact. I think she said this because at least one other person had claimed an acquaintance, even an intimacy, for which there was no basis. I should explain that I was not being absurdly modest; it was simply that I felt that, from an official point of view, I ought to take a back seat. Eliot then stayed with the Harvey-Woods, who found him rather withdrawn at first, and even apologetic at putting them to the trouble of entertaining him; but he soon made friends with the younger of the girls, and wrote her a letter containing an amusing poem ('Cat Morgan introduces himself') and an invitation to tea at Faber's. The prolongation of Eliot's stay was due to the fact that the University of Paris gave him an honorary degree.

My departure from Paris, and the sadness of leaving friends such as Pierre Emmanuel and Henri Fluchère, two of the most prominent of Eliot admirers and experts, presented accommodation problems. It was Cyril Joad that took me in; I lodged with him at his large house at 4 East Heath Road, Hampstead, until his death in 1953. He was then under a cloud because of a charge of bilking the railways; but owing to his performance in the Brains Trust he still possessed national fame. He was also a Faber author, well known both to Eliot and to Geoffrey Faber, and his sales were huge, because he wrote well and with remarkable clarity. Although a bit of a bounder, he could be a warm and generous friend. Of him I could say what Dr Johnson said of Thomas Hervey, 'He was a vicious man but very kind to me. If you call a dog Hervey, I shall love him.'

As head of a department in London, my life became busy; but I occupied every moment of spare time with writing. The first production was the book on Simone Weil, published in the series edited by Erich Heller, then at Swansea, in which Iris Murdoch's *Sartre* (1967) remains the outstanding volume. Both Eliot and Herbert Read encouraged me in this work – the first in English on that remarkable young woman – most of which I carried on in the library of the Reform Club. But Eliot very much wanted me to produce a book on philosophy as near to being original as possible; and in January 1952 I signed a contract with Faber's for the book which became *Living and Knowing*. Eliot took the most minute interest in it, and without his encouragement, I could never have brought it to a conclusion. I had outlined to him the argument I proposed to adopt in a session with him at Faber's on Monday, 11 August 1952, suggesting at that time a title such as *Natural and Supernatural*. He listened as usual with his head tilted, so that I addressed my remarks to the impeccable parting, all except the times when, some remark striking him more forcibly than the rest, he would look up with an expression of pleased assent. The mentioned of a name like Max Scheler especially gratified him, because he had published Scheler's work in *The Criterion*, the only place save for specialist journals where his name had appeared in England.

'I had come under the influence of several other continental thinkers, above all Raymond Ruyer, then and indeed now unknown to the British public; and to Eliot this was refreshing, because he had found the analytical philosophers as uncongenial as the latterday Hegelians whom they claimed to discredit. In fact, as the interesting preface which he wrote at this time to Pieper's *Leisure the Basis of Culture* (1952) showed, he had long abandoned 'philosophy' in favour of theology. To me it had seemed that philosophy could be abandoned only by demonstrating that it had abandoned itself, and therefore needed to revert to what it originally was, namely metaphysics – the study of the implications of 'physics' or the sciences of life and nature. But I am not sure that Eliot would have agreed. I made a false start, in the sense that, by working every night until 1 o'clock after a heavy day in the office, I ended by producing an outsize manuscript. For if we are in a hurry or have insufficient time, we run to excess. With his experience of spotting straightaway what was wrong, Eliot, without (as I hope) going to the labour of reading the entire work, declared that I had been trying to write two books at once. I saw he was right. The surgical task of detaching the two, which was far more complicated than mere separation, proved the most excruciating literary job I have ever undertaken. There were moments when I almost decided that I must scrap the whole thing, but the thought of telling Eliot as much put me to shame. In the end, the book emerged the better for being much slimmed down; but that is to anticipate.

During 1952 Cyril Joad was suddenly taken ill, and it became clear after a month or two that his condition was grave. Eliot and Geoffrey Faber were in constant touch – I need not mention many others such as Rose Macaulay, Elizabeth Jenkins and Father Hood – and Eliot called one afternoon to talk by the sick man's bedside. Although he knew that he had cancer Joad was as mentally resilient as ever, and, partly through my encouragement, he had begun to take interest and pleasure in Eliot's poetry. The art to which he was devoted was music; poetry was a late discovery. I suppose that Eliot was the most 'difficult' poet that he had encountered, and his reaction was a combination of exhilaration (for he welcomed an intellectual challenge) and bafflement. Little excerpts intrigued him for hours or days on end, such as

> Highbury bore me. Richmond and Kew
> Undid me. By Richmond I raised my knees
> Supine on the floor of a narrow canoe.

Being unfamiliar with Dante, and always somewhat literal minded when it came to art, he expended much energy on speculating why Richmond should be singled out for attention, and on the mechanics of the posture described, which he contended – if it implied what he thought it did – would upset the canoe. When Eliot called, he did not raise this particular point (which had worried him almost as much as the rending of the veil of the Temple at the time of the Crucifixion) but one or two others. I had prepared him to find Eliot a little laboured in any explanation he might give, or that perhaps he might adopt the ploy that he had used on other such occasions and say that he was the last person qualified to give an explanation; but I proved to be quite wrong. He was both willing to elucidate and fluent in doing so; and he obviously found the task of exegesis much more congenial than having to voice a series of platitudes or generalized sympathy, or, perhaps worst of all, to provide 'religious consolation', which might have been expected of him. In fact, the visit proved, so far as I could judge, a most successful and rewarding one for all parties. When in the end I took Eliot to the door, and he whispered that he hoped he had not stayed too long, I was able to assure him that this was far from being the case.

It was not long before he came to see Joad that I attended a meeting of the Institute of Contemporary Arts, which had undergone a revival in the 1950s. Eliot took the chair. There was a poetry reading, but I cannot now recall who participated. Eliot's task was far from easy, not least because the programme was interrupted by outbursts from the bar, which was to the right of the platform but concealed by a partition: so that the anonymity of the roisterers was preserved. From the distinct accents if not the distinct words, however, they seemed to be Highland Scots. A generation accustomed to the drilled laughter off-stage of TV comedies, anonymous applause and comment are nothing unusual; but the yells, yawps and roars on this occasion had no relevance to what was taking place. All Eliot could do, short of personally going behind the scenes to break up the party, was to look annoyed, or to give that this-is-how–I-should-appear-if-I-were-angry-look, which was the best he could muster. Fortunately, there was an interval during which the delinquents were out-numbered by other members of the audience, and either obeyed remonstrances to be quiet or meanwhile drank themselves into a stupor. There was at this time, I gathered, much commuting of poets or would-be poets from Scotland to London; but as a rule the return journey had to be financed by well-wishers, such as Alan Pryce-Jones, a man whose kindness was equal to his wealth. I have already mentioned how Eliot was repeatedly sponged on by young writers.

The interval left Eliot standing on the stage, his hands in his pockets and trying not to notice the people crowding round him.

Ronald Bottrall, an even taller figure, acted as his bodyguard; and for some time – for Eliot was not loquacious – the two stood silently side by side. I was able to have a quick word with Eliot, because he wanted to know about Joad. But my general impression of the evening was that he was not happy in such surroundings, and was awaiting the moment to escape. By contrast, John Hayward, who was there in his wheelchair and with whom I spoke in person for the first and last time, enjoyed any social occasion.

Joad, who was lucid until a few hours before his death, often talked about the visit Eliot made. Eliot attended the funeral at Hampstead Parish Church, being ushered in to a pew immediately in front of mine and of Margaret and Chris Ingram, who inhabited a flat on the top floor of Joad's rambling house. As the coffin was carried past him for the committal he hastily crossed himself. Then, mingling with the following concourse, he was lost sight of.

A few days after Joad's obsequies (16 April 1953) he wrote to me:

> My dear Tomlin,
> Thank you for your letter, and thank you also for having suggested to me coming out to see Joad when I did. I did not see you after the funeral, but I had to get away as quickly as I could for another engagement.
> I should like to get you for a meal as soon as we can manage it. What about lunch on Tuesday, the 28th? In any case, let me know where you are if you move your quarters.
>   Yours ever,
>   T.S. Eliot.

I duly met him at the Garrick on 28 April. I noted that in that club, which he began to favour from then on, he felt somewhat more at home than at some others. Perhaps it was that his privacy was more respected, or that so many more members knew him for what he was. No nudging whispers – 'That's T. S. Eliot' – occurred, as they tended to do elsewhere. To begin with, we talked a good deal about Joad. No two people could have been more unlike than Joad, the hedonist, and Eliot, the puritan. But they had come to be fond of each other; and Joad's gradual shedding of a kind of rationalist hedonism for the embrace of Anglicanism obviously appealed to Eliot. He was in any case remarkably charitable in respect of official 'sinners' as Joad had for years made no disguise of being; and he was in advance of his time in condemning some of the hypocrisy of those who, in the words from *Hudibras*,

> compound for sins they are inclined to
> By damning those they have no mind to.

For Joad had suffered social ostracism following his conviction of the kind which today would not have visited the commission of far graver sins. Joad's death meant, among other things, that I was again without a home; but after some searching, I managed to find accommodation in Courtfield Gardens, Gloucester Road, where I took a small bedsitter at no. 55. Eliot was most interested to learn of my new address, because, as he told me, he too had lived in a boarding-house in the adjoining street, Courtfield Road (no. 33), before moving to 9 Grenville Place, the presbytery inhabited by Father Cheetham. Back in 1933, this was probably the worst time of his life, as it was mine twenty years later – but that is by the way; yet he was able to see the funny side of it all. On his arriving to enquire about accommodation, the proprietress, Miss Bevan, said that she took only public school men. She had not the least idea who he was, though the owner of the place, an Old Catholic 'Bishop', knew Father Cheetham; and he had some difficulty in persuading her to accept him.

I thereupon entered upon a period when I not merely saw much of Eliot but received from him a great deal of kindness and generosity, some of which was extended without my knowledge. When I say that I saw much of Eliot, I am referring in particular to my contacts with him at St Stephen's, where he was Vicar's Warden. That Eliot attracted to that church many young men and women (they were mostly young) who came merely because he officiated there and simply in order to glimpse him, is true, and no one was more aware of the fact than Eliot himself. It made him acutely uneasy. On occasion be rebuked people, however kindly, when it became obvious that they attended with no other motive. Of this I was very aware, and therefore I would to begin with creep in as surreptitiously as possible and hurry away at the Angelus. But he was bound to spot me in the end, and he did. Usually the celebrity-hunters would disappear after a Sunday or two, having had their curiosity satisfied and their taste for the Anglo-Catholic liturgy more than sated.

Years after I would meet people and was tempted to say: 'Didn't you at one time attend St Stephen's, Gloucester Road?' – a question which often brought a faint blush to their cheek, and, if the conversation were prolonged, the admission that they had gone with the intention of seeing T. S. Eliot. In my case, having examined my conscience, I was obliged to admit to myself that *one* of the reasons why I became a member of the congregation was because Eliot was there. But I had been a churchgoer all my life, to the quiet amusement of some of my colleagues. I was intellectually convinced, if a trifle unorthodox; and when I lived in Courtfield Gardens, St Stephen's was the nearest church with the kind of service I found congenial, and where I was made to feel welcome.

Much of the work Eliot did at St Stephen's was behind the scenes. I had been told that he was to be seen sitting in the porch doing the accounts, but never did I come across him thus engaged. There was a very large vestry, and that was where he would have discharged business of that kind. He liked Father Cheetham, but he suffered from his irrepressible loquacity, which he attributed to his being a confirmed bachelor, with no one regularly to talk to. True, the single state meant much to him, and he sacked a curate who went so far as to express the wish to get married. He preached against women wearing lipstick. He was probably one of those men who, without being homosexual, had an aversion for sexuality as such; for he repeatedly inveighed against 'amorous old men', and then, as if to issue a special warning to the other half of the congregation, he would add, with a knowing look, 'and amorous old women are just as bad'. Some, not all, of the dear old things to be found in every such concourse must have wondered what he was talking about. In addition to his dedication to celibacy, he was a good and conscientious priest, with a gift for scrupulously following the church calendar; and, as Eliot said in a tribute in *The Church Times*, he was a master of ecclesiastical pageantry. He also entertained a devotion to the Queen which was almost touching. In fact, he seemed to place the Queen of England on a level with the Queen of Heaven. Eliot found that he could work with him, or he would not have served him faithfully for twenty-two years.

In those days, in addition to a 'liturgical choir' in the chancel or in the organ-loft, there was a 'people's choir' which occupied the back seats of the nave on the right. Of this Eliot was a member, and one could often detect his clear tenor voice. He always took the offertory on the right-hand side; and when he did so he assumed an undeviating solemn and austere look, as if he were wrapped up in himself – his lips tightly pursed, and his hands, once the bag had been sent on its way, clasped firmly together in front of him. Just as he looked clerical in his office, so he looked the businessman in church. Presumably at his suggestion, the verger would sometimes ask me to take the offertory on the opposite side; and this meant finally delivering the weighty bag, full of silver in those days, to Eliot. When I handed over my burden for the first time, I suppose I must have given him a faint smile; but I saw at once that this was not in order, for his features remained fixed, and I never tried such familiarity again.

At the conclusion of the service, he would either disappear to the Vestry, or visit certain parts of the church, especially the Children's Corner, which was then not far from where his memorial plaque is now fixed. On one occasion, I came across him kneeling on one knee with his hand over his brow on the stone floor. Possibly after fifty years I remain ignorant of certain aspects of Catholic practice, but I assumed that this was some kind of penance. He went to confession regularly. I think he deliberately remained aloof during the services in order to disassociate himself from his great reputation, and he sought desperately to practise the humility which came no more easily to him than to anyone else. Once out of church, however, he was a different man. He may have felt that he was less likely to be bothered in the conspicuous role of churchwarden than in the precarious anonymity of the pews. As for Father Cheetham, he was immensely proud of his famous layman – the most renowned in the whole Anglican Communion – and, when Eliot was away, he wold refer to him with almost mystical respect. What he would have made of some of the King Bolo poems, I cannot imagine.

When in youth I had read, as a result of the remark of William Temple, about the conversion of the avant-garde writer, T. S. Eliot, I had conjured up images of the notorious converts of the 1890s, like Lionel Johnson or, in France, J. K. Huysmans : men whose religion seemed largely to consist in, to adapt Eliot's own phrase, a prolonged flirtation with the liturgy. Such changes seemed not so much an entry into a genuine *vita nuova* of faith and morals as a different way of experiencing essentially aesthetic emotions in the context of icons, tapers and statues of the Virgin, all enveloped in a cloud of incense. I was later to meet on my travels the Christian equivalent of Kerouac's 'dharma bums' (though they were products of the 1960s), that is to say, 'holy' young men talking at once of vestments and vices, and contriving to follow a way of life which permitted liberal indulgence in both.

I believe that Eliot joined the Church, first because he had attained intellectual conviction, and secondly, in order to effect 'a discipline and training of the emotions' (again to use his own words), which, in the past, had been partly the function of education, but only because education had been an ecclesiastical responsibility. In a secular age, this training had ceased to be provided, even by those public schools which were supposed to engage in character-building and of which some foreigners still believed them to be the guardians. Sometimes I would wonder what distinguished Eliot, in his general demeanour, from so many others, and what made him more like the disciplined devotees of the Buddha, at least in his calm, if slightly austere, exterior (and it is known that at one time he was much attracted by Buddhism). The explanation lay, it seemed to me, in precisely that discipline which a full liturgy helped to guide and promote, and which non-liturgical religious practice so often failed to do. A ritualistic formality, far from obliterating or etiolating emotion, protected and even nourished it: and the 'soul in pain' of which Oscar Wilde spoke in *The Ballad of Reading Gaol* and which Eliot, for different reasons, likewise harboured, could be eased by the therapy of the impersonal Mass more effectively than by an uprush of personal evangelical fervour.

Eliot was right in his theory of 'the objective correlative' as the only means of expressing emotion in art: he could have gone on to say, what indeed he implied, that some form of objectivity or distancing was the only effective means of expressing emotion at all, if the emotion were to emerge in a healthy state. I believe he felt that this aspect of religion had been almost lost sight of, and that religious observance had become as casual and perfunctory as turning up to some ceremony out of group loyalty or habit. No modification of conduct was any longer involved, and participation in the ceremony was somehow an excuse for doing nothing else. And for those who engaged in no religious observance at all, there was little to control emotion, which therefore enslaved itself to irrational, crypto-erotic and sometimes downright evil forces. Of senseless violence, violence that could not be 'explained', there was an obvious explanation, as the years following Eliot's death have served to make clear.

What Eliot most dreaded, but feared might come about, was the decay not merely of belief – which was far advanced – but of religious *feeling* itself. 'A belief in which you no longer believe, is something which to some extent you can still understand; but when religious feeling disappears, the words in which men have struggled to express it become meaningless' ('The Social Function of Poetry' in *On Poetry and Poets* (1957)). Paradoxically, it might be said that the way to regenerate feeling was by way of the liturgy itself: because feeling may decay in consequence of relying on too much feeling alone, as in the case of some extreme protestant sects: for, to quote again one of Eliot's most trenchant adaptations, 'The spirit killeth, but the letter giveth life'. Of religiosity he was entirely free.

Naturally, if the church were to resume its traditional role, there needed to be a more dedicated priesthood and episcopacy. More than once Eliot expressed apprehension to me about the relaxation of faith and morals not merely among the laity but among the clergy themselves. When Father Cheetham announced his retirement, Eliot was much exercised about his replacement: for Cheetham had lived into a world almost unrecognizably different from that in which he had sought ordination. Never shall I forget the moment at the Athenaeum after lunch one day when, lowering his voice to evade the attention of nearby members, some of which were high ecclesiastics, he said glumly and with a half-despairing shake of the head: 'I hope we don't get one of these homosexual types.'

As my work sometimes took up weekends – those were the days when the work came first, whatever the 'unsocial hours' involved – I would miss a run of Sundays, and in any case I wanted to avoid giving the impression that attendance at church was conditional on my meeting him. But there were other ways of keeping in touch. I took a friend to see *The Confidential Clerk*, which had come to London after its opening at the Edinburgh Festival in August 1953 and about which we could not quite make up our minds. I think more highly of it now. Then in November 1953 I went to hear him talk at the Central Hall, Westminster, on 'The Three Voices of Poetry'. Harold Nicolson, unhealthily rubicund, was in the chair, and, with his slightly soap-box oratorical style, provided a complete contrast to the stately lecturer. Eliot had in fact become a really accomplished speaker, and his habit of bowing to the chair and the audience had assumed an almost Japanese smoothness. Given the fact that he was just recovering from the chest complaint which was to grow more serious with the years, he gave a most professional performance. Ironically, this expertise was attained just when he was beginning to think that public addresses were a futile exercise.

On 24 November 1953, not long before he was to set out on a second trip to South Africa, he wrote to me:

Dear Tomlin,

Thank you very much for sending me your essay on Collingwood, which I look forward to reading.

I have thought about you very often, and have hoped that we might be able to arrange a meeting. I am going away for two months after Christmas and am accordingly very busy until then, but if I can find time, will you be able to come and lunch with me one day?

                Yours sincerely,
                T.S. Eliot.

This was the kind of letter which, despite its brevity, rallied my spirits. I felt grateful and, now having a club of my own, I wrote to say that I hoped he would be able to have lunch with me instead. Valerie Fletcher wrote back on 3 December 1953, asking whether Tuesday, the 22nd, would be suitable, and on 7 December whether, owing to a mix-up, I could keep the 24th as well. The latter date was finally arranged. Lunch meant much to him, perhaps because, with regular exceptions, his supper (for that was all that it could be called) was at that time often taken in his dingy room with a tray on his knees. He also felt that other people must set store by the mid-day meal. Back in the 1930s, he had mentioned to me that Leon Daudet, the founder with Charles Maurras of *L'Action Française*, had come over to London, and, because he could not speak English was not too popular with his compatriots, 'had no one to have lunch with'. This Eliot regarded as a real deprivation, so he felt obliged to entertain him for days on end, which, as he said, 'came expensive'.

When as my guest I took him into the large dining-room, he asked me with some earnestness whether we might sit in a corner, as much out of sight as possible. Although he could escape notice in public places, he was well-known in clubland, even if not by everybody; but he disliked the sensation of being stared at, especially at times when he considered himself off-duty. Once I had managed to secure a secluded table right up against the wall on the extreme left, he perceptibly relaxed.

He used often to begin with salami, or some other highly seasoned hors d'oeuvre, and he was inclined to make comments of some acerbity on the menu, comparing one club with another. When he and John Betjeman put me up for the Athenaeum, he remarked that although it was an excellent club, the food was 'cheaper and nastier' than at the Reform. (It has improved out of recognition.) Having relieved his feelings on the subject of gastronomy, he would set me talking, and unless directly interrogated, he would rarely discuss what he himself was doing. I was at the time working on the Simone Weil book. He and Herbert Read had already done a good deal to make the posthumous work of that remarkable woman, who had died in Ashford during the war at the age of thirty-four, better known in the English-speaking world. We talked, I remember, of people like Simone, who, though academically trained, were not admitted as academically respectable, and were never likely to be. Nevertheless, they subtly influenced the direction of thought. The same was true of Teilhard de Chardin, whose influence had quite overshadowed that of Simone Weil, possibly because – and this was why Eliot found him the less attractive figure – much of his writing consisted in a kind of incantatory mysticism, for which there was always a public. His very name seemed to convey the incandescence of an exploding supernova of esoteric wisdom.

This brought the conversation round to the occult in general, which Eliot regarded with deep distrust, because, like many genuine believers and unlike many unbelievers, he held his views with a certain degree of scepticism. Indeed, he was the least credulous of men, the last person to be taken in by the bogus and the fraudulent. Whether he had had any so-called 'occult' experience himself, I could not persuade him to admit. I suspect he had not, though he had certainly had moments of significance, from the 'moment in the rose garden' to 'the moment of sudden loathing', and these had gone into the poetry. He did tell me on this occasion, however, one of the best ghost stories (if it can be called that) I have ever heard. It was retailed by a friend whose word he trusted implicitly. A guest at a house-party given by this friend had one evening suddenly been wracked by toothache and retired to his room. A year or so later, another guest occupying the same room, had come down to breakfast pale and drawn and somewhat shaken. Asked by his host whether he was unwell, he replied: 'I just couldn't sleep. All night long there was somebody walking up and down the room, holding his face.' As I say, Eliot could vouch for the truth of that, since he knew the host extremely well. Moreover, the agitation of the guest was nothing if not genuine.

I am not saying that Eliot disbelieved in the existence of occult powers or supernatural or paranormal influences; he could hardly accept a supernatural religion and believe otherwise. However, he distinguished between the Christian supernatural and the kind of beliefs, such as those entertained by Yeats, in 'folk-lore, occultism, mythology and symbolism, crystal-gazing and hermetic writing', which he regarded as 'the wrong supernatural world', i.e., the world of 'Madame Sosostris, the famous clairvoyant'. It was 'not a world of real Good and Evil'.

That the Christian (or 'right') supernatural gave access to malign as well as to good forces he certainly believed. Many years later Theresa Eliot, his sister-in-law, told me that on the few occasions when he discussed his first marriage, he ventured to suggest that Vivien might have been a victim of demonic possession. For there had come a point when mental disturbance had seemed to give place to something more horrible and intractable. This was surely what had left him with such feelings of anguish as some thought must be the result of a 'guilty secret'.

After we had discussed the paranormal, we moved on to literature. He expressed puzzlement that some of his fellow-writers should be so keen to attend conferences, especially international conferences. One of his younger contemporaries, who was in the habit of doing so, had thereby acquired a reputation on the strength of regularly turning up. I chimed in by saying that the man in question had, on the strength of a few poems written in youth, earned perhaps excessive literary fame. Eliot slightly back-pedalled, because he had published the poems in question – a fact which I had momentarily forgotten. Looking hard at the table, he said he thought the poems 'rather moving'; and he added, looking up 'he's a sweet person'. Of that I had no doubt and could confirm it; but I realized that I had struck a false note. He went on to say that, so far as conference-going was concerned, he had been surprised to find that a poet from the East, who had settled here and become virtually British, had suddenly turned into an official representative of his country, complete with elaborate uniform and well-provided with funds. Eliot had always been slightly suspicious of 'official' culture; and although he had undertaken several tours for the British Council, he had reservations on what that organization thought it was doing – a matter he had raised at the beginning of his *Notes towards the Definition of Culture* (1948). Consequently, as I had been for many years in the service of that organization, he was always curious to know what it was like from the inside. This I did not always find it easy to explain. What he distrusted was the amount of bureaucracy involved, and I was obliged to agree that it was increasing.

The other subject upon which we embarked was health. He admitted that he had been warned to cut down on smoking; I was glad to hear it, because my impression – based to some extent on the discolouration of his teeth before most of them were summarily extracted – was that he had been smoking to excess for years; and this must have harmed his chest. The result of abstention, which cost him a great effort of will and (if Ronald Duncan is to be believed) the taking of an occasional oath not to light up until lunch-time, was that he began to put on weight. This is revealed in later photographs, where he assumed a slightly chubby and avuncular appearance; but, as he mentioned, the most tiresome thing was that his always well-cut suits became too tight for him. He was in fact allowed one cigar a week for the rest of his life, and later on his wife had a special cigar-holder made for him at Dunhill's. A habit he had developed was that of taking snuff, emptying it carefully on the back of his hand and sniffing with great concentration.

After lunch we adjourned to the gallery, where, in contrast to some other clubs, conversation of the most private nature could be conducted without being overheard, as the small tables were well-spaced. Over coffee, we found ourselves sitting beneath the portrait of Macaulay. This inspired Eliot to level some severe criticisms against the once popular historian (now chiefly remembered for the *Lays of Ancient Rome*, and in particular for 'How Horatius kept the Bridge'). Appointed chairman of the Committee of Public Instruction of the Supreme Council of India in 1834, Macaulay laid it down that Indians should be taught European literature and science, to the exclusion of their own heritage, so that a generation grew up ignorant of the Hindu scriptures – i.e., the Vedas, Upanishads, and Sutras. The same would apply to the Moslems. Eliot gave it as his opinion that this was a reversal of what a true education should be. His point was of considerable interest, because Englishmen such as Sir William Jones had, by contrast, already pioneered the revival of the study of Sanscrit; yet, coming down to our own times, many Westernized Indians had gained more insight into the Hindu classics from references in *The Waste Land* than from anything their own education had provided. In other words, English Literature, increasingly secularized, had been introduced to plug the gap left by the neglect of the oldest spiritual tradition in the world : a disaster of which the results were now making themselves felt. By the seriousness of his tone, I could see that Eliot was puzzled that so few people seemed disposed to share his concern for what had happened – and above all in India.

He was in a serious and concerned mood altogether. He told me that he had been having conversations with the Inland Revenue concerning the huge royalties which had accrued from *The Cocktail Party*. He had wanted to use the bulk of it in order to make provision for his two sisters in the United States in their old age. One was in fact already in poor health. Although the young man with whom he discussed the matter in the Treasury had been charming, Eliot considered that the financial regulations, with their swingeing imposition of tax, were, in a case of this kind, unjust. Perhaps because I gave a weary smile at the Inland Revenue's familiar lack of understanding, he insisted: 'I *really* mean that'. He went on to remark that justice in more than one field was being increasingly ignored in favour of expediency : this was to indicate that he was not simply complaining about his own treatment. As if to emphasize this in turn, he admitted that his career had recently entered into 'quiet waters' as compared with the 'harassment' he had suffered over so many years. But then he suddenly said, with reference to the strange pattern his life had taken ('It seems, as one grows older, that the past has another pattern, and ceases to be a mere sequence'): How does one set about *dying*?' He was already ill, and I think he realized that, as things were going, he might not have long to live. His question, though half-rhetorical, was answered by neither of us. I was nonplussed by its unexpectedness, and he, by the fact of asking it, showed that he had no ready reply. A friend who knew the doctor he was consulting about this time, told me that, when informed that he might be facing grave illness (presumably advanced emphysema), he reacted with a calmness which, for one haunted by the idea of death, was exemplary.

We said goodbye as usual at the foot of the steps of the Reform. He heaved a sigh and said, a propos of Christmas, 'I won't wish you blessings, but' – realizing that this was rather a cold way of parting – 'shall we say, such blessings as there are'. It came home to me then, and increasingly later, that he was intensely – even wretchedly – lonely. At the same time he had a distressingly 'stricken' look. I had rarely parted from him with feelings of such foreboding.

CHAPTER EIGHT

After a good deal of writing and re-writing, I finished the *Simone Weil* and sent a copy to Eliot, which Valerie Fletcher acknowledged on 15 September 1954, as he was then in Switzerland. On 22 September, he wrote to me:

Dear Tomlin,
    I returned from Geneva to find your letter of the 13th, and your little book on Simone Weil which I am happy to have, and shall certainly read as soon as I can. I shall be most interested to see what you have to say on this subject. It is an excellent series and I have great respect for Erich Heller. I took Holthusen's essay on Rilke for reading on my holiday. Do you know anything of Holthusen's work? He seems to me one of the ablest of the younger literary critics today.
    I learn to-day that you should be hearing from us very shortly about the problem of reducing your script, so I do hope that it will be possible for you to do the necessary operations in time to get the book out in the Spring.
    I have indeed heard from your colleague, and am sorry to say that I have given the expected response. I do less and less public lecturing and must really concentrate on the few things that I shall want to do that may possibly be of more permanent importance.
    I am delighted to hear that you are quite well again, and I shall look for you any Sunday now at St. Stephen's.
    With best wishes,
        Yours ever,
           T.S. Eliot.

The reference to 'your colleague' was to do with a request from the British Council that he should lecture at one of its high-level Modern Literature Courses, which were attended chiefly by foreign scholars. (These presented problems, as more than one British author, considering that he or she represented Modern Literature, would complain about their exclusion, and in one case tried to get this excellent annual course abolished.) I had told Eliot of the likely invitation, and I knew he would feel obliged to decline it, as indeed I had warned my colleagues; but he was such a good catch that the request was made all the same. The reference to my health was prompted by the fact that in June 1954 I had been rushed into Guy's Hospital suffering from a kidney-stone. He had been good enough to send me flowers with a card saying 'Best wishes for a restful convalescence', which, spotted by members of my staff who visited me, made a great impression. To the charming nurses, however, the name meant nothing, any more than did that of Wyndham Lewis, on whose behalf and on her own Froanna had telephoned. The otherwise apparently trite message was no doubt composed with some knowledge of what, in those days, could be an excruciating experience, both in the having and in the removing, so that a reposeful aftermath was much to be welcomed.

After my *Simone Weil*, I had toyed with several titles for my more substantial personal book, to which Eliot had referred. There was a good deal of correspondence with Faber's, from which I received a series of letters each signed by a different person. When I learnt in March 1954 that Eliot had gone into the London Clinic, I wrote to him to wish him well; but I repent of having made some allusion to the book, which, had I known at the time that he was suffering from tachycardia – a condition to which I myself was no stranger – I would never have dreamt of doing. I had become dissatisfied with *Natural and Supernatural*, though the content of the work reflected this theme, but from a point of view very different from that of the conventional Gifford Lecture treatise. Back in harness after illness, Eliot wrote to me on the subject on 8 and 22 September 1954, rejecting as misleading my suggestion that the book should simply be called *Life* (because that is what it was really about). He contended that it might induce people to think it had something to do with the well-known periodical of that name, 'which gives an unfortunate connotation to the word', but he agreed that 'life' should be in the title. A decision was urgent, as his letter of 2 December 1954 made clear:

> Dear Tomlin,
> You will, I trust, have inferred from my not having followed up my letter about the title, that my Board were entirely in agreement with me that *Life* was not a satisfactory title. I now have the unwelcome task of writing to urge you to let us have an alternative title, or a choice of several alternative titles as soon as you possibly can, for if we are to advertise the book in the spring list, we should have the title very soon indeed. Actually the original title, *Natural and Supernatural* seemed to most of my Board quite satisfactory.
> Finding a title is often one of the most vexatious details of publication. Often, in my experience, the kind of title the author wants is one which only appears appropriate after reading the book, whereas the kind the publishers suggest is apt to be one which seems interesting and arouses curiosity, but which has less appropriateness after the book has been read.
> Yours ever,
> T.S. Eliot.

On receipt of this letter, I racked my brains, and then, as so often happens, the problem was solved in consultation with a friend. My colleague, Renée Tickell (Haynes), suggested *Living and Knowing*, and I at once perceived that this was right. The conflicting views referred to in Eliot's last paragraph were thus brought into harmony. A letter from him dated 9 December 1954, agreed that *Living and Knowing* was preferred as being 'more out of the way and stimulative of curiosity'. As the argument of the book was new, at least to the English-speaking public, and as I was aware that any work seeking to tackle what were called, even by hostile critics, the 'great' problems, would arouse antipathy in the philosophical establishment (the review that appeared in *Mind* I could myself have drafted as a spoof), I wrote to ask Eliot whether he would consider writing a Foreword. I was only too well aware that this was presuming on his good nature, as he was in constant demand for sponsorship of this kind. He wrote at length on 4 July 1955, first of all apologizing for the delay in replying ('as I absent myself from this office on Fridays, I leave over until Monday letters arising out of business discussions on Thursdays'), and pointing out that the publishing plans had already been worked out, and that if he were to write anything of value, he would need to read the book, the original and lengthy version of which he had perused some time back, as if he had never read it before; and this would mean delaying publication by a whole season. He concluded:

> In consolation, I can say that my Board, including the Sales Manager, agree with me that a preface by myself to a book of this kind, is hardly likely to carry the weight which you are so good as to attribute to it. I may be known as a philosophical poet by a good many people who are not philosophers but I have no standing whatever in the philosophical world, and while a preface from me might induce some book-sellers to order copies who otherwise would not, or to increase the order which they would give in any case, I don't believe for a moment that it would make a particle of difference to the attention of the reviewers.
> With regrets and cordial good wishes.
> Yours ever,
> T.S. Eliot.

I am still not sure about that, but his practical sense was always uppermost. No long after receiving this letter, I happened to meet him in the street – hardly a coincidence, as we had both emerged from different departments of the British Council where he had been recording – and he again expressed regret about the Preface. I said I quite understood, but mentioned that, some time before, I had asked him whether he would consider writing something, and he had replied, in his careful way, not ruling out the idea. In reminding him of this I wanted to account for my forwardness. He put his hand on my shoulder, and said that this had quite slipped his mind. He had such a way of speaking gently that I felt that this made everything satisfactory. I had caught him up, as he was walking with meditative slowness, no doubt complicated by the arthritis from which he had begun to suffer, and aided by the now indispensable walking-stick,

The deliberately plied stick forms part of my memory of an extremely hot day about this time, when I saw him approaching St Stephen's by way of Southwell Gardens with two elderly female members of the congregation. Heavy garments being intolerable, he had looked out a linen suit, which had no doubt been put to much use in the United States; and this, because it was over-large and despite his increase in weight, was ballooning about his person, so that he seemed to be borne along by some imperceptible zephyr, using the stick to plot his course. On another occasion, talking of St Stephen's,

I saw him in quite different character. He was walking much quicker and with more determination, turning his slightly-bowed head this way and that, so that his spectacles (which he had begun to wear more frequently) seemed to be emitting rays of their own, according to some medieval ocular theory. The stick was rapidly striking the pavement, and under his arm was a copy of the *Collected Translations of Ezra Pound* (1953). It had been some time since he had been to St Stephen's, and, when I enquired after his health, he said that he had been feeling better than for some time. He insisted that we must meet, and when I made some formal reply about its being kind of him, he said, almost gaily, 'It's not kind: I want to see you'.

Another occasion, in bad weather, he was in just the reverse condition. He had arrived early at Emperor's Gate, as had I; and seeing that he looked both tired and ill, almost alarmingly so, I persuaded him to come and have some coffee at Dino's restaurant near Gloucester Road underground station. He was reluctant at first to assent, pleading that he had some business to do in the vestry; but I managed to persuade him, as I felt that even a few minutes sitting down in that warm and friendly place (which, alas, has now gone) would do him good, We had to cross the street, and noticing some traffic approaching rather quicker than expected, he surprised me by almost skipping the last few steps on to the kerb. I had never seen such agility on his part, hernia and all. That he was perhaps a little touched that someone should have been solicitous of his welfare (for at home the solicitude was lavished on John Hayward), I was pretty sure. Nevertheless, he was determined to get his business done, and fortunately we arrived back at the church with five minutes or so to spare. Of stray meetings I give these instances, because they illustrate something of his basic toughness, of will if not of constitution.

To return to the previous April: on the nineteenth of that month I had gone to the Overseas League, St James's Street, to hear him lecture on 'The Literature of Politics', under the auspices of the London Conservative Union. The lecture seemed to me brilliant, with some of his best witticisms (Shaw, 'by persuading low-brows that they were high-brows, and that high-brows must be socialists . . . contributed greatly to the prestige of socialism'). And he was in excellent form, even, in contrast to some previous appearances, debonair. In the Chair was the Rt Hon. D. Heathcote Amory, MP, but, perhaps because I was concentrating on the lecturer, I remember nothing of what he said by way of introduction. Anthony Eden was originally to have taken the Chair but cancelled at the last moment. At the end Eliot answered questions, and found himself defending, among other things, Disraeli's novels, of which he thought more highly than I had realized, especially praising their literary style. One young man, who must have been ignorant both of the occasion and of Eliot's work, arose and said: 'Mr Eliot, from what you have been saying, I get the impression that you vote Conservative.' To which he replied, with the slightest smile and the usual measured tempo: 'I should be quite content . . . for that inference . . . to be drawn.' which occasioned a good deal of jubilation.

After the questions, it was announced that Mr Eliot would be happy to autograph copies of his books, a pile of which had been assembled at the back of the hall. As I had gone up to greet him after the lecture, he asked me to stand by while he discharged what he called 'this rather sordid business'. He would laboriously strike out his name on the title page, and even more laboriously inscribe 'T.S.Eliot', so that the session took up a good deal of time. To one young man, who produced a copy of *The Family Reunion*, he remarked; 'That's my best play' – an interesting judgment seeing that it was the one with which he was said to have been dissatisfied. While this routine business was going on, I noticed a female journalist and also another rather earnest-looking woman hovering in the background, though they appeared to have no connection with each other. The journalist asked him whether he had ever been inclined to go into politics. He replied in the negative, saying that his mind worked too slowly for him to shine as a politician, and that he considered he were better employed in reflecting on theoretical matters.

In the speech he had described himself as 'a detached contemplative', but I notice that this does not appear in the printed version. Coming forward, the other lady announced that she wanted to work out his horoscope. At this he looked a trifle alarmed; but, on her assuring him that all she needed to know was the time of day he was born, he replied readily that it was early in the morning. She said she would get to work, on which he interjected with an earnestness to match her own, 'Mind, don't show it to me!' Horoscopes and the other superstitious practices – 'pastimes and drugs', as he called them in *The Dry Salvages* (1941) – were antipathetic to him, as was anything that suggested that his life, or anybody else's, were at the mercy of malign or arbitrary forces. As it happened, the lecture had another consequence which he related to me later. He had sent the typescript in advance to Anthony Eden, as the Conservative Political Centre had invited the latter to write a Foreword to the published version. Apparently Eden had merely signed the text and returned it, as if Eliot had been a young aspirant seeking his autograph. He had been extremely hurt by this arrogant behaviour. I told him that Eden, who had become Prime Minister on 6 April, with all his merits, had a reputation for vanity, due partly perhaps to his 'golden boy' reputation as a young man. Eliot cited some fairy story – about 'chicken-licken', I think – to the effect that pride comes before a fall, which within a year or so proved prophetic in Eden's case. In fact, the short Foreword that he did write was itself slightly condescending. It asserted that Eliot's dwelling on politics was to cast him in 'an unfamiliar role', which showed an unfamiliarity on his part with an important aspect of Eliot's work. A lengthy book such as Russell Kirk's *Eliot and his Age* (1971, 2nd edn 1984), to cite but one, was evidence enough of his constant preoccupation with politics and social questions, about which he had written much more profoundly than Eden ever did.

Having taken leave of the Conservative organizer – one of those fair, light-blue eyed earnest young men in a very dark suit – we strolled back together. He propounded his method of capturing the attention of a general, uninstructed audience. You must start with some pleasantries, then define the scope of what you are going to say, and then, once you have got into your stride, you should manage to slip in two or three fundamental points, and finally, if you can, you should end up on another lighter note. He was firmly of the opinion that no audience, unless a very specialist one, can be expected to take in more than two or three 'fundamental matters' in a lecture lasting an hour, just as no play, at least in the case of a modern audience, should last for much more than two hours. If Greek plays were longer, it was because they were elements in a full-scale religious festival.

Living and Knowing was published in the autumn of 1955. I am pretty certain that Eliot personally paid for my excessive proof-corrections. The authors of the Faber books issued at that season were invited to a party in October. This was much on the lines of the old *Criterion* evenings. Our books were lined along the mantelpiece. Of these, William Golding's *Lord of the Flies* achieved the greatest fame, and I remember the youngish Golding, who was a contemporary of mine at Brasenose, with a very russet beard. Eliot had just come out of hospital, where he had been treated for athlete's foot. My impression was that, having spent longer there than he expected, he had more or less decided to discharge himself. Perhaps as the result of the rest, one of the welcome by-products of hospitalization, he struck me as looking fit; he was certainly in a genial mood. One of the initial difficulties of communicating with him was that John Davenport, then in the BBC, a hefty man who liked it to be known that he had been a champion heavy-weight boxer – the knowledge being sometimes conveyed by practical demonstration – got steadily drunk. He decided to station himself near Eliot as a kind of Cerberus-watch-dog-guard. I had entertained him to lunch a week or two earlier, because he appeared to want me to give a talk on the Third Programme; but, despite his being benign on that occasion, his mood had changed, and it changed more menacingly when Eliot, spotting me, engaged me in conversation. This and the effort of others to have a word in the same quarter, so inflamed Davenport, already primed, that he staggered violently, barged into Geoffrey Faber, not me, and caused a near-rumpus. Every effort was made to remove him, which, in view of his bulk, proved difficult.

How much of this Eliot observed, I am not sure, because he had already had his statutory talk with Davenport. This, as he told me afterwards, had included a series of disparaging remarks about St Louis, Missouri, Eliot's birthplace, which Davenport had recently visited, and, no doubt a cause of his low opinion, where he had received less attention as a 'famous critic' than he presumably considered he merited. Eliot had found this on the whole rather amusing, but he obviously regarded the guest as exceedingly tiresome, as he did boorish behaviour in general. He enquired about St Stephen's, from which he had been absent for some weeks, and I described to him a demonstration against 'Popery' which had taken place outside the previous Sunday. A group of elderly men, with white drooping moustaches, in dark overcoats with velvet lapels, and white silk scarves, like so many pious clones, had assembled in silence. They carried rather tatty banners, brown from frequent use, denouncing the Mass and other High Church practices. They were in no sense a menacing group – they seemed to come out of the past – but I am glad that Eliot, as churchwarden, did not have to be confronted with them, or with a man who, on a previous Sunday had shouted 'Shame on you' from the pews at the visiting Archdeacon, after which, the

Service proceeding, he lapsed into disgruntled silence. Eliot said that such protests were not uncommon, but he intensely disliked them.

Apart from the interruption caused by the removal of John Davenport, the party was a most enjoyable one. There was an unremitting flow of alcohol; but, as on previous occasions, Eliot, though he seemed always to have a glass in his hand, remained, so far as I could see, totally unmoved. He liked a bit of banter, and he seemed to be able to keep this up the whole evening. I left while the conviviality was in full swing, to find two Faber young men still trying to induce John Davenport to get into a taxi. He was engaged in refusing to do so for so long as I kept the group in sight.

At this time I was seeing a good deal of Wyndham Lewis. I had taken him and Froanna to see *The Confidential Clerk* when it came to London in the autumn of 1953. Contrary to the impression sometimes given he was not, and never was, completely blind. He could see vaguely where the characters were standing on the stage. But although he had always been greatly interested in Eliot's work, he found the plays difficult, and this one most of all. At the Ivy afterwards we tried to work out its meaning. Eliot had several times called on the Lewis's, and had been taking a close interest in the ambitious successors to *Childermass*, the entire work being given the title of *The Human Age*. Lewis showed me the annotated typescript of both *Monstre Gai* and *Malign Fiesta*, in which I noticed that Eliot had put Lewis right, among other things, on questions of dress and of etiquette, on which he was something of an expert. In his piece on Eliot in the Seventieth Birthday *Festschrift*, Lewis spoke of the way in which, on arrival at the Notting Hill Gate flat, he would rub his face with both hands as a means of generating a little spare energy. As so often with Lewis, the description was exactly right: indeed, as Lewis became more incapacitated, his writing achieved a new precision. He was very fond of Eliot; but the occasional needling remark conveyed the impression that he sometimes found the discrepancy between Eliot's world fame and his own modest recognition difficult to bear. With friends like Betjeman, on the other hand, there was no such feeling. Betjeman, satisfied with his own reputation, rejoiced in the extent to which Eliot's, deservedly, as he thought, eclipsed it.

The English Literature course at Cambridge, to which I have earlier alluded, gave rise to more than one tricky problem. In a lecture, F. W. Bateson had cited the 'King Bolo' epic as evidence that Eliot had written a quantity of obscene poetry, and that this would be found after his death. A lady, whose name I do not recall, wrote to protest to the British Council; and, no doubt because the reply was in her view unsatisfactory, wrote to Eliot himself enclosing the Council's letter. Eliot telephoned me about this and I accordingly went to see him, but not before consulting our legal adviser. The latter expounded to me a subtle distinction between a 'contract for service' and a 'contract for services'; and he gave as his opinion that our employment of Bateson, being a one-off affair, constituted a 'contract for service', and therefore exempted us from responsibility for what he said. Having offered the Council's apologies to Eliot for the distress he had been caused, I outlined this distinction, which convinced him no more than it did myself, but I was merely acting as an emissary. Eliot then told me that he had already had some correspondence with Bateson over an article by John Peter in his magazine *Essays in Criticism*, declaring *The Waste Land* to be a homosexual allegory. As he related this, he shook his head sadly, and merely exclaimed 'Good Gracious!' He had felt obliged to discuss the matter with Counsel, and he had written to the young man to say so. John Peter had replied with a touchingly contrite letter. After Eliot's death, however, the article was republished, with further reference to Jean Verdenal. It has also been suggested that Eliot's threat of legal action was due not to his outrage but to a desire to suppress the truth. And as in our venereal age it is thought inconceivable that a man, however sincere his wish to do so, can live a life of continence, Eliot has been credited with more than one *sub rosa* liaison, and with the extremes of hypocrisy in trying to pretend to be what he was not. Lack of proof is not enough for the detractors; the lack itself generates suspicion. A new law is thus brought into service : that which cannot be proved can be used to fill the gap left vacant by the absence of proof.

To the letter which he had written to Bateson, he had received a reply which he described, drumming his fingers on his desk, as 'pert'. He repeated the word as if to prove to himself that it was the one he needed. Bateson had declared that he regarded Eliot as 'The Enemy'. I could see that Eliot was not only hurt but also puzzled by this letter : for so far as I could gather – I did not see it myself – Bateson gave no cogent reasons for fixing on Eliot this epithet, usually employed of Wyndham Lewis. The mild insult rankled, and echoes of it appeared in a later lecture, delivered in America to an unprecedently large audience, on 'The Function of Criticism'. Here, in speaking of Wordsworth, Eliot referred to a theory of incestuous relations between William and Dorothy as having been put forward by 'a' Mr Bateson. This would have offended Bateson in his turn, for he considered himself sufficiently well known. Eliot had repented of the slighting phrase, because, in presenting me with a copy of the text, he remarked rather uneasily that the 'a' was a 'mistake'. At any rate, he removed it when it was reprinted in the volume *On Poetry and Poets* (1969).

Save for a few lines, none of the 'King Bolo' verses have been published, and they were certainly not written for publication. I have read some of this or similar work, and it left me a trifle puzzled. In speech Eliot could be frank, and occasionally – very occasionally – ribald. This was either when he wished to express moral indignation or when he considered the subject genuinely amusing. His talk contained none of the expletives of which Belloc in private made use, not did I ever hear him retail anything in the nature of 'the one about' sort of bawdy story. In *After Strange Gods* (1934) he made his position quite clear: 'the only disinfectant which makes either blasphemy or obscenity sufferable is the sense of humour: the indecent that is funny may be a source of innocent merriment, while the absence of humour reveals it as purely disgusting'. My slight perplexity was this: that whereas some of the verses I have seen were certainly not disgusting – I could not conceive of Eliot composing anything of the kind – I did not find them particularly funny either. But some friends who have read more of the King Bolo 'epic' than I, tell me that much of it is very funny indeed. It may be that the Puritan strand in Eliot's character (to which he referred in particular in the essay on 'Goethe the Sage') was responsible, as in the case of many Puritans, for an occasional attraction to its opposite. I do know that at the time of the *Lady Chatterley* trial, he was not only asked to be a witness for the defence, but expressed willingness to stand for that purpose. It was Jeremy Hutchinson who felt that some of his written statements might prove difficult to reconcile with the way he felt now.

During the *dégringolade* of taste which followed, when publishers vied with one another to issue books of obscene and pornographic character for their supposed 'literary' merit, Eliot was invited to give his imprimatur to one or two pieces which, as he told me, he rejected as at once worthless and disgusting. Such was not the reaction of some other literary figures, both male and female, for whom the scabrous and the literary were suddenly found to be identical.

In the autumn of 1955, after an exceptionally busy season, I downed tools and left on holiday for Morocco. Inspired by Wyndham Lewis's *Filibusters in Barbary* (1932) and with other ends in view, I crossed the High Atlas and arrived in Marrakesh extremely grubby but much refreshed. Making my way to Tangier, then in ferment, I received a telegram c/o the British post office there (one of those anachronistic institutions which made travel up to a few years ago so fascinating), which read:

> Eliot suggest (*sic*) you might write leader about 1200 words on Wyndham Lewis for Christmas Number deadline November 17th stop Would like written around The Human Age which could post immediately stop Would be so delighted stop Literary Editor Time and Tide Tydantym Westcent London.

I had of course outlined to Eliot my proposed journey. The ultimate aim had been to venture into the Rio de Oro, while that Spanish-owned territory remained virtually unknown. I did not succeed, because the whole area of Spanish and French Morocco was in a state of rebellion, and the frontier, with its Beau Geste forts, had been closed. For that same reason, I was glad to be able to sit down to write an article on Lewis, and grateful to Eliot for putting forward the idea. It was a pleasant alternative to getting shot at. When I returned, Eliot was most interested to hear of my adventures, such as they were; and he questioned me closely about the situation in that part of North Africa, the Magreb, as it was once called. He did not share the horror (or pretended horror) of colonialism which has become almost statutory among the Western intelligentsia. Not that he believed in any permanent hegemony of a powerful state over one less developed. Morocco above all fascinated him, because it was the country which Charles de Foucauld, patrician turned missionary, first explored and then made his home, and where he was martyred. Echoes of that saintly man, with his 'care over lives of humble people', are found in *The Family Reunion* (Part II, Scene 2), and he gave a broadcast on Foucauld early in the war. In fact, Eliot believed that the only final justification of Empire was the spreading of the Gospel; and although I once heard an academic figure chortle helplessly with laughter at this idea, the interesting thing is that Christianity, while apparently declining in the West is spreading more rapidly in Africa, the great ex-colonial continent, than anywhere else. In the case of Algeria, where the crisis came to a head five years later, he lamented that a territory which had become formally part of France, should have wished to break away in so violent a manner. He had not only a great and abiding admiration for France, but also an appreciation of French political realism; and it grieved him that a man of the stature of de Gaulle, with his almost mystical belief in France's *mission civilisatrice*, should have surrendered both to the Algerian rebels, and, in the role of the Foreign Legion and its parachutists, to French rebels too.

I noticed that thenceforward his interest in politics, but above all the general movement and tendency of events, became increasingly keen. Some of his remarks in *Notes towards the Definition of Culture* (1948) contain a good deal more political wisdom than he has been given credit for. That a kind of mutual irritability between nations is one of the best guarantees of peace, seems to me a much more acute remark than some of the fatuous statements of the unilateralist peacemongers. Toynbee was the kind of thinker in whom he took interest, though he could not accept some of Toynbee's short-term political views; Toynbee, as I knew, had great respect for Eliot and much admired his poetry. To what extent Eliot's views were taken note of by practical politicians I do not know; I suspect not at all. It was on political issues that Herbert Read – a firm friend, if not exactly a close one – now began to move away from him. Read proclaimed himself an anarchist, whereas Eliot maintained his stance of radical conservatism, believing that socialism was not a new liberating doctrine, but merely the last stage of capitalism. As a practical doctrine, socialism was already superannuated. Of the two viewpoints, Eliot's has shown itself to be the more realistic. The idea that Eliot had fascist leanings, as Michael Hastings was to suggest in the play *Tom and Viv* (even to the point of fabricating a fascist speech), can have been made only by one who had failed to read such important articles as 'The Literature of Fascism' (*The Criterion*, December 1928). And what about *The Rock*? Nobody seems to have read *The Rock*, Part 1. Eliot was a democrat, maintaining what every true democrat has maintained, that there must be some limits placed upon the democratic process, not in order to weaken it but rather to preserve it.

In the summer of 1956, having been invited to be a British delegate – the only one, as it happened – I went to Switzerland to attend the Rencontres Internationales de Genève. I had twice before attended this conference. Hearing that I was going, Eliot told me that he planned to be in Switzerland too at that time, and he asked me to spend a day with him 'in the vineyards'. He liked Switzerland, and had already visited the same place two or three times. Moreover, he needed a holiday, because on the journey back from America in June 1956 he had a severe recurrence of tachycardia, for which in March 1954 he had been taken into the London Clinic, and he went in again, with bronchitis, at the beginning of 1956. On 12 June, his picture appeared on the front page of the *Evening Standard*. It showed him being wheeled into the French Hospital in Shaftesbury Avenue by two nuns, who, from their habit, might have been characters out of *Murder in the Cathedral*, one being of seraphic beauty. The caption reports that he had 'had a heart attack in the liner Queen Mary when two days out from New York!'. It was not a heart attack, but, as I say, severe tachycardia, no doubt severe enough to bring to his mind the danger of a coronary – 'the sudden thrombosis'. I much looked forward to seeing him in these new Swiss surroundings, but, alas, on telephoning the address he had given me, I found that, due to further illness, he had been obliged to cancel.

This was indeed a disappointment. Throughout the Rencontres, with its slightly heavy atmosphere of earnest academics, I had looked forward to the chance of a *villeggiatura*, and into company that I knew I should find stimulating. I guarded my secret appointment, because Alan Pryce-Jones, a veteran conference-goer, who knew just about everybody, had warned me that, once the news of Eliot's propinquity became known, there would be a rush to commandeer him for interviews, lectures, or simply for public exhibition : all of which he detested. For he was now as much a public figure in Switzerland, as he was in so many other countries. I began to fear for his health as never before, and I realized how protective of him I had become. This apprehension had been increased by my having described to my brother, who had just qualified as a doctor, the gasps and sighs that came over the telephone with almost stethoscopic volume, when Eliot had been speaking. My brother had diagnozed emphysema, and he proved to be right.

Not long after my return, Eliot asked me to lunch at the Athenaeum, and I was amazed at his renewed resilience: but I notice that when he was filling in the form with our orders, he semed to scratch the paper by a kind of *raturage*, in the most toilsome manner: an indication of his slowing down. He confessed that he was feeling rather worn out; and, as a way of making some positive suggestion, I cited Bernard Shaw's contention that, after middle life, everyone should take the opportunity every ten years of going to bed for a month or two. (Shaw seems to have cured himself of angina in this way.) I believe he either thought I was trying to be facetious or else that anything that Shaw said was not to be taken seriously anyway. He gave the jerky grunt that often did duty for a laugh; but at the same time he seemed on second thoughts not to dismiss the idea as altogether preposterous. What was going through his mind, I suspected, was the doleful prospect of being confined for anything like so long to his dingy back bedroom: so that the proposal, attractive in principle, had to be dismissed as out of the question.

This was the occasion when we had the conversation about Anthony Eden. We talked a little about Spain, as I had paid a visit there for the third time on my way to Morocco. He had been there in 1952, but I think he preferred Portugal, a country he knew rather better. That he should have regarded bull-fighting as 'fascinating' came as a surprise to me; but he explained that his Portuguese guide, drawing attention in particular to the matador, had counselled: 'Watch his feet!' This and not the bloodier aspects of the sport was what held his attention; for 'moving in measure', as some formal verses in *The Family Reunion* and of 'Little Gidding' indicated, was a subject that had always preoccupied him. When I told him that my revulsion from bull-fighting had arisen from being informed that the old horses, sometimes used as targets for the bull and therefore ripped open, had their vocal cords cut to prevent them from screaming. He agreed that this was a repulsive practice. On the whole, he enjoyed skill in sport, and even enjoyed a boxing-match, for he had taken up boxing at Harvard. His enjoyments were very much of the people: I think he much preferred the music-hall and the pantomime to ambiguous 'refined' arts like the ballet. To the cinema, however popular, he never became addicted. It was with difficulty that he was persuaded once to go to see a film about General Gordon, 'with all those fuzzy-wuzzies', as he put it: which he thought amounted to a great deal of expense for very little effect. And, as he said in another context, the cinema 'interfered with his day-dreams.'

It was at this meal that, probably at my instigation, the subject of women came up, not for the first time in our exchanges. I think I must have said that the company of women meant a lot to me (which it did), because, like many single men, I would grow tired of going to theatres, concerts, and not least having meals by myself;

but unfortunately, one's companion would sometimes – indeed often – resent the fact, if she had ascertained it, that one liked to vary one's company. Looking hard at the table, Eliot agreed that whereas a man could enjoy a woman's company up to a point yet remain unwilling to push the friendship any further, a women *tended* to demand one's full and exclusive attention. He then made the remark, on which he seemed to have been ruminating for some time: 'Some women think that if they want a thing hard enough, it must be right.' When I first reported this remark in *The Listener*, I brought down on myself the fury of a women's libber, who wrote a letter to that periodical denouncing something called 'the gospel of E. W. F. Tomlin', and declaring that by quoting this statement I was doing a disservice to my friend. All I can say is that I was performing a service to the truth, which cannot do the friend any harm. In the light of what I now know, I believe, in saying this, that he had in mind both Emily Hale and Mary Trevelyan, and it is no derogation of their characters to say so. He may have been thinking of others too, though how much he suspected the devotion of Brigid O'Donovan I have no idea. I then quoted Nietzsche's somewhat more lurid statement: 'It is better to fall into the hands of a murderer than into the dreams of an ardent woman'; and this seemed to plunge him into deeper reflection still, for he went on staring at the table without venturing a reply.

It was in following out this slightly perilous theme that the subject of continence and the possibility of the celibate life arose; and he stated emphatically, placing both hands flat on the table, as he often did when stressing a capital point: 'Well, it *can* be done, as I know.' This was the only time I heard him refer directly to his sexual life, or the absence of it. I was convinced that he was sincere; but having referred to sex in *Thoughts after Lambeth* as 'the most imperative of our instincts', the inference was that he had found this, understandably, no easy task.

There did not seem any reason, short of risking indiscretion, to pursue this subject; but I record it because I remember so well a young poet, now dead (not Dylan Thomas) saying that he assumed that Eliot, despite his pious pretensions, had 'something on the quiet', either female or male. Some people have even gone so far as to identify the individuals with whom, since Jean Verdenal of the Paris days, Eliot is supposed to have had sexual relations. I have seen a letter making a definite assertion in one case; but as I happen to have known the writer, I would not attach to it the slightest credence. The trouble is that when people hold the view that sexuality 'will out', their obsession with identification is unappeasable.

I raised the subject of correspondence, and he confirmed that in his case this had grown in such volume as to be beyond satisfactory handling. Fortunately, he had a most efficient secretary, who dealt not merely with most of his letters but with his engagement diary, which was filled up months ahead. He saw a great variety of people. On the whole, in spite of an occasional sharp remark, he referred to individuals, especially his fellow-poets, with charity; but one he described as 'that *difficult* man', followed by 'I have to say, that *difficult* man'. And when Eliot expressed himself in that fashion, he left the impression that his patience had been severely tried.

This occasion was memorable for me by another of his remarks, one of the saddest he ever made. We had alluded to regrets at past actions and at remarks one wished one had never made, leaving the most painful recollection; and how there seemed no way in which this could be expunged, since although one can struggle to remember, one cannot resolve to forget. This thought seemed to strike him forcibly, and, again bending his head, he said in a low voice: '*I* can never forget anything.' The failed marriage left him unhappy and, until his second marriage, inconsolably so.

We had spent rather longer over lunch than usual, and at the end I made some conventional comment about detaining him, to which, despite his pensive mood, he murmured: 'It has passed very pleasantly so far as I am concerned.' It was one of those kind rejoinders which gave to the younger man the feeling that he has not irreparably wasted a great man's time.

He needed a taxi when we emerged, and, with the usual liberal flourish of his stick, he hailed one which was passing on the other side, almost stepping off the pavement to cross over towards it. The taxi-driver steered round to where we were standing. He said: 'I wanted to save you the trouble.' Despite thoughtful acts of that kind, there were occasions when he was misunderstood. Eliot was one of the most unhurried of men. Unhurried men (and women) are reassuring. How different was Ezra Pound, always in a tearing hurry, and in consequence slightly unnerving. That might account for Arnold Bennett's annoyance, as recounted in his Journal, at being detained once by Eliot in the street discussing the situation of *The Criterion*. Bennett says: 'He could see I was in a hurry.' That, I think, is more than doubtful. Being unaccustomed to haste, Eliot, otherwise so percipient and patient, could fail sometimes to detect impatience or restiveness in other people. Another case was related to me by an American girl, Linda Hilles, daughter (if I remember right) of a General, who knew Eliot's work well and to whom I had propounded the judgment that one of the great lines of poetry was from 'Phlebas the Phoenician' (*The Waste Land*, Part IV):

He passed the stages of his age and youth
Entering the whirlpool,

so much more evocative than the French version from 'Dans le Restaurant,' which becomes 'repassant aux étapes de sa vie antérieure'. However, she told me that a friend, having paid a visit to Faber's and finding himself with Eliot on the doorstep in pouring rain, had expressed surprise that Eliot did not arrange for a taxi to be called. Instead, they both stood there until the American, a trifle annoyed, decided to make off. I do not consider that this necessarily showed inconsiderateness on Eliot's part. He used to go to Mass, wet or fine, at home or overseas, every morning; and I suppose that he assumed in a fellow-American a similar degree of independence and initiative. But I am not here concerned with whitewashing Eliot's every action. A memoir which amounted to nothing but hagiography would make insipid reading.

It was during 1956 that I learnt that I was to be posted to Turkey, this time as head of the British Council there. I had continued to see Eliot regularly at St Stephen's, though sometimes for no more than a few minutes' chat. Now I called at Faber's for tea to tell him about Turkey and my preparations for departure. This meant giving up the room in Courtfield Gardens where I had done so much writing, often late at night after a hard day in the office. He began by presenting me with a copy of his 'Goethe the Sage' lecture, gracefully inscribed.

I told him how I had not long before lectured on his work to a group of German teachers, and had referred to the Geothe prize, and how they had expressed their appreciation not by the customary clapping but by pounding the desks at which they sat. This was evidently the custom, though unfamiliar to me; but the racket, perhaps on account of their enthusiasm, was tremendous. He was amused, as he always was by some quirky situation; but I could see that even so he was low in vitality.

Although he had been assured that spasmodic tachycardia implied no serious organic trouble, he was still worried about it. Perhaps one reason was that in some medical dictionaries it is classified under Heart Disease. He remarked that, once the trouble started (which, as every sufferer knows, is without warning), the only thing to do was to go straight to bed. I could only tell him my own experience, which was that, since a paroxysm often came on at work, a few simple techniques, combined with a relaxed but upright posture, were often just as effective; and I was surprised to find that he had not been instructed in such methods, which could produce instant results. This could be done by holding the breath under pressure, a firm grasp of the wrist, or, more effective perhaps, applying pressure below the angle of the jaw over one of the carotid arteries. As I then and there demonstrated these methods, which had become second nature to me, I hoped that they may have been of some help to him. He had given the impression of momentarily not knowing quite where to turn; and I suspected that, since I had never seen him so distraught, this had been one of his 'bad days'. Besides, he looked as if, by the operation of an accelerated time-machine, he had been forcibly aged by at least ten years. I myself felt in a minor panic of helplessness in face of someone in need of authoritative reassurance. Finally, trying to think of something positive to say, I hazarded: 'Why not take a holiday in the South of France?' It may be hindsight (but I think not) that makes me recall that he had a special tone in his voice when he commented: 'My secretary is in Menton.'

Not so very long after my arrival in Ankara, where I was to meet old and to make many new friends, the news came through that Eliot had married again. I found a draft of the letter I wrote to him on 19 February 1957, of which I reproduce the greatest part. In retrospect, it shows a degree of personal solicitude which might invite the comment that I felt he had had no other friends to turn to. All I can say is that I was genuinely delighted at the news, for I had feared that overwork, dejection and deteriorating health would kill him before I had the opportunity of seeing him again.

Dear Mr. Eliot,
I was so pleased to hear – though naturally after some delay – the news of your marriage, and I hasten to send my warmest good wishes to you both. I felt very happy about it. I had been worried, during the last year or two especially, about the fact that you seemed to be wearing yourself out with work, and the strain was obviously telling on you; and yet I felt quite helpless

to do anything. But now you will have someone to look after you properly, and this is a great relief to me.

I wonder if the suggestion is fantastic that you should have a delayed honeymoon in Turkey. I believe you have never been here, and it is certainly one of the most interesting countries in the world, and you should see it. It is only a day's flying distance from London, and I have fortunately been able to find a large and comfortable flat where you could have a restful and undisturbed time. As a matter of fact I am putting on *The Cocktail Party* here in April, and if you could come for that, it would of course be magnificent – I need not emphasise what a tremendous thing it would be for everyone concerned; but if you wished to come unofficially or incognito or at any other time, it would be equally pleasant as far as I am concerned. I know you would like the Turks (who are a quiet and charming people, very different from the legendary 'barbarians'); and a trip to the South of Turkey would be as climatically pleasant as the French Riviera – and of course it is much more unspoiled. I do beg you to think of this seriously; I could promise you both a really interesting as well as a restful holiday.

And if you have a play to finish, or one to begin, this is the place to do it.

If you do not wish to fly, you could come at leisure through the Mediterranean either to Istanbul or to one of the southern ports, where I would meet you. Politically, I may add, the country is absolutely calm, and there are not likely to be any disturbances in the neighbourhood for a long time to come. I would not wish to seem so pressing except that I *know* you would enjoy your time here. Please do think about it.

But in any case, I repeat how delighted I was with the news.

His reply, dated 21 February 1957, was charming, and by no means as dismissive of the idea of a Turkish jaunt as I had been afraid it might be. As a matter of fact, the British Council, to which I had already put the case, was prepared in this instance, but so far as I know in no other, to bear the expenses of both husband and wife: an earnest of the immense respect in which he was held, and the influence which his reputation was considered likely to wield.

My dear Tomlin,

Your letter of February 10th has given me and my wife much pleasure and we were particularly touched with the concern you express for my health over the last year or two. I am very glad to assure you that there is no longer any need for such anxiety.

I am very much pleased at the suggestion that we should visit you in Turkey but we are now occupied with all the details of getting settled, and are not likely to be able to take another holiday this year as we have used up nearly all of our travel allowances on our honeymoon. Any further travels outside the sterling area can only be conducted at the expense of the institutions like the British Council, and I doubt if the Council would pay for my wife to accompany me even if I could give the time to preparing lectures. But I should indeed very much like to consider a visit to Turkey and should like to consider the possibility of combining a Turkish holiday with some British Council work in a future year.

I do not suppose you will be back in London for a long time, but remember that you are often in my thoughts and regularly in my prayers, and that I hope that in spite of the handicaps and the burden of administration you may be able to devote some time to your own thinking and writing.

    Ever yours,
    T.S. Eliot.

Frederick Tomlin Esq.,
c/o The British Embassy,
Ankara,
Turkey.

The reference to his health was indeed reassuring; I gather that just before his marriage, the doctors informed him that his chances of surviving much longer were fifty-fifty. In fact, so great happiness was brought by his marriage that he recovered almost boyish spirits, and his last years were the idyll that most people experience, if at all, in the first flush of youth. Nor need I assert – except that many people ridiculed the idea, including, I regret to say, such friends as Allen Tate – that the marriage was a full and complete one.

My reply to his letter is worth reproducing in part, for reasons which the reader who has come thus far will understand. On 23 March 1957, I wrote him from Ankara:

Dear Mr. Eliot,

I was very pleased to receive your letter of February 21st. I quite realise the difficulties of coming out here this year, but I am very glad to learn that you might feel inclined to pay a visit here next year and to combine a holiday with a lecture tour. I really think you would enjoy your time, and I am sure that the British Council would agree to pay the expenses of Mrs. Eliot too.

I think I told you in my last letter that we are putting on *The Cocktail Party* soon – on the 15th April, to be exact. (The London Office has dealt with the matter of fees.) This will be the first performance of the play, so far as I know, in the Middle East. I believe it will be a success, especially as we have some trained talent among the British colony here. I want to ask whether you would consider helping us in the following way. The Turks feel very cut off from the culture of Western Europe, for which they have very great respect. A short message on a tape recorder, to be played before the performance, would have an effect here which, if one does not know the country, is difficult to grasp; I can only use a cliché and describe it as likely to be 'electric'. You might not care for the idea and there may be complications of which I am unaware, and in any case time is short. But I give below the kind of thing I have in mind. Our Recorded Sound Department would arrange for the recording any time and anywhere you wished, and I don't suppose the whole operation would take more than 20 minutes. But I hope you will realise that I should perfectly understand if you were reluctant or unable to do this.

I suggested something as follows:

I am happy to learn that my play, *The Cocktail Party*, is being performed in Turkey as part of the British Cultural Week which the Turco-British Association and the British Council have organised. This will be the first time that my play has been performed in Turkey and indeed in any of the Middle East countries. I hope that you will enjoy this performance, and I send my greetings to the Turkish people.

My letter concluded:

May I leave it to you to do with this passage what you wish, or to lengthen or even shorten it if you care to? It may strike you as very simple, but I do not think this matters. If you feel able to make

the recording, perhaps it would be possible for your secretary to telephone the Recorded Sound Department of the British Council (the Director of which, Mrs. Dennison, I think you know), and the tape could be given to one of the lecturers who will be coming out here about April 8th by air (Mr. Pryce-Jones, for example).
   Yours ever,

 It was extremely good of him to proceed immediately with the task of recording the message. (I wish in retrospect that I had worded a sentence in my letter and the penultimate sentence of the message slightly differently, as Turkey regards herself as a Western and not a Middle Eastern country; but I was at the time working under pressure, and the point escaped me.) On 1 April I received this letter:

My dear Tomlin,
 I received your letter of March 23rd and have just made a recording of my brief speech with Mrs. Dennison who tells me that Alan Pryce-Jones will be bringing the tape out. I am very grateful to you for saving me so much trouble by telling me exactly what to say. Of course I have altered it a bit in order to save face with myself, but it is substantially what you told me to say and not very much longer. I do hope it will produce the effect you look for. I will be most interested to hear a report of the performance and should also welcome a more personal letter about yourself.
   Ever yours,
   T.S. Eliot.

Frederick Tomlin Esq.,
c/o The British Embassy,
Ankara,
Turkey.

 In fact, the performances were more of a success than I had dared to hope. We had two professionals, in the sense that Molly Lake (Mrs Travis Kemp) and her husband were well-known ballet dancers: and Molly, whose death at the age of 88 occurred a week or so before these words were written (1986) had had a very distinguished dancing career indeed. But the important point was that they proved a success on the stage; and if their acting was slightly stylized, as their art dictated, this was not perhaps a disadvantage in the circumstances. Celia was acted by a British teacher from Ankara College who combined beauty and poise with an intuitive understanding of the part. I think she was the best Celia I have seen among the three or four productions I have attended. Sir Henry Harcourt Reilly was acted by a professor from Ankara University, Arthur Sewell, whose knowledge of drama and understanding of Eliot were a great asset. All this I duly reported to Eliot in a letter written some weeks later, and of which I reproduce the salient paragraphs of my draft:

Dear Mr. Eliot,
I must first of all apologise for my long silence, but the Cultural Week took almost as long to wind up as it did to prepare. Nevertheless, I ought to have written to you sooner to thank you for going to the trouble to record the message about *The Cocktail Party* in time for Alan Pryce-Jones to bring it out here. It was extremely kind of you, and as you can imagine it made a great impression.

The play was performed on the evening of April 15th. The theatre (it is called the Small Theatre and holds about 615 seats) was packed; in fact tickets were sold out within a day or two of the opening of the box-office, and we could have filled at least two more houses. What was especially gratifying was the fact that most of the audience was Turkish, and included Minsters and Deputies as well as ordinary working people. There were also members of foreign missions.

We arranged to diffuse the message during a pause just before the curtain went up. We had transferred it to another tape, adding some introductory words in English and Turkish, and the message itself was followed by a Turkish translation. It came over well; the only blemish was that owing to a common fault in the theatre audiences a number of people were still trying to find their seats while the broadcast was being made. The message was read over the Radio the next day and published in a number of newspapers, so that its impact was not confined to a particular audience.

From the very beginning the play itself went admirably; the audience got point after point, including some subtleties which I should have thought beyond them. People were impressed by the efficiency and ease of the acting; we were fortunate in the fact that Celia, Lavinia, Alex and Julia had all received training at drama schools, while Professor Sewell, the producer (he is head of the English Department of the University here) had been responsible for twenty or so productions in the course of his career. I myself confess to have got more out of the play than I did from the London performances; but then all the rehearsals took place at my flat and we worked sometimes until 2 or 3 a.m. You will receive some idea of the 'set' from the photographs I enclose: I am sorry that they are not very well printed, but if I can obtain better ones I will let you have them.

By the middle of the play it was evident that we were holding the audience, and the acclamation at the end was most rewarding. The Turks are not given to wild demonstrations, but they were really enthusiastic. We have received repeated requests to put on other performances, but I am concentrating now on a performance in Istanbul, and I was in fact holding up this letter in hope of being able to report progress on this front. I should add that as a dress-rehearsal we put on a special performance for students on the day before the performance, and again we were amazed to see how much they were able to assimilate. I am very glad that we had this preliminary run-through, as we were able to learn a good deal from it.

As you know, the Cyprus crisis broke just as our Cultural Week was beginning, and the Prime Minister refused to allow a military band to come over from Cyprus to 'open' the proceedings. There was a moment when I feared that the whole thing would collapse. In fact all went well, and considering how pained the Turks were by the turn in our policy over Makarios, I think it showed great magnanimity that this was so. We had hoped that the President and the Prime Minister would attend some of the functions, but they stayed away presumably in protest; but members of the President's household came regularly, and also the Prime Minister's wife.

I expect Alan Pryce-Jones will have been able to give you some account of the various events, including the play itself. Meanwhile, I enclose some programmes. You may also have seen a reference to the Week (and the play) in Peterborough's column in the *Daily Telegraph* for April 25th. Sir James Bowker, the Ambassador, gave his full support and encouragement to the venture, and he very much hopes that you may be able to come out here while he is still in office, though I fear he may be leaving in the autumn.

On 15 May, he replied to my letter at, for him, some length, as I had given him a good deal of the personal news that he sought. The reference to Josef Pieper, the German philosopher-theologian, was prompted by my resolve, given the limited time at my disposal, to write something succinct in the manner of that author whom Faber's had published. Eliot's reference to his work remains of the greatest interest, but more fascinating still in some ways are the political references and the allusion to his new way of life.

My dear Tomlin,
Thank you for your good long letter of May 7th together with three photographs and the programmes of *The Cocktail Party*. I am delighted to know that the production was so very successful and hope that you will be able to realise the aim of taking it to Istanbul. That is should be well-received in spite of the release of Archbishop Makarios is very agreeable. To me it seemed a mistake in the first place to whisk him over to the Seychelles but, having done so, another mistake in the second place to release him without any guarantees or promise of amendment.

I have not seen Alan Pryce-Jones since his return, which means, of course, that I have been living a rather quiet domestic life.

I think that you are sensible in trying to find a form in which you can write to the best advantage in the adverse circumstances in which you find yourself. After all, it was war-time conditions which produced three of my *Four Quartets*. *The Family Reunion* was produced in the spring of 1939; when I saw it on the stage and realised all the errors and defects of technique, I was determined to start another play which should be free of the same faults. The war prevented this owing to the impossibility of sitting down morning after morning to a task which would occupy me for perhaps a couple of years. The quartet form was the solution because I could concentrate on the five sections of each poem separately: so I think that an essay in the style of Pieper is very well worth trying. How far it reduces the labour is another question but I think it does ease the problem of writing in an interrupted life.

I look forward to seeing you in July. We shall be here from the 6th July pretty well straight through the month and into August.

I do not know whether it is possible to obtain any copies of the sermon, so-called, which I was obliged to deliver in Magdalene Chapel, but I know that Valerie has a copy of it and I might be able to get it typed out for you.

        Yours ever affectionately,
        T.S. Eliot.

The final paragraph referred to my remark that I thought I possessed every publication of his except the Cambridge sermon. I had finally read it in the Houghton Library at Harvard, where the Eliot Collection was housed.

I had written to him saying that I should be on leave in July, and he wrote again on 17 July trying to work out a day for us to meet in his usually busy schedule. The letter was addressed to Winchester, where I was staying with my sister:

Dear Tomlin,

I should love to see you, but I haven't really much to offer this week and next week and up to the August Bank Holiday are very crowded. The time is all the more restricted as I have to be away both this week-end and the following week-end. You speak as if you were leaving England at the end of the month. My difficulty is that literally the first day possible for me is Wednesday, the 31st, if I cut a committee altogether. Would Wednesday, the 31st, be a possible day for you to lunch with me and my wife? Alternatively, it would be much better if you were to be here during the first week in August, Bank Holiday week, as I have no engagements at all from then on except a short week-end away on the 10th and 11th. If the 31st is impossible for you and you are not to be in England after that, then all I can offer is a little while at the end of the afternoons of the 23rd and 24th, if you can look in here at the office.

I am anxious to have your news.

        Yours ever,
        T.S. Eliot.

In fact, my leave extended into August, as I explained, and I received a card dated 23 July 1957, followed by a letter dated 25 July from his temporary secretary, Natalie Balck-Foote, which ran:

Dear Mr. Tomlin,

As Mr. Eliot is not in the office today he has asked me to write to you for him. He and Mrs. Eliot are extremely sorry that they will not be able to entertain you at their flat on Tuesday, the 6th, but Mrs. Eliot has pointed out that it will be the day after Bank Holiday and there will be very little food in the shops. They would be extremely glad, however, if you would lunch with them at the Russell Hotel, at 12.45 p.m. as there is a very good lounge there where one can talk quietly over coffee.

This meeting was noteworthy from my point of view as it was the occasion of my first meeting with Valerie. I was already at the hotel, well in advance of the time of appointment, as usual, and witnessed his arrival on the arm of this most striking young lady. His whole deportment, expression, spirits, were transformed, as if a great weight had been lifted from his shoulders. After he had introduced me, he perceived that I was carrying a dispatch case, and, taking hold of it for inspection, he verified that it lacked the leather tag-loop at one corner (of the kind that usually contains a lock), which he pronounced to be essential for both carrying and safety. He was right. Such little matters seemed to be part of a new delight in life.

At table, Valerie, who looked very happy, sat on the other side of him, and on this first occasion she left him to do almost all the talking. He began by alluding to the international situation; for foreign policy – especially that of the governments of Britain and the United States, for which he appeared to feel a kind of remote responsibility – had become one of his preoccupations: witness the remark about Archbishop Makarios. Of John Foster Dulles, US Secretary of State since 1953, he had come to form a very poor opinion, and he quipped: 'Whenever Valerie finds me looking glum, she knows it's because I'm thinking about Dulles.'

As he considered that office work had become much more of a burden as a result of the proliferation of business machines (as compared with the slower and more natural tempo of the past), he was always anxious to enquire how I found bureaucratic or administrative life abroad. His new lighthearted mood broke through when he referred to his own office life, one of the complications of which had been that his secretaries tended to fall for him. He rather implied that secretaries were bound to do this in any case, which Valerie found rather impish of him. There were, I knew, exceptions, for he had referred to Ann Bradby's marriage at the time with a kind of wistful amusement, as he noted her mounting elation. This must have led us on to Wyndham Lewis, who in his turn had been very much of a *coureur*; and I remarked somewhat unkindly that I had found one of his early friends, Agnes Bedford, among the ugliest women I had met, though she had been exceedingly kind-hearted, especially when the Lewis's Notting Hill studio was being refurbished. Eliot always derived a certain amount of amusement from gossiping about Lewis, especially his habit of keeping Froanna, his attractive wife, in purdah, until he became blind and helpless. 'That reminds me,' he said, turning to Valerie: 'we must have Froanna round for a meal.'

We talked about St Stephen's, and, as I had been absent for so long, it was from him that I learnt of Father Cheetham's death. He had gone on a long voyage to India after retirement, and, as I knew, he had long suffered from a heart condition, and no doubt did not expect to return.

Settled in armchairs in the lounge, we moved on to the subject of the British Council. It was soon clear that he still very much minded, and no wonder, the imputation, made in an article by John Peter in *Essays in Criticism*, that *The Waste Land* was a homosexual allegory. Owing to absence abroad, I was not *au courant* with the later developments, nor had I read John Peter's article. But I now realise that correspondence had taken place in May of 1957 with Father Curtis, the Mirfield Father, who had forwarded to him a long, meandering and, in my view, somewhat inaccurate account from Bateson; that Bateson had written a long letter to Eliot; and that Eliot had replied to the one saying that he wanted 'the case to end there', and to the other simply that he found his letter 'interesting'. It seems clear that he had heard from Bateson *before* receiving the letter and enclosure from Father Curtis, or I do not see how he could have told me about the Bateson *contretemps* when he did. At any rate, the matter though closed in one sense, was still on his mind, and he repeated, with a similar weary shake of his head, the absurdity of the interpretation. Indeed, his repudiation was conveyed in a tone which suggested that anyone who had known him and Jean Verdenal could not possibly have placed that construction on the poem.

He also referred to unfortunate indiscretions of other kinds, including one of which I did not learn the details, but which concerned a priest about whom Eliot was asked to give his confidential opinion – which was not a favourable one – whereupon his letter was promptly shown to the cleric, with embarrassment all round. I capped that by citing a case in my experience in which, in order to secure the resignation of an unpopular colleague, his confidential file had 'in error' been marked to him. This had had the desired effect. The incident occurred before the days when dismissals, even for extreme incompetence, were rendered difficult.

When Eliot had alluded to the *Essays in Criticism* episode, I noticed that Valerie had begun to look concerned; and, once the subject had been mulled over, she determinedly grasped the sides of her armchair : which I took, rightly I believe, as an indication that her husband was not to be put to further exertion or worry. Her solicitude for him was touching. We therefore rose and moved to the exit. He reiterated his hope that I would be able to get some of my own writing done in Turkey, and I then ventured to raise again the question of a visit. He still found the idea attractive, and Valerie asked a question about the climate and the best season to come. His last remark was that, if I felt that a visit from him would really serve the national interest he would do everything possible to make the journey. I assured him that it would.

CHAPTER NINE

Once I had returned to Turkey and again consulted with London, I decided to write to him in general terms about a visit; and, in order to make clear that I knew he was often pressed with such invitations and to demonstrate that I was not badgering him to the point of importunity, I will reproduce the business part of the letter, which was written at the end of August:

Dear Mr. Eliot,
 I expect you will have guessed one at least of the motives I have in writing to you immediately on my return to Turkey, so I will come to the point forthwith. You know how keen I am that you should pay a visit here some time, but I naturally realise that you have at present heavy commitments in the way of foreign travel, and I do not want to bother you with propositions that may for the moment be impracticable. At the same time, I understood from our recent conversation that you would not altogether rule out a visit here next year. What I would like to ask, therefore, is whether you would care to receive an official invitation from the Council, couched in general terms, so that you could consider it at your leisure. I know that London would be only too willing to extend this invitation (with such conditions as you would, I think, approve); but I do not want you to be troubled with it unless the prospect definitely appealed to you and unless you could come here at the time most convenient to yourself and with as little fatigue and exertion as possible.
 We had some discussion, I remember, about the best time of the year for a visit of this kind. Although any time would be convenient from our point of view, I should like to feel that you

were coming at the best time from the point of view of weather, travel and comfort. I think I must say that in order to fulfil all these requirements such a visit should take place between the beginning of May and the end of June. I am naturally thinking in terms not merely of official business but of sightseeing; for you would want to see Istanbul as well as Ankara, and perhaps Izmir and the South, at their best. (On the other hand, if you felt disposed to come in any case and could manage only the early part of the year, I should explain that Ankara between January and March is cold but dry, and therefore invigorating, though there is the height to consider. Istanbul, on the other hand, tends to be rainy and windswept. In that case, you might wish to confine your visit to Ankara.)

It goes without saying that any visit that you paid to Turkey would be a great event here and that you would have the warmest reception. I likewise will not conceal that your visit during my Representativeship would be most gratifying. On the other hand, I would like your decision to be based on whether you would really enjoy coming and were able to do so without a lot of inconvenience. For this reason I will ensure that you are not troubled with the formalities of an invitation unless you would like to think the matter over on the basis of a firm proposition from London. Naturally, I would see to it that any such invitation automatically included Mrs. Eliot . . .

He replied on 13 September 1957, and I perceived that my hopes, which had in any case been tempered with caution, were unlikely to be realized, at least for the time being.

Frederick Tomlin Esqre,
c/o The British Embassy,
Ankara,
Turkey.

Dear Tomlin,

Thank you for your letter of August 31st. I wish that I could hold out any prospect of a visit to Ankara in the coming year, both for personal reasons – my wanting to make such a visit while you are in charge of the British Council there, and because of the general political reasons which you advanced – but I do not see what promises I could possibly make for 1958. We are almost certainly paying a visit to the United States in April and May, a visit which is due for personal reasons, as my wife has never visited that country, and I wish to introduce her to it as soon as possible. It would be very unwise, as these visits to America are always very fatiguing for me, immediately to embark for Turkey, even leaving out of account the desirability of a prepared lecture. In the early autumn I am obliged to pay a visit to the University of Rome which I would have paid last spring if possible, and which has had to be postponed again. So I think there is no point in inciting London to make a formal offer at the present time. If the situation next year should allow of an interval such that I could both prepare myself for a visit to Turkey, and give the time itself, I would certainly acquaint you with the possibility.

I am sorry that the matter must be left completely in the air.
    Yours ever,
    T.S. Eliot.

P.S. My wife sends her good wishes with mine.

In spite of this, and in view of the fact that he had always in mind the use which might result from a visit, I did not abandon the idea altogether, as will be seen. Nor could I dismiss the thought, which he had once mentioned to me rather ruefully, that he had never travelled East of Suez. I remained convinced that a journey eastward would greatly interest him, as from an early age he had reflected a great deal about the oriental mind; and I think he had come to the conclusion ahead of many of his contemporaries, that the East was stirrring in a way that might alter the course of history. Toynbee had of course long proclaimed his conviction that this was going to happen. Indeed, people only write books with titles like *The Triumph of the West* (a well-know TV serial), when that triumph is beginning to be put in doubt, just as they produce books with titles like *The Bible to be Read as Literature* when, as Eliot himself stressed, its literary influence has seemingly come to an end.

The thought of Eliot's happy marriage had left me with the feeling that, if there were silence between us, it was in itself a kind of reassurance, a guarantee that all was – not just 'shall be' – well. This was the difference between being friends and being merely acquaintances. And in any case I had news of him from other friends, like Herbert Read, or through Faber's, or indeed through Ezra Pound, whom I met near Tirolo in the Italian Alps – *venti anni doppo* (as he put it in a dedication) our original encounter in

Kensington before the war. But it was gratifying, if surprising, when he wrote out of the blue, as he did on 10 April 1958, concerning the request I had made about his Cambridge Sermon:

> My dear Tomlin,
> I am terribly ashamed of myself for my long silence. It has been on my conscience for so long that you wanted to see a copy of the sermon I delivered some years ago in the chapel of Magdalene. I have not been able to turn up a copy anywhere and am writing as a last resort to one of the Fellows of the College to ask if there are any still available, but I doubt whether there are any left. If I could I would borrow a copy and have the text copied out for you. I know John Hayward has one but I should prefer not to approach him on this point.
> We are sailing for New York on the 12th and shall not be back until 3rd June. I hope to get in touch with you on our return and am anxious to know how things are going with you and whether you have any time for thinking and writing.
> Yours ever,
> T.S. Eliot.

I was duly grateful for this letter, and I trust that I showed my appreciation of his conscientiousness. On 23 July, when I knew he would be back from the United States, I wrote him a long account of my various activities. As the post of Representative of the British Council and Cultural Counsellor at the Embassy was one of the busiest I knew – so that I wondered that I managed to reach retirement age without a breakdown in health – I was glad that I kept him posted at intervals. It never ceased to surprise me that, with his wide acquaintanceship both at home and abroad, and his huge correspondence, he was able and disposed to communicate as often as he did. His reply was dated 29 July 1958:

> Frederick Tomlin Esq.,
> c/o The British Embassy,
> Ankara,
> Turkey.

> Dear Tomlin,
> Your letter of the 23rd is very welcome after not being in communication with you for such a long time. I expect to be returning from Edinburgh, where my new play will have been

produced at the Festival, about September 1st and shall be in London until the beginning of October when we have to pay a short visit to Paris, so I hope to see you during your home leave.

It is good news to know that you have been making even very slow progress with your book. I had feared that your time would be so fully occupied by duties and responsibilities in Ankara that you would have no time at all for thinking and writing.

With most cordial good wishes,
Ever yours,
T.S. Eliot.

The book, which had begun to crystallize, was now to be called *The Concept of Life*; the play was *The Elder Statesman*, which was to open in London at the Cambridge Theatre on 25 September 1958. I was determined to attend the First Night, and was glad to find that a box was available. My sister and I and Michael Cullis, in whose rooms in Oxford we had entertained Eliot over twenty years earlier, occupied it, and found ourselves looking across the auditorium to the box opposite, which was occupied by Eliot and Valerie, together with Henry and Pamela Sherek, a couple whom I was later to come to know well. Fortunately perhaps, the distance across was too great to permit an exchange of greetings, and in any case I knew that Eliot was usually on tenterhooks on these occasions. Indeed, before the play had ended, he quietly slipped out, so that there should be no question of his responding to the calls of 'Author, author!' Afterwards I learnt that our box had originally been reserved for a well-known dramatic critic, who decided that he could just as well write his piece without going to the trouble of seeing the play; which caused him to commit at least one colossal howler. The other explanation put about for his omitting to see it was that he had spent the evening on the floor of the box in question making love to a woman; but I can be practically certain that there was no basis for this allegation.

In reply to a letter of mine written in the autumn, Eliot's secretary, Susan MacEwen, wrote on 17 September, inviting me to dinner with the Eliots at the Garrick on Tuesday, 23 September. It had always seemed to me, though this may be surmise on my part, that, of the clubs Eliot belonged to, the Garrick was that in which he felt most at home. Even in the Athenaeum he seemed something of a stranger and apart, despite the presence of Anglican clerics, some in a garb so rarely seen today as to be walking anachronisms. But the

Garrick, with its associations with writers and actors, and its warm décor, suited him perfectly: and, not a minor matter, it was a place where he was known to the members as he was not always known to that extent elsewhere, and therefore he was left undisturbed, as his fellow-writers wished to be left undisturbed themselves, except for a minority pining to be 'noticed'. Thus, when Eliot, Valerie and I were walking across the vestibule to the restaurant, I observed out of the corner of my eye an actor in a cloak – I think Ernest Milton, but I am not sure – arriving at the front entrance. As he caught sight of Eliot, he stopped and gave a low bow. This, I am sure, was not in order that Eliot might see, because he had by that time passed on, but by way of a private gesture of respect.

On arrival, he had parted temporarily from Valerie, and Eliot turned to me with that searching expression of his, remarking how the new regime had transformed his whole life. As to the earlier alliance, he summed it up, not so much in bitterness as though trying to get across what it had in fact amounted to: 'Seventeen years of married misery!' This was said with an almost bewildered emphasis on the final word, by way of pointing to his present happiness. I confess I felt just a twinge of pity for that poor creature Vivien.

There followed one of the pleasantest evenings that I remember. Possibly because of the acoustics or the disposition of the tables, no distracting chatter plagued us. Moreover, Eliot was feeling thoroughly at ease. No doubt I was too; for Valerie told me, after her husband's death, that I may sometimes have tended to give the impression of perhaps too respectful seriousness in his presence. I could well believe it: for, as I have said, I never ceased to experience a sense of awe therein. This did not so much exasperate as cause slight amusement: but then men who command such a degree of respect must not be surprised when it is elicited. And I on my side could argue, though not exactly complain, that he over-estimated my powers. Perhaps that is why I never showed him any of my poetry: and when I once ventured to enquire whether he had seen a piece of verse of mine in the *New English Weekly*, 'Nalut, Libya', he simply asked: 'Why?'

I ought to interject here a point that might otherwise be missed. In the early days especially, we – that is to say, myself and a few friends – had mixed our veneration of Eliot with a good deal of lighthearted fun at his expense and the occasional imitation of the deep, measured tone of voice. Not for a moment was our discipleship, mine least of all, a matter of solemn or fawning obsequiousness. It was very much the reverse. As John Betjeman pointed out in his seventieth birthday tribute, Eliot was in many ways a funny man. And he was fun to recall – he is still – that is why he was so endearing.

At any rate, as here, we always had plenty to talk about. Despite high spirits and even merriment, there was, I realized, something on his mind : for it must not be thought that his last years were unclouded with anxieties, still less devoid of wounding attacks. For instance, apart from the tiresome homosexual insinuations, there were accusations of anti-Semitism. But what used to hurt him as much as anything were the occasional assaults on his literary achievement, of which the most recent salvo had been launched by Raymond Mortimer in the *Observer*. Mortimer had tried to imply, following the example of Edmund Wilson, who had initiated the anti-Eliot crusade, that Eliot had enjoyed immunity from criticism for so long that it was time someone took him down a peg. It was much like saying that Shakespeare, having for centuries been classed as distinct from other writers in that he was 'free', whereas they 'abide our question', ought, simply for the sake of shuffling reputations, to be questioned in his turn. 'He says I can't write prose,' Eliot muttered a trifle sardonically. 'He's jealous of you, Tom,' Valerie commented. I have no doubt he was; but I believe I said something not altogether polite to the effect that Mortimer was a 'pip-squeak' whose views did not matter anyway. That seemed to set the matter in perspective. Of course Eliot was not immune from criticism, and never for a moment did he think that he was; but even Bateson was obliged to admit that, as well as being a distinguished poet, he was a master of prose. I do not know how anyone sensitive to language can dissent from that judgment.

I remember that this led us on to reflect briefly on the changing vogues for writers, and how reputations were acquired sometimes for reasons other than purely literary ones. Dylan Thomas was a case in point. It would be interesting to be able to judge how far his high reputation was due to his low antics. I said that some of Dylan's poems – 'Death hath no more dominion', for example – gave me the impression of a bonfire kept alight by the repeated throwing in of synthetic inflammable material, such as highly-charged phrases like 'Christ's blood'. Eliot remarked that he had never cared for Dylan's work, but that Valerie tended to disagree with him. This was one case among others that I noticed where Valerie was prepared to take her own line, and to make no bones about doing so; and I believe Eliot, far from being stung by such dissent, found it rather exhilarating, especially as, like much else in his second marriage, it was a novel experience for him.

I further recall a moment in the meal, such as occurs only on the best such occasions, when I felt I could make a request. This either had not occurred to me before or had seemed hitherto too venturesome. It was that I should henceforth address him by his first name. In the present days of extreme informality, such timidity may sound childish; but the reader must bear in mind that Valerie herself referred to him as 'Mr Eliot' until her engagement. This was at first secret; and it was in his room at Faber's, after he had proposed in writing, placing the paper among the signed letters, and she had replied the next day, that he said to her quietly, 'What is my name?' She had never called him Tom before that. Until quite recently, you were obliged to ask of a friend, or of someone with whom you had established a particular rapport, 'May I call you' – whatever your first name was? (Hence the amusement I derived from a young woman I had met a few times who wrote me a letter beginning 'Dear Frederick, or may I call you Tomlin?') Eliot at once agreed that, so far as I was concerned, I was to call him Tom; but, strangely enough, when I sat down to write to him next from Turkey, I discovered that I simply could not break myself of the old habit, and so I found myself calling him 'Mr Eliot' until the end, for 'Mr Eliot' he was and, in that sense, always would be.

It was Valerie, indeed, who towards the end of the meal, suggested that I should be one of the guests at the small party they were shortly giving at home to celebrate his seventieth birthday. This naturally meant a great deal to me, and it proved to be one more occasion that I would not have missed, and of which I retain almost every detail. If at the last hour the mind resolves to hold on to a few scraps of recollection, this one would certainly be among them.

The party, a small one, which made it more interesting, was held at 3 Kensington Court Gardens on the day following the opening of *The Elder Statesman*. Among those present were Jacob Epstein and his wife, Mr and the first Mrs Martin Browne, Rupert Hart-Davis and Ruth, a young self-effacing girl, Betty Harries, a school-friend of Valerie's, and a teacher of English and drama, and myself.

It was a tribute to Eliot's vitality that, despite the fact that he and Valerie had returned home at 5 a.m. that morning from a celebration party with the cast at the Ecu de France, he was in buoyant spirits. In fact, they found *Life* magazine photographers awaiting them at that early hour, and the result was a much-treasured photograph.

The large ground-floor flat, which was approached through a rather dark vestibule and of which there were no details on the board indicating the occupants, was as warm and well-lit as the Eliot-Hayward ménage was, so far as I had been able to judge, bleak and uninviting. Eliot's sanctum was immediately on the left and the entrance to the sitting-room beyond it. It was a very bright and comfortable room, the mantelpiece crowded with photographs, a Wyndham Lewis on the wall opposite the door, and books, most of them new, on shelves around. As befitted what the Vicar of St Stephen's, Father Jennings, called 'that serenely happy home', the atmosphere was cheerful. We placed our presents on the table. I had discussed with John Betjeman what Eliot might like to receive, and he had suggested a book dating from the 1920s, to remind Eliot of the atmosphere of his first great creative period. Unfortunately I could not find what I wanted. In the end, after consultations at Bertram Rota's, I obtained a copy of Bernard de Fontenelle's *A Plurality of Worlds*, in John Glanville's translation of 1688, published by the Curwen Press. The book was about new astronomical theories, but is so stimulating and diverting to read that I thought Eliot might like it. The slipcase had an attractive silk cover; and when Eliot handled it, he remarked that it was 'like a caress' – a description he would hardly have employed, I fancied, in the days of his enforced bachelorhood. I quoted to him the last words of Fontenelle, who, dying in his hundredth year, and asked what he was feeling, is reputed to have replied: 'Je sens ... une certaine ... difficulté ... de continuer ... de'être', and thereupon died. That it was an appropriate sentence to quote at what was for him a moment of intense living, I am not sure; but he relished the wit, and as he had concluded *The Elder Statesman* with the avowal that death had 'no terrors' for him, it cannot have struck a false note. At one point I found myself sitting next to Mrs Martin Browne, who remarked, what indeed was evident enough, that as a result of the marriage, Eliot was 'happy as a sandboy'; but she added darkly, when the animated conversation made it safe to do so, that 'not everybody' approved of the match. I assumed she was referring to John Hayward, who was describing himself as 'the widow', though later I was to hear some snide remarks from those such as Eric Newton, the art critic. There are some who, out of a kind of general *Weltschmerz*, resent the happiness of others. They wanted to retain the old stereotype of 'unhappy Eliot, choosing his words', of Auden's poem.

Naturally, there was talk of *The Elder Statesman*, and someone – I cannot remember who – remarked how Ivor Brown, in his critique, had expressed the view that no character in real life would have experienced such an intense sense of guilt as Lord Claverton, the protagonist, at having run over a man later found to have been already dead, and in particular at not having stopped (Act III). At least, *he*, Ivor Brown, would not have done so. To which Eliot, after a pause, speaking with his head almost sunk on his chest, murmured slowly: 'Lucky Ivor Brown!' After this, he looked up with a slight smile, which released, like so many of his considered comments, a good deal of merriment.

As the champagne had been flowing steadily, it was time to cut the birthday cake. This had been specially ordered from the Queen's confectioner, with a tribute to 'the great poet'. It was good to think that the purveyors were aware of the presence among them of a great man, as I hardly think those of Notting Hill Gate were aware of Wyndham Lewis. Rupert Hart-Davis proceeded to light the seven candles; and, as the cake had been placed on a low table, Eliot, stationed behind it, promptly dropped to his knees – a movement in which he had had some liturgical practice – and blew them out in quick succession. In his brief account of this gathering in the famous correspondence with George Lyttelton, Rupert Hart-Davis says that he invited Eliot to blow them all out at once. The attempt again elicited applause, and, looking delighted, he exclaimed: 'That's what comes of breathing exercises!' Prompted, I think, by his attractive brunette of a wife, Epstein then proposed a toast. He too seemed to be as happy as a sandboy, because he too had sailed into quiet waters after a somewhat stormy career. One of the women, in a surge of affection, then advanced to put her arms round Eliot, who was on his feet again, and would have landed a smacking kiss, by way of expressing the sentiments of the company, had he not retreated in embarrassment, endeavouring in mock struggle to unwind her arms. I believe he was gratified all the same.

After this, seated in his high-backed chair, he looked cursorily through the book published in his honour for the occasion, edited by Neville Braybrooke, and specially bound in leather. Bending back the covers so as to align the facing pages, he made a token inspection, not without a look of wonder that his work should have given rise to still one more volume of eulogy: for I suppose no poet had had more books written about him in his lifetime.

Eliot, who never liked to be parted from Valerie for very long, insisted on coming to the door with her to say goodbye to us all. But on the way we were taken into the sanctum. He commended it above all for the fact that he had sufficient room to walk about and to reflect: in which respect, it differed from his room at Faber's, and the dreary quarters at Carlyle Mansions. A silver cross in a glass case rested on the mantelpiece, and indeed, in contrast to the sitting-room, the study had about it something of a 'dim religious light'. It was Valerie who, conducting us towards the more secular part of the room, indicated, pinned to some photographs, a certificate and a stetson, which he enjoyed wearing and which signalized the fact that he was an honorary deputy sheriff of Dallas. In other respects the room was a good deal tidier than that at Faber's. I had once mentioned to Eliot, before the war, that Wyndham Lewis's studio in Notting Hill Gate was more ordered than I had expected from one of Lewis's temperament and habits: which prompted him to say that it was certainly tidier than his own room at Father Cheetham's. One wonders how may people did see that room, where he must have spent some of the loneliest hours of his life. Most people, Lewis included, had no idea where he lived; and this all added to the air of mystery which enveloped him. So ended what Eliot described as 'the happiest birthday I've ever known'.

I still did not despair of persuading Eliot and Valerie to come to Turkey, and, as I have said, I may have pressed him a little too hard, as no doubt I underestimated his physical stamina. There is a slight note of reproach in his letter of 18 March 1959, though this was more than balanced by the conclusion:

My dear Tomlin,
    I must apologize for the long delay in answering your letter of the 2nd February, which is the less excusable as my secretary forwarded it to me in Nassau. I was, however, living a very lazy life. I had no typewriter with me and much dislike having to rely upon penmanship, and I hoped that you would realise by my absence that a visit to Ankara in April would be impossible. I am very sorry about this. For public reasons I should particularly like to be able to pay a visit to Turkey at the present time, but I am

afraid it is quite out of the question. And I am arranging to pay another visit to the United States next October, so the whole of this year is impossible for other engagements abroad. I do realise the importance of such visits to Ankara at the present time and am deeply regretful that I cannot come.

With most affectionate and cordial good wishes,
    Yours ever,
      T.S. Eliot.

In reply, I stressed how glad I was to learn that he was living 'a lazy life', because he had more than earned it. I explained, not perhaps in the most convincing manner, that I had once more raised the subject of a Turkish visit on the off chance that he might be returning from Nassau 'by a route within reach of this part of the world'. In the years when, so far as physical energy is concerned, nothing seems too difficult, one does not pause to reflect that a man twenty-five years older and not in the best of health, cannot be expected to undertake such an extra excursion. Indeed, it may have been unfeeling and selfish of me even to have hinted at the idea; but I knew he had a conscience about public service, and, if I played on it, it was from what I thought to be the best of motives.

Not long after there arrived a copy of *The Elder Statesman*. It was inscribed:

With affectionate greetings
T.S. Eliot.

In the same letter I had announced that in June I was to pay my first visit to the United States. This was to attend the Harvard International Seminar, which was directed by a man with a growing academic reputation but scarcely known to the outside world, Henry Kissinger. In his next letter, dated 4 June 1959, Eliot provided me with the opportunity of meeting relations and friends of his; and this was to prove so rewarding and pleasurable as well as informative, as to add an extra dimension to this memoir.

Dear Tomlin,

I must apologize for my delay in thanking you for your letter of May 11th, the last paragraph of which gave me much pleasure. If you have not already left for the United States and are to be at Harvard, I should like you to look up my sister-in-law, Mrs. Henry Ware Eliot of 84, Prescott Street, Cambridge, Massachusetts, who is extremely hospitable and would like to introduce you to other friends and relatives. I blame myself for not having answered your letter at once, but it arrived while I was away for a week in Yorkshire and the accumulation of arrears even in that short time produced confusion.

There are other people I should like you to meet if they are in Cambridge or Boston during that sultry period, when most of the people who can, go away to the mountains or the sea.
        Yours sincerely,
        T.S. Eliot.

Not long after the arrival of this letter, I received another. Although in length it was one of the briefest, in content it was one of the most gratifying that I was to receive from him. To reproduce it may seem an exercise in vanity, but its omission would amount to false modesty, though I still think that he somewhat overestimated my achievements. On 17 June, he wrote:

My dear Tomlin,
    I am delighted to see your name in the Honours List, but having some information of all that you have done in the service of the British Council and thinking of your other merits and achievements of which officialdom is perhaps ignorant, I wish that it might have been a higher honour.
        Yours ever,
        T.S. Eliot.

I sailed to Boston in high spirits and expectations. Nor were these disappointed. On Theresa Eliot, I paid an early call, and found that Eliot's description of her as 'very hospitable' was no exaggeration. I still think of her as possessing as sunny a temperament as almost anyone I have known; and well past middle life, she remained an extremely attractive woman. Within a short time she had introduced me to the 'Eliot circle', as well as to a group of people, young and old, of immense vitality and shared interests. Were this my autobiography, I would give abundant reasons for describing my stay at Cambridge, Mass., as 'a golden time', in Wordworth's sense. Theresa enjoyed nothing so much as talking about her brother-in-law, and it was obvious that they had always go on extremely well together. From her vantage-point on the other side of the Atlantic, she gave me a new insight into his background, his character and the growth of his reputation, of which she was very proud. For example, she described how in St Louis, Missouri, the Eliot who first made a name for himself was Henry Ware Eliot, her husband, who took up archaeology after retiring from business; but then there began to trickle back from Europe news of another Eliot who was being talked about in drawing-rooms and even in the papers as an advanced writer, a new voice in literature. And not merely did Thomas Stearns Eliot become increasingly known in St Louis, which even so never quite grasped even at his death what a great man he was, but wherever writers were talked about in the United States and in the English-speaking world and beyond.

At the same time she told me that the brothers never enjoyed quite the rapport that can make fraternal relations so fruitful, even though Henry came to take pride in his brother's success and was convinced of his genius – hence the letter he wrote to the authorities at the time of the Blitz. Eliot was also much attached to his sisters, of whom one, Marian, survived.

As I spent hours in Theresa's company, and as I became convinced that her word was to be relied on, what I record of her conversation enjoys a particular authenticity. Of Emily Hale she told me a good deal. It would seem that at one point Eliot did give her to understand that, if Vivien were to die (but in no other circumstances), he would marry her. Consequently, she began to go about as if she were his fiancée presumptive, and she would dutifully kiss the members of the Eliot family – at a time when the bestowal of kisses was by no means so free as it is now – almost as if she were already an in-law. Theresa, otherwise the kindest of souls, found this conduct rather irritating. In fact, so insistent was Emily that she was to all intents and purposes the next Mrs T. S. Eliot, that Henry felt obliged to write to his brother not merely to report her behaviour but to enquire whether there was any basis for it. Somewhat to his surprise, he received a reply confirming that there was. This letter has not survived. So incensed was Henry by it that he tore it up, making the comment, 'Tom has made one mistake, and if he marries Emily he will make another'. At any rate, the testimony it contained may explain the terms of one at least of Eliot's letters to Mary Trevelyan, in reply to her suggestion, the second of its kind, that they should get married. He wrote a lengthy answer, hinting at an earlier attachment, which cannot be other than that with Emily Hale.

There must have come a moment, however, when the relationship

– at one time semi-idyllic, as some references in *The Family Reunion*, a play in which she claimed to have a hand, show – began to turn sour. Theresa described occasions in which the two 'got across' each other in conversation, so that when Emily left, Eliot would frown theatrically and clench his fists in mock irritation, conveying by exaggeration the very real exasperation he felt. This made me recall his remarks about women wanting a thing and therefore considering it right, and that friendship with women was delightful up to a point, but that the point was so often in advance of that which the man considered desirable.

Although Eliot liked to keep closely in touch with Theresa – as the stream of postcards she showed me signified – she expressed disappointment on two matters. He had shared with her so many confidences – often over washing-up, which he seemed to enjoy sharing with her as well – that she confessed to being hurt at not being admitted to his confidence on the subject of his engagement. In fact, secrecy was paramount. The only Americans he told beforehand were his sister Marian and Emily Hale herself. In England, he did not even tell the Fabers.

The other disappointment was even more personal. She had arranged to take Henry's ashes to the cemetery – I do not remember whether for depositing or scattering – and she had assumed that Eliot would accompany her. Perhaps some misunderstanding had occurred. Not long after, Eliot preparing to go out, announced: 'I've got to get something over with'. He then departed with no further explanation. When he returned late in the day, he told her of his mission. He had nerved himself to tell Emily that all thought of marriage between them must be forgotten. Theresa enquired how she had reacted, and he answered that on the whole she had taken it very well. No doubt she had for some time noticed a change in his manner. The news of his second marriage could not therefore have been the shock to her it has been made out to be. Eliot avowed to Theresa that he would be prepared to 'kill himself' (those were his words) if Emily insisted on marriage. But Theresa felt a trifle disappointed that he had not accompanied her on her own mission. 'But then', as she exclaimed with a shrug, 'he's not like other men'. How true. One day he had said to her, as if out of the blue: 'I want someone to love me for myself, not because I am T. S. Eliot'.

She once told me to try, if I could, to have a look at the letters exchanged between the two brothers, because she felt these would throw an interesting new light, especially on Tom. I asked her where they were to be found, and from her slightly enigmatic answer I gathered that she had meant 'when they become available'.

When Henry Eliot came to England in the summer of 1921, preceding by some weeks the arrival of his mother and his sister Marian, he found, according to Theresa, that his brother was paying rent for at least two other forms of accommodation, apart from the flat in Clarence Gate Gardens. Although the marriage had not collapsed, its conduct had been distributed over several locations. Again according to Theresa, Henry had wound up more than one of these *pieds-à-terre* and had paid off the landlords. This might suggest that Eliot was an unsystematic muddler, who needed someone to put his house or houses in order; but the truth was that Vivien – and I am told that this is a well-known psychological condition – had developed the habit of repeatedly moving house, with the result that her husband became increasingly 'harassed'. That was the word he used to me when speaking of this period. Henry was a source of strength to him at this crucial time, which was that of the gestation of *The Waste Land*. When Theresa spoke of her husband's qualities and generous character, tears would sometimes come into her eyes.

It was through Theresa, and at Eliot's express wish, that I met two other women of the circle, the inner circle. The first was Marian Eliot, his surviving sister, who lived at 83 Brattle Street, Cambridge. On meeting her, the first thing that struck me was that she was a typical Eliot with neither the anguish nor a spark of the genius. She was a tall, rather plain yet serenely-aging spinster, who seemed content with her limitations of mind and resource. I first called on her on one of the sultriest of sultry Cambridge days of which Eliot had spoken in his letter; and she was sitting in statuesque manner beside a contraption which seemed to do duty for air-conditioning. It purred by her side much like a substitute pet. On my remarking how well it functioned, she said quietly: 'Taam gave it me.' It was as if she had sat there day after day enduring the heat until he had arrived, the beloved brother, to provide her with welcome relief. She spoke of him straightforwardly, without a trace of fulsomeness, but with obvious admiration, even though she did not appear fully to understand how his great reputation had descended on him and the family. Cambridge, as the street signs indicated, was already famous for its Eliots. The quality which she shared with him was simplicity – the simplicity that Alec Rowse had tried to define at our first meeting, if not quite successfully; for it is assumed that a great intellect must at the same time be a complicated character, whereas Eliot was very much the reverse.

From Marian I learnt few new facts about Eliot, nor did I go to see her with a view to ferreting out information. But from the unaffected way she talked about him, I formed a view of him which was compatible with my own observations and which directly contradicted some of the notions he had put out about himself. The aboulia or emotional remoteness from which, in a letter to Richard Aldington at the end of 1921, he maintained that he had long suffered, and the 'dry stick' picture of him which others had circulated, and upon which some of the obituaries were to draw: these were, in my view, myths. That Marian's account should stress his Americanism was perhaps inevitable; and it was interesting that, late in life, Eliot, who was devoted to England and had served his adopted country so well, should have laid emphasis upon the essentially American sources of his poetic inspiration. I always liked to think of him as an Anglo-American.

The other friend from childhoood I met was a very different character. His cousin, Eleanor Hinkley, lived at 1 Berkeley Place, Cambridge. She was highly talented, witty, vivacious, sophisticated woman, herself an author (she had written a play on the Brontës), who today might have become a familiar face on television. From her I saw the other side of Eliot, the vanished side: that of the lively good-looking young man, who enjoyed good company, picnics, boating, charades, theatricals, as well as the boy who would 'curl up in the window-seat, behind the *Encyclopaedia Britannica*'. Whereas Marian seemed somewhat lacking in humour, except of the quiet kind that tended to go unnoticed, Eleanor was most amusing company. In talking to her, I realized that she viewed him almost exclusively from her own side of the world, and that the problems he had encountered as a married man over on the distant, 'decadent' continent were beyond her comprehension. When I spoke of the unhappiness, the *ayenbyte of inwit*, which had gnawed at him until his second marriage, she looked a little blank and did not respond (not that I used that Anglo-Saxon phrase). It was an Eliot she could only with extreme difficulty reconcile with the youthful figure who had moved in with his family to New England from St Louis, Missouri. For our view of people tends to remain fixed at the point of our most vivid encounter.

Although Theresa put so much time at my disposal, there were several other 'New England ladies', as I found myself calling them, who gave me hospitality and, in the American manner passed me on to others: so much so that if I were to record every Eliot association or allusion this memoir would become inconveniently long. I ought not to forget Fanny Butcher (Bokum) of the *Chicago Tribune*, something of an Eliot expert: for after the Harvard Seminar I endeavoured to cover as much of the United States as I could; and penetration of Chicago society proved more difficult than that of Cambridge, Massachusetts. Similarly, Henrietta Buckmaster, the novelist, entertained me in New York with conversation about Eliot which I found interesting for its revelation of how America and Americans liked to feel that they possessed Eliot.

Finally, there was Marianne Moore, born the year before Eliot in St Louis, Missouri, for whom he had a particularly tender spot. I saw her on only one occasion, but this visit extended to a long afternoon at her humble one-room flat at 260 Cumberland Street in the heart of Brooklyn. She thought the world of her fellow-townsman, and seemed content to spend the whole of the time talking about him. As she had just suffered a minor stroke, she was taking the advice she had been given not to concentrate too much on herself, the result being that she talked of everything but her own work, to which I had endeavoured to divert the conversation. I recalled Eliot's disappointment that his edition of her poetry had had poor sales; but at the end of her life, she deservedly became something of a national celebrity; and I was glad that, despite her fears about health, she lived into her 86th year, which was a decade longer than Eliot, who, according to Stravinsky, had hoped that his own life might be correspondingly prolonged. And so it went on, as in America, with so many warm-hearted people around it does.

Before returning to Turkey, I gave Eliot an account of my stay; and on 24 September 1959, he wrote me a letter which much reassured me, as the recipient of kindness and hospitality sometimes wonders whether he or she has managed to earn even a small part of it.

My dear Tomlin,
   I have just received two days ago your letter of the 20th. I heard much of your visit to Harvard from my relatives and gather that you were a popular visitor there, so I had hoped that you yourself had enjoyed your stay. I am dreadfully distressed that we cannot see you while you are here, but your visit is so very brief and unfortunately we are going to the seaside on Friday until next Tuesday which leaves no time at all; and we have to sail to New York on the 8th October. But I gather that you are leaving on Wednesday next in any case, and that leaves the margin not narrow but invisible. I am so very sorry and hope that you will write and let me know how your work is progressing and when you will next be in London.
      Ever affectionately,
      T.S.E.

The truth was that, once having tasted life in the United States and especially in New York, I was anxious to return. I wanted to complete the successor to *Living and Knowing*, and naturally I wished to be able to place it before Eliot while he remained at Faber's and this, it seemed to me, could not be for very much longer. Three steps had to be taken: I needed to apply for a sabbatical year; I needed to finance myself; and I needed somewhere to undertake research and to work. The British Council was generous about the first; Herbert Read and Allen Tate were kind enough to back me for a Bollingen Fellowship, which would cover part of the cost; and Eliot, with his valuable contacts, more or less fixed me up with the third. His letter of 18 December 1959 set out the possibilities, after definitely and understandably closing the door on a visit to Turkey. I had by that time surrendered to pressure, while realizing that I was virtually asking for the impossible, which is why I did not seek a reply to my October letter.

My dear Tomlin,
   I took you at your word in not answering your letter of the 23rd October. I find it almost impossible to write letters when in America as the fatigue of seeing so many people without intermission is very great, and the conditions of a visit such as I pay not favourable to calm thinking. I am afraid that your appeal again is in vain, and I am beginning to wonder whether I shall ever wish to face official visits of any kind again. I dare say that

occasions of necessity will occur, but I tend to avoid travel when I can. I am sad, however, to think that in all the time you have been in Ankara I have never once backed you up in this way in your British Council work.

If there is anything I can do to help you get a suitable invitation to America do let me know. I don't know whether the Institute of Advanced Studies in Princeton would consider that your work was of a kind which they should promote, or whether the Committee on Social Thought at Chicago University would be interested. Do let me know whether you get the sabbatical year, and if so what steps you propose to take to turn it to the best advantage.

With most cordial and affectionate good wishes from both of us,
>> Yours ever,
>> T.S. Eliot.

I gave him the information he wanted in a letter dated 3 January 1960, and I was touched that, despite his poor health, he should forthwith have taken action. It is now clear that he was very much indisposed, and the Morocco visit, with all its promise, was ruined by the effects of the Agadir earthquake. On 28 January 1960, he wrote:

My dear Tomlin,

We have just got back from a few weeks at the seaside, not very satisfactory on account of bad weather, and are just off for several weeks in Morocco which, I am told is the ideal climate for people with my bronchial weakness. I have written to my friend Professor John Nef, the head of the Committee on Social Thought, at the University of Chicago, and also to Dr. Robert Oppenheimer at the Princeton Institute, commending you and expressing the hope that your studies are such as the Institute desires to promote. I can't tell you anything about the Yale University Press, but it would be certainly worth while your approaching them or any one you know in that University, with suggestions. I do think that some institution in America ought to find a place for you for your year of leave.

In haste,
>> Yours ever affectionately,
>> T.S. Eliot.

In due course, I learnt that I had been granted the prized Bollingen Fellowship, which rendered the visit feasible. On 20 July 1960, I received the following letter:

> Dear Mr. Tomlin,
>
> Mr. Eliot has asked me to write to you on his behalf, since he is away from the office at present, to thank you for your letter of July 12th, and to express his warm congratulations to you on receiving a grant from the Bollingen Foundation. He is delighted to hear this news.
>
> He very much hopes that there will be an opportunity of seeing you when you pass through London.
> > Yours sincerely,
> > Angela Miles.
> > Secretary to Mr. T.S. Eliot.

The day before my second embarkation for the United States I dined with the Eliots at their flat. Having them to themselves was a particularly interesting and illuminating experience. Already in the United States Theresa had told me of the little ceremony which, in the Eliot household, preceded every meal; and so when at table Valerie rose to her feet, I followed suit. Placing his hand on her shoulder and reciting a grace familiar from my youngest days – 'Bless this food to our use, and us to Thy service' – he kissed her on the cheek with studied precision. Indeed, all through the evening the signs of mutual affection were so obvious as, paradoxically, not to intrude, still less to embarrass. He needed her presence. When she occasionally absented herself, in connection with serving the meal, she stroked his hand several times in succession, in order, so to speak, to build up a credit of reassurance on which he could draw until her turn. 'Holding each other by the hand which betokeneth concord', he had quoted in *East Coker* in surely one of the most beautiful passages he ever wrote. With him the concord was meant literally 'of one heart' or 'heart to heart' which, as I know from something Valerie later showed me, he was convinced would endure beyond the grave. Otherwise he declared that he would have preferred 'extinction'. He had never before been really in love, or could have imagined that, in his lifetime, he would enter upon such a *vita nuova*.

Not for a moment must it be thought that this final idyll bereft him of his old down-to-earth commonsense. After alluding once more to the letters he had received from relatives about my Harvard visit, he gave me some very sound advice about the one which lay ahead. There had been no place vacant for me at Princeton, despite Eliot's letter to Oppenheimer, but I had been fortunate in securing one at the University of Chicago, in the rather oddly named Committee on Social Thought, of which the Director was a friend of Eliot's, John Nef. Eliot knew the latter's habit of making use of his protégés for lectures and other activities – 'rather like Middleton Murry', he said – because that generous man wished to turn the Committee into a kind of intellectual brotherhood; whereas, as Eliot said to me, looking earnestly across the table 'You want to get on with your work'. He was right : I did. In point of fact, John Nef was most kind to me throughout my stay, and I pushed on with *The Concept of Life*, in which Eliot continued to show interest.

The conversation touched on lawyers, and he ruminated on the need to arrange matters so as to leave Valerie with an ordered estate and the minimum of worries. To express one's wishes in a detailed and intelligent way had not proved easy. The subject of Lawrence Durrell coming up, he spoke of Larry's impish habit of sending slightly unusual presents through the post. One, a wedding gift, had consisted of two ceramic figures of French peasants who gave the impression that they were about to – here a peculiar psychological black-out overtook me; for although I fancied he said 'fuck', the unexpectedness of such a word coming from his lips somehow momentarily deleted it from my consciousness. In fact, the word he used was 'pee', because he went on to say: 'All you could see were two pink bottoms', pronouncing those last three words in plosive staccato. Valerie had looked round at him as he entered into that description, as if mildly surprised at his frankness. It must also be remembered that all this took place before the 1960s, with their cult of explicitness in speech and writing, much of which was, however, a form of prudery *a rebours*. I still cannot envisage what sort of toy this was, but it must have been what used to be called *risqué*, because Eliot expressed mild apprehension as to what the porter or the refuse-collectors might think of it. In fact, the porter, thinking that it had been thrown out by mistake, returned it, which gave them all a good laugh.

Since the *Lady Chatterley* case, Eliot had been pressed by certain publishing houses to lend his name and authority to the issue of certain books which no publisher would formerly have dreamt of touching. He had been surprised by the bizarre works which some literary editors, scenting the possibility of huge profits, had hope he might grace with his imprimatur. One in particular, submitted by a well-known director, he described as absolutely disgusting and totally lacking in literary merit; a reaction which greatly disappointed that would-be social benefactor. He had told me years before that he could not abide the post-war American 'realistic' novel.

Realizing that I should be away for some time, though in the land of his birth, Eliot began to reminisce about our first meeting. I was amazed at his recollection of the handwritten wad of paper I had sent up to Faber's in youthful ardour, excoriating Rowse's book, and I said so. I also stressed how much his reference to my Lawrence essay in *After Strange Gods* had meant to me at Oxford, and he commented that the book had done rather badly, and he was against its being reissued. Bearing in mind Leavis's description of this volume as 'Eliot's book on whoring', I suggested in lighthearted vein that had he had given it the fuller title, it might have done better. He failed to take in quite what I meant; and there was another occasion, when Valerie had to intervene with a 'No, Tom', that I realized for the first time that his memory was beginning to deteriorate. We talked about Hugh Kenner's book *The Invisible Poet* (1960), which neither of us had read; but it led to his saying apropos of some comment: 'I am *not* a scholar', looking straight in front of him, as if announcing the fact to the world at large.

I did not in any case wish to stay late, because I needed to be off at the crack of dawn, and I noticed that he tired easily; but I said I wanted to send him a record I thought he would enjoy. Although I was starting off in Chicago, I hoped to spend a little time in Cambridge, Mass., and to see my friends again. This led Eliot to remark that it was people like Theresa, originally from Kentucky, who had enlivened his Puritanical New England family. 'They warmed us up', he said, followed by his chuckle. The phrase pleased him so much that he repeated it.

I kept him informed of my various peregrinations, for after leaving Chicago, I spent some time in California. It was there that news arrived from the British Council of my appointment to take over the work in Japan. On 14 July 1961, Eliot wrote to me at the California Institute of Technology, Pasadena, where I was doing some research for *The Concept of Life*:

Dear Frederick,

Thank you for your good letter from California. I had no idea that your travels were going to extend so far. I am delighted primarily for your sake but also for the sake of John Nef's Committee that your visit to Chicago was so very satisfactory.

It is refreshing to hear from you that you have been getting on with your book and I look forward to the manuscript turning up at the moment when you feel it is ripe.

I doubt if we are likely to meet on American soil. We are leaving for New York on the 5th October at the earliest, but it may be that we shall arrange to go much later and be there into December. I do wish however that we could have a talk about your experiences, but when can that be? We hope to arrange again to have two winter months in the Caribbean if I can finance it and it rather looks as if you might be off to Japan by that time. In that case there would be no hope of seeing you for a year or more. So do let me know if you can how long you will be in England on returning before leaving to take up your new post.

With all best wishes,
   Yours affectionately,
   T.S. Eliot.

Meanwhile, shortly after the dinner at 3 Kensington Court Gardens, I had arranged with my sister, Esther, who had met Eliot at Wychwood all those years ago, that a record called *The Best of Sellers* – which was indeed Peter Sellers at his best – should be sent to him. I knew that he would like it; for, except for the occasional umbrella, which he appreciated, he tended to be presented with things – books especially – of a solemn nature. It was therefore delightful to learn that the Sellers record proved such a success with him. But above all his extreme kindness and solicitude in penning a letter at a time when, as he had previously made clear, longhand was becoming laborious to him, was something both of us could never appreciate enough. As to the final sentence, my work, such as it is, must make its own way. I would not have missed my life, and the question is whether there will be time to add what I still want to say.

JAMAICA INN
Ocho Rios Jamaica, W.I.

17 Jan. 1962

Dear Miss Tomlin,

I hope you will excuse my delay in writing to thank you for sending us the Peter Sellers record. We left England on December 28, and with the usual Christmas occupations and duties and our preparations for two months' absence, we are only now beginning to write our thanking letters. Do please let Frederick know, when you next write, that we have enjoyed the record very much; it will amuse us and our guests for a long time to come.

I do hope your brother is enjoying his stay at the University of Chicago, and particularly that he will be able to get on with his own work. It has grieved me that his original contributions to philosophy, which I value highly, have been so hampered by his official life.

With best wishes and thanks from my wife and myself,

    Yours sincerely,
    T.S. Eliot.

Miss Esther Tomlin,
27B St. Swithun Street,
Winchester,
England.

CHAPTER TEN

As my sabbatical year drew to a close, I duly returned to Cambridge, Mass., and spent some time in the two great Harvard Libraries, the Weidener and the Houghton. The latter housed the Eliot collection. With the permission of the custodian, I was there made free of a mass of correspondence, notes, diaries, etc. – the only ban, which I strictly observed, being that placed on the typescript of the Clark Lectures on the Metaphysical Poets, with which Eliot had declared himself dissatisfied. There were some interesting discoveries. I came upon a letter to Harriet Monroe, written in the early days of the first marriage, which spoke ironically of 'my happiness with Vivien'. I also came across a typescript of *The Waste Land* – not the famous 'lost' one which turned up some years later from John Quinn's collection in the New York Public Library – but evidently an intermediate version. Here I spotted a line which had not been included in the first printed version – 'The ivory men make company between us' (from 'A Game of Chess'), which the Librarian reported to Eliot by letter. I learnt later that this had been deleted at Vivien's request, but Eliot remembered it. Some diaries – that is to say, of the commercial variety, with a small space for each day – contained notes of his first continental visits; I observed how much detailed attention he had given to works of art, and how frequently he had recourse to such phrases as 'superior to' and 'inferior to', as one value-judgment displaced another. A long letter from George Saintsbury on *Homage to John Dryden* must have made fascinating reading, save that its illegibility, raised to the level of fine art, totally defied decipherment. No greater contrast could there have been with Eliot's own hand, which, from one end of his literary career to the other, maintained an elegance few other great writers could parallel, and which on the calligraphic plane seemed the ideal notation for a prose so shaped and spare.

Before leaving for New York and home, I said goodbye to Theresa and to the Eliot circle. With her I remained in contact for years. So did my sister – who met her a little later – until, as age dimmed her memory, she seemed to compound us both and sent to Esther regular Christmas greetings right into her nineties. The last full letter she wrote me, conveying congratulations on my appointment to a professorship at the University of Nice, concluded: 'I remember your visits here with joy'. She was a rare and radiant spirit, and she was ageless. One could easily have fallen in love with her, had not one found another American taking precedence.

All my luggage and notes on philosophy, science and on Eliot, were sent direct from Los Angeles to Tokyo. Japan opened a new world for me, and a new approach to Eliot too; for here was a land which revered his work even more than some European countries. Although in certain respects the *oeuvre* presented great difficulties for the Japanese, their extraordinary intuitive and empathetic gifts made other aspects immediately accessible. From the start I found myself in demand for lectures, readings, elucidations and recollections. Japan, with its Wasteland Publishing Company and other associated bodies, was an Eliot country, just as she was a Shakespeare, a Toynbee and a Blunden country; and so although we were parted by thousands of miles, I felt I had entered upon a new kind of proximity. And the fact that Valerie was looking after him in a manner that must have seemed to him little short of a daily miracle, afforded a comparable contentment to his friends.

Of course I wrote to him of my experiences; but I knew enough about the precarious state of his health not to suggest that he should reply or any longer that he should pay a visit to a country that otherwise would have fascinated him. It was true. This was a time when, as some exchanges with Philip Mairet make clear, he was taking increasing interest in such subjects as Zen Buddhism. Some of my colleagues urged me to make one last plea that he should be asked to come out to give some readings; but I knew that it was out of the question. True, he was the greatest living writer in any language, and everybody wanted to meet him; but from visitors like Alan Pryce-Jones and Henry and Pamela Sherek (a mine of information about the Eliots) I was confirmed in my surmise that he should no longer be disturbed, even by the kind of adulation that he had not merely never sought but for which he had long passed beyond caring.

It was sufficiently satisfactory for me to receive, apart from the regular Christmas card, such letters as that written by his secretary on 7 February, 1963:

> Dear Professor Tomlin,
>
> Mr. Eliot has asked me to write and tell you how very interested he was to receive your letter and to say that he is sorry to be unable to write himself for the time being. Unfortunately he was unable to escape the rigours of this winter and he has been in hospital for five weeks. However, he is now making a good recovery while convalescing at home and is enjoying your Peter Sellers records particularly at this time.
>
> He asked me too, to send you a copy of his essay on George Herbert which I now enclose.
>
> Yours sincerely,
> Pamela Barker.

This was followed by a similar letter dated 28 March, which confirmed that he and Valerie were in Bermuda, but that they hoped we might all meet in the summer, when, as I had informed them on 7 March, I was due for home leave.

Meanwhile, I had enjoyed the opportunity of paying official visits to the Philippines, to Korea, to Vietnam, and to India; and in all of these highly receptive countries, I lectured, among much else, on Eliot. On All India Radio on 6 June 1963, I gave what I believe to have been one of my best efforts in that sphere. But then India was a special case, as I soon discovered. Never was it brought home to me more compellingly how much these peoples, not least the Vietnamese in their heart-breaking struggle against an oppressor with whom many 'intellectuals' among their American allies expressed their sympathy, valued the arts, and above all the art of poetry: not as a snobbish distraction but as a psychic need, a nourishment of the spirit. Many years later, when I wrote a book called *Psyche, Culture and the New Science* (1985), I based my advocacy of what I called 'psychic nutrition' largely on the experiences I underwent in the turbulent countries of south-east Asia. I realized that art either promoted the sacred view of life – which was to give life the only meaning that renders it worth living – or it was not art at all, but rather a disguise for what I called neg-PN (negative Psychic Nutrition), usually a compound of the violent and the erotic, the staple fare of the media in most Western countries. It seemed to me that Eliot's poetry was the most powerful counterweight in my time to this ugliest of trends, and his whole outlook a reassertion of the traditional values by which the great writers and artists have lived and worked.

As this is a memoir but not my memoirs, I forebear to enter into detail about a new development, namely the beginning of my slow but profound disillusionment with the direction my organization was taking, and in due course, after the departure of Sir Paul Sinker, with the authority that presided over its activities. These matters can be safely left to the other volume I have long contemplated, in which Eliot's ideas, rather than recollections of the man himself, will play their part, unless death should meanwhile overtake me.

A letter dated 23 August 1963, handwritten by Eliot's secretary, signalized the arrangements for the next meeting; a very special one.

> Dear Professor Tomlin,
> Mrs. Eliot would be delighted if you could dine with them on Wednesday, 4th September at 7 p.m. – no dinner jacket. The Allen Tates are going to be there and Mr. and Mrs. Eliot very much hope you will be able to dine as well.
> Yours sincerely,
> Pamela Barker.

Since meeting him at Harvard in 1959, I had seen Allen Tate several times, and, now that he was to come to England in 1963, I was able to meet him for the first time on my own ground. So far as I was concerned, he was a kind friend; but I soon realized that he had many enemies, and there were scandalous tales circulating about his sexual adventures, which his conversion or reversion to Roman Catholicism had done nothing to curtail. Whenever I met him, from Harvard onwards, he was either winding up a marriage or embarking on a new one. Yet for one who had acquired such expertise in the field, he seemed strangely imperceptive about the intimate life of others.

His Catholicism entailed a naively empirical view of transubstantiation which would have satisfied the most ultramontane Counter Reformation theologian; and from a reference he made to a conversation with Eliot on the subject, the latter had shown mild surprise at such a literal interpretation. But although he made some joking remarks about Eliot's reincarnation as a beach-boy on the sands of Barbados, Bermuda or Jamaica, he sincerely revered

Eliot both as a man and as a writer, as his published remarks after the poet's death testify. He told me that he had once asked Eliot how he personally accounted for the immense impact he had made on his contemporaries, and Eliot had replied that it was largely a matter of technique. Allen could not agree; nor could I. It was infinitely more than that. Eliot initiated an intellectual and spiritual change of *Weltanschauung*.

As Peter Ackroyd has pointed out in his biography, from the year 1962 friends had begun to notice a change in Eliot's physiognomy; and when I saw him on that Wednesday, in September 1963, the alteration was indeed a shock. This could be attributed to cortisone. But it was not so much the physiognomy as the posture, which was a good deal more bowed. True, his face was fuller and much less lined that I remembered previously; and to that extent he looked better. He still insisted on accompanying Valerie to the front door, partly because he disliked being separated from her, even for a moment, but also perhaps because, even in his weakness, he wanted to show that he would be ready to defend her against any form of assault. I recalled his vehement exclamation against the attacks by Greeks on English women in Cyprus, which seemed to him to disqualify anybody from saying a good word (as I had) for that tormented but beautiful island. I then realized that, on his own, he walked with difficulty, holding on with each hand to the high beading, which by happy chance ran at a convenient height along the corridors of the flat.

The change of posture from the tall, impressive figure to one that appeared to be breaking down beyond recovery was in some measure modified when he took his usual seat to the right of the hearth. This permitted him to resume the inclined, meditative posture which had become habitual to him, just as over the table he leaned forward over his plate, though at a more pronounced angle. What I noticed once again on the positive side was that, apart from an encroaching greyness, his hair was as abundant as ever, seeming to be disposed at several levels, which the absence of hair-oil, long discontinued, served to accentuate.

My fellow-guests included Lady Epstein as well as the Tates. Valerie had begun to tell me of the alarming evening of the previous November, when, four days before they were to leave for the Caribbean, he had been taken desperately ill. It was during one of the worst spells of smog in London (a problem that had been building up over a decade); and the miasma had evidently penetrated even through closely-shut windows. It was night and she was all alone. She put him to bed, finding him confused. For hours she was obliged to hold him up. Although she tried to kick the telephone off the mantelpiece in order to summon help, without letting go of him, his great weight (something the hospital remarked upon) made this impossible. Moreover, his doctor was away, and it was not until morning that she succeeded in getting through to the Brompton Hospital. It was the obvious place to take him. It was an extremely anxious moment, and she never thought he would pull through. But an ambulance soon arrived. He rallied and spent weeks in hospital, breathing oxygen. Even so, he had been well enough in March to go to Bermuda.

Although Valerie later told me that during the last two years of his life, she had more or less taken over everything, it was certainly not true that he had become a vegetable. Even if his memory showed signs of faltering, his mind was still active, and on this occasion he was in good spirits. He tried to make some comparison between Heine and Hölderlin, quoting Heine in German; but he seemed to lose the thread of what he was saying, and none of us present was sufficiently instructed to help him out. Possibly it had been connected with automatic writing, because he went on to relate how Herbert Read, compiling a new volume of his work for Faber's, had wanted to include some of his own efforts in that category, but 'I said, "*No*, Herbert" ' Eliot enunciated decisively; and the proposal had been (fortunately, I think) dropped. In the course of the evening Eliot and Allen Tate, by a series of perverse synchronicities, initiated a remark at exactly the same moment; and this would prompt Isabella to issue an admonitory '*Allen*!', so that Eliot might be allowed priority. This, to his credit, Allen, though slightly irritated by his wife's interventions (they were soon to part), acquiesced in with a good grace.

Little escaped Eliot's attention, and his hearing was still remarkably good. I was saying something to Valerie about Japan – a subject of which I was full – and he caught the words 'tea ceremony' across the table. His interest was immediately aroused. I think I explained briefly what it was all about; and I again realized how, if the opportunity had arisen, he would have been enthralled by that beautiful country, as Japan in turn would have taken him to herself. That she has now done so I realized when I returned there in 1986.

After the meal, I wandered down, as on the day before my second visit to the United States, to the recesses of the flat, and washed my hands in the matrimonial bedroom. I noticed the large oxygen cylinder beside the bed on the left, and I realized that the emphysema had reached a stage where a crisis, perhaps the ultimate crisis, might occur at any moment. The remarkable circumstance was that not merely was Eliot to pay another, if final, visit to the land of his birth, but that he was to live another year beyond that.

He certainly kept up with the news. He spoke bitterly of the case of Stephen Ward and the Profumo scandal, then the talk of the town, which seemed to him to reveal evidence of serious corruption in public life; and, when the women were absent, he was scathing about Kenneth Tynan, whom he found it difficult to forgive for reviewing *The Elder Statesman* and quoting lines not in the acting version. He also berated Tynan and Angus Wilson for the letter they had written defending Ward. In fact, his judgments were much more forthright than in the days when he tended to issue pronouncements with perhaps excessive caution. (There was a story circulating before the war that, when asked in company to make a statement on some contentious issue, on which most of the intelligentsia had come down on one side (the left), he had lowered his head, studied his shoes for some time, and then declared after seemingly immense cogitation: 'It is very difficult ... to form ... an opinion.') That evening his choice and flow of words were still remarkable, and there were touches of the old dry wit. He returned to the theme of Leavis and Lawrence. This had given him a good deal of concern in his last years, because Leavis, who had virtually deified Lawrence, never forgave him for describing that writer as spiritually sick. Indeed, this hostility had gone so far that Leavis, backed by Queenie, had issued instructions that Eliot was never to be admitted to the house, as if Eliot would conceivably have arrived on their Cambridge doorstep without prior notice. What Eliot complained of was that neither Lawrence nor Leavis had any sense of humour; and in this I think he hit the nail on the head.

One minor subject that arose after dinner, I forget how, was the quality of American beer. This especially livened Eliot up, as a relief from the sustained intellectual conversation of which he grew increasingly tired. Declaring that he had never acquired a taste for Budweiser, he began, much to our surprise, to break into verse – doggerel (the lines must be familiar to Americans), of which he could recall only scraps. One which I remember, enjoined the listener not to

> . . . . . tarnish
> Your palate with such varnish.

But again, though he enjoyed light verse and had a marked talent for it, he found, after repeating the fragment several times, that he could recollect no more. This caused him exasperation, though fortunately not distress; and so it went on through the evening. We were prevented from feeling awkward because he was obviously enjoying himself in his quiet way, and there were never any agonizing pauses.

What presented a rather touching sight was Eliot, though unsteady on his feet, moving slowly round the table and pouring out the wine. Otherwise I saw that Valerie had begun to treat him as an invalid. She was a most cheerful hostess; and I could see that he lived off her infectious *joie de vivre*, which must have sustained him years longer than the doctors had believed it possible for him to survive. She told me that she was hoping to install some kind of air-conditioning as a precaution against another smoggy winter.

In describing the evening, Allen Tate speaks of Eliot standing in the vestibule, and supporting himself on two canes, as he bade us farewell. I have no recollection of his leaning on a stick, let alone two. In fact, before we all left, he had stood stolidly in the lobby, beside the picture commemorating Coleridge, his hands in his trouser pockets, and launched what was for him a minor tirade against Ezra Pound for his so-called 'campaign of silence'. He thought he was being a 'silly ass' (Eliot always pronounced this more like 'ahss.') Pound, he maintained, never understood *people*, and he believed that the present mood of recantation was merely the obverse or depressive pole of his former exuberant fanaticism. We let Eliot give vent to his indignation, which soon spent itself: for I think he was implying that Ezra, however repentant he might be about his anti-Semitism or even about his having 'botched' the *Cantos*, was not going the right way about it.

Before leaving, I expressed the hope that we might keep in touch, because I could not for the moment think what better to say. I was glad that he did not treat this as a mere cliché, but he said that it was just the right way of putting it and that this was what we must certainly do. When I stepped out into the dimly-lit hallway, there he was, side by side with Valerie. It was the last that I saw of him.

To have returned disconsolately to the Athenaeum straight away would have been too painful. Lady Epstein, a woman of quiet charm and feline attraction (which description, now that *Cats* has achieved such triumphs, should convey no derogatory nuances), took us back to her late husband's studio. I was glad of the respite. Then I ran the Allen Tates home. That, too, was the last I was to see of them. Allen died, a divorce later, in 1976.

I returned to Japan to begin one of the busiest periods of my career. Sometimes, in a moment of respite, I sat down to write to Eliot, but I never succeeded in framing my letters to my satisfaction: that is to say, to give him the kind of news that would be of interest to him while making it clear that he was not to reply. From friends I had fairly regular intelligence, some of it depressing. I learnt of his breathlessness, his difficulty in climbing stairs (Josef Chiari has spoken of him as great climber of stairs: the *som de l'escalina* was one of his archetypal images). Keeping in touch meant for me, among other things, reading his work. It also involved preparing, with the help of two friends, Father Peter Milward, SJ, of Sophia University, with which I had close relations, and Professor Masao Hirai, a distinguished English scholar, a book which finally came out from Kinkyusha as *T.S. Eliot: A Tribute from Japan* (1967). This contained some fine essays by Father Milward, Frank Tuohy, Kenichi Yoshida, Nicholas Hagger, Roger Matthews, Masao Hirai, William Johnson, Tsuneari Fukuda, and Japan's best known poet, Junzaburo Nishiwaki. My own essay, entitled 'The Master of Prose', sought to establish Eliot as not merely the major poet but the greatest prose-writer of the age: an opinion to which I still adhere. I also wrote a long Introduction to Father Milward's excellent commentary on *The Four Quartets*.

It must have been on the afternoon of Tuesday, 5 January 1965, that Alan Baker, my deputy, whose office was adjoining mine in the large building in Shinjuku from which one looked across to Mount Fuji, told me of the news of Eliot's death, which had just come over the BBC Far East network. I finished the day's work as usual, though perhaps in more subdued fashion; but when I got home that evening and opened the *Collected Poems*, I had a strange sensation, for which I can recall no parallel, of the words jumping off the page. It was as if they were temporarily charged with an added meaning and dynamism, or as if they were saying: 'Here *we* are, even if he is gone. From now on it is to *us* that you must look'. My sister told me that she had a similar experience. Ezra Pound's admirable tribute, published a few days later, chimed in with such a notion, ending with '*Read him*'. By 12.15 a.m. on that same Tuesday, I had drafted an obituary article to the *Japan Times* to appear on the Friday.

Some Japanese poets held a special wake on the same evening, and the next day I had some callers, among them Nicholas Hagger, who was later to publish some of my books. The incumbent at St Alban's Anglican/Episcopal Church, the Reverend Bob Smith, at once set about organizing a memorial service. As I had preached the Shakespeare Sermon at a service there in 1964, to commemorate the quarter-centenary, so I preached the Eliot sermon on Sunday, 31 January 1965. This way to pay homage, as I put it, 'to a great Englishman and a great American but also to a man who may be said to transcend nationality and to belong to us all'. I went on to observe how difficult and delicate it was to discuss another man's personal faith : for 'by indulging in edifying platitudes, the man becomes an effigy in a niche: and by expounding doctrinal views, he survives only as a disembodied intellect'. After quoting the superb opening lines of 'Little Gidding', with their reference to 'midwinter spring', I proceeded:

> I hope I shall not be thought to indulge in sentimentality when I point out that it was precisely at this season and (as I learn from reports from home) on just such a day as that described, that the poet himself died, shortly after the Feast of St Stephen, the Church's first martyr and the Patron Saint of his own Parish Church. That is why it is appropriate that we should render him homage today here at St Alban's, dedicated to England's first martyr, and in Epiphany, the season of 'showing forth'.

And I ended by recalling the apposite words taken from the lesson read earlier in the service (Ecclesiasticus, Chapter 44):

> Let us now praise famous men..
> Leaders of the people by their counsels,
> And by their understanding, men of learning for the people;
> Wise were their words in their instruction:-
> Sush as found out musical tunes,
> *And set forth verses in writing.*

When I next was home, I saw a good deal of Valerie. Sometimes we talked into the small hours, before I returned to my club. She told me things, and showed me material, that she may not perhaps have made available to others: I do not know. And, as she spoke of Tom (as he thereafter became between us), she exhibited a radiant look that I shall always remember. Accordingly, it is to her that I dedicate this book.

She invited me to sit in the high-backed chair, his favourite; and in due course I learnt the details of his death. Most of the accounts so far given are highly inaccurate. What happened was that the end came after several days when he was in bed at home, and it had become obvious that he was failing. On the morning of 4 January 1965, his doctor gave Valerie a prescription which she took to the chemist in Thackeray Street, just across the road (it has now gone). She had slipped out without his knowledge. Her mother stayed with him, gently stroking his head. Valerie could not have been away for more than four minutes; and, hoping that he might be sleeping, she crept in as quietly as possible. Even her mother did not hear her entry. He appeared to be unconscious; but, without opening his eyes, he called across that distance almost triumphantly, 'Valerie!'. This quite startled her mother. After a few hours, during which he did not utter another word, he died.

The tributes poured in, many of the official obituaries being, in my opinion, hopelessly astray in assessing the man. A verse tribute I particularly liked, however, was that quoted by Canon Demant in his fine address at the Requiem for Eliot at St Stephen's on 17 February 1965. It was by a Liverpool poet, Adrian Henri (I have never seen the complete version):

> I'd been out the night before and hadn't seen the papers
> or the telly,
> And the next day in a cafe someone told me you were dead.
> And it was as if a favourite distant uncle had died.

Although for me it was much more than that, the line – 'someone told me you were dead' – somehow exactly fitted. You could not imagine such a thing being said in quite that way about Wordsworth or Tennyson or Hardy or Yeats. The truth is that Eliot, instead of being the 'dry-stick' intellectual he was often described, was much nearer to the people than most poets, just as one felt that Shakespeare himself must have been. Eliot would have liked the verse, just as he would have enjoyed and approved the success of *Cats*.

For myself, I can say without hesitation that he was quite the greatest man I have ever known, and, to many more than myself, one of the kindest. At the time of his death, and during the twenty years that have followed, the words of *Murder in the Cathedral* have repeatedly come to mind, that, in losing him, 'we can rejoice and mourn at once and for the same reason'.

For Product Safety Concerns and Information please contact our EU representative GPSR@taylorandfrancis.com
Taylor & Francis Verlag GmbH, Kaufingerstraße 24, 80331 München, Germany

www.ingramcontent.com/pod-product-compliance
Lightning Source LLC
Chambersburg PA
CBHW060559230426
43670CB00011B/1884